D0804469

A full understanding of human action requires an understanding of what *motivates* people to do what they do. For too many years studies of motivation and of culture have drawn from different theoretical paradigms. Typically, human motivation has been modeled on animal behavior, while culture has been described as pure knowledge or symbol. The result has been insufficient appreciation of the role of culture in human motivation and a truncated view of culture as disembodied knowledge. In this volume, anthropologists have attempted a different approach, seeking to integrate knowledge, desire, and action in a single explanatory framework. This research builds upon recent work in cognitive anthropology on *cultural models*, that is, shared cognitive schemas through which human realities are constructed and interpreted, while also drawing upon insights from developmental psychology, psychoanalytic theory, and social theory.

Most of the research described here was conducted in the United States and deals with some of the pressing concerns – romance, marriage, parenthood, and success – of women and men from different class and ethnic backgrounds. A study of gender roles in Mexico provides comparative cross-cultural data. Several of the chapters deal with oppressive social ideologies, exploring cultural models of gender and class. The careful, in-depth case studies and innovative methods of discourse analysis used here turn up findings about the relation of ideology to people's thought and action that challenge any kind of simple social determinism.

Human motives and cultural models

Publications of the Society for Psychological Anthropology

Editors

Robert A. Paul, Graduate Institute of the Liberal Arts, Emory University, Atlanta

Richard A. Shweder, Committee on Human Development, The University of Chicago

Publications of the Society for Psychological Anthropology is a joint initiative of Cambridge University Press and the Society for Psychological Anthropology, a unit of the American Anthropological Association. The series has been established to publish books in psychological anthropology and related fields of cognitive anthropology, ethnopsychology, and cultural psychology. It will include works of original theory, empirical research, and edited collections that address current issues. The creation of this series reflects a renewed interest among culture theorists in ideas about the self, mind–body interaction, social cognition, mental models, processes of cultural acquisition, motivation and agency, gender, and emotion.

The books will appeal to an international readership of scholars, students, and professionals in the social sciences.

Human motives and cultural models

Edited by
Roy G. D'Andrade
University of California, San Diego

Claudia Strauss
Duke University

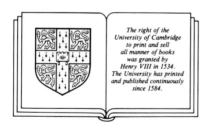

The right of the
University of Cambridge
to print and sell
all manner of books
was granted by
Henry VIII in 1534.
The University has printed
and published continuously
since 1584.

CAMBRIDGE UNIVERSITY PRESS
Cambridge
New York   Port Chester
Melbourne   Sydney

Published by the Press Syndicate of the University of Cambridge
The Pitt Building, Trumpington Street, Cambridge CB2 1RP
40 West 20th Street, New York, NY 10011–4211, USA
10 Stamford Road, Oakleigh, Victoria 3166, Australia

© Cambridge University Press 1992

First published 1992

Printed in Great Britain at the University Press, Cambridge

A catalogue record for this book is available from the British Library

Library of Congress cataloguing in publication data applied for

ISBN 0 521 412 33 1 hardback
ISBN 0 521 423 38 4 paperback

UP

Contents

Illustrations

Preface

The impetus for this volume began with an invited session of the Society for Psychological Anthropology and the Society for Cultural Anthropology at the meetings of the American Anthropological Association in 1986, organized by Naomi Quinn and Roy D'Andrade. The symposium was titled "The Directive Force of Cultural Models." All of the contributors to this volume gave papers at the symposium. Alan Fiske also contributed a paper which later became the basis of a book-length monograph.

The basic idea of the symposium was to investigate the theoretical and ethnographic usefulness of the concept of "directive force." Robert Weller and Edwin Hutchins were discussants, and grateful acknowledgment is made for the assistance given by their good critiques.

R.D.
C.S.

Contributors

Roy G. D'Andrade
Department of Anthropology
University of California, San Diego

Sara Harkness
Department of Human Development and Family Studies
Pennsylvania State University

Dorothy Holland
Department of Anthropology
University of North Carolina, Chapel Hill

Constance H. Keefer
Harvard Medical School

Catherine Lutz
Department of Anthropology
State University of New York, Binghamton

Holly F. Mathews
Department of Sociology and Anthropology
East Carolina University

Naomi Quinn
Department of Cultural Anthropology
Duke University

Richard A. Shweder
Committee on Human Development
University of Chicago

Claudia Strauss
Department of Cultural Anthropology
Duke University

Charles M. Super
Department of Human Development and Family Studies
Pennsylvania State University

1 Models and motives

Claudia Strauss

Why do people do what they do?[1] To address this question the papers in this volume take a new look at the nature and sources of human motivation. Human motivation has to be understood as the product of interaction between events and things in the social world and interpretations of those events and things in people's psyches. In this introduction I argue that models of motivation need to reject not only psychobiological determinism but also sociocultural determinism, if the latter is taken to mean that private interpretations are replicas of public messages.

This point may seem obvious, but it runs counter to earlier research paradigms in psychology, which have explained motivation primarily in terms of universal needs and drives, and to currently dominant social and cultural theories, which would make human action a direct precipitate of cultural constructs. In contrast to these approaches, the research presented here shows, on the one hand, that motivation depends on cultural messages and is realized in social interaction, but on the other, that motivation is not automatically acquired when cultural messages have been imparted. Knowing the dominant ideologies, discourses, and symbols of a society is only the beginning – there remains the hard work of understanding why some of those ideologies, discourses, and symbols become compelling to social actors, while others are only the hollow shell of a morality that may be repeated in official pronouncements but is ignored in private lives.[2] Our key question thus becomes: How do cultural messages get under people's skin (both literally and metaphorically)?

It is particularly important to address this question now, because anthropological descriptions of culture are changing. In earlier decades it was conventional wisdom to think of cultures as integrated, stable sets of meanings and practices unproblematically reproduced through socialized actors. Now, anthropologists are beginning to stress conflict, contradiction, ambiguity, and change in cultural understandings – the way cultural understandings are "contested" and "negotiated," in current jargon.[3] These new models of culture are driven in part by theoretical currents, but also by the undeniable evidence that the social order is not a master

1

programmer in any simple, straightforward way. Even though any two middle-class North Americans are more likely to share concerns than either would be with a Nuer or an Ifaluk Islander, there are enough social resisters and amoral hustlers in any society to show us that culture is not "loaded in" to us the way it is into a computer. As this is being written, at the beginning of the 1990s, examples of both ideological resistance from around the world and of domestic fallout from the continuing modernist crisis – if there are no absolute truths, why be good? – should be enough to give the questions of this volume motivational force for social researchers.

Fortunately, the people whose lives inform these studies show little of the postmodern exhaustion that is currently a subject of much elite intellectual interest. The people we talked to were sometimes torn between conflicting desires, but they did not lack deeply motivating concerns. Their stories urge us to find the missing links that would explain how ambiguous, conflicting, and potentially impotent social messages become a basis for someone's action.

The remainder of this introduction presents a brief discussion of our dispute with traditional psychological studies of motivation, followed by a longer discussion of weaknesses of some other sociocultural approaches to motivation. Next, I summarize the papers in this volume and, finally, outline its organization.

It should be noted from the start that although most of the contributors to the volume are cognitive anthropologists, we do not believe cognition is a realm that is separate from affect. When we speak of "mind" or "cognitive representations" we refer to psychic processes and states in which thought and feeling are linked. New models of mind that are particularly conducive to integrating what nineteenth-century psychology took to be the separate faculties of cognition, emotion, and motivation (Lazarus, Coyne, and Folkman 1984, Isen 1984) will be presented later in this introduction. Taking a suggestion from Wikan (1989), I will use the phrase "thought-feeling" to emphasize the interdependence of these aspects of psyche.

Traditional psychological models of motivation

Psychological theories of motivation have been largely concerned with "the biological needs and psychological drives that influence the behavior of organisms" (Bock 1988:12). Thus, a psychology text might introduce motivation by talking about an animal's physiological *needs* for food and water, the *drives*, i.e., urgent subjective states of hunger and thirst, to which those needs give rise, and the consequent *motivation* animals have to eat and drink because they have learned that those activities satisfy hunger and thirst. After this starting point, specifically human needs (e.g., the desire for achievement, affiliation, and self-esteem) would be discussed and proposed to work analogously, producing motives that explain human action across cultures and throughout time.[4] On this model needs and drives built into the human personality can be canalized (that is, steered toward cross-culturally varying ends) and may exert varying degrees of pressure (for example, some cultures foster a high, others a low, need for achievement), but otherwise the motivational pool is the same for all humans.

As D'Andrade's first essay in this volume explains, the tradition of motivation research described above is no longer dominant in psychology because its proponents were unable to specify a limited set of universal motives, identify them in behavior, and explain situational variance in their expression. D'Andrade proposes that a more promising alternative may be to investigate how cognitive schemas learned in specific cultural contexts are linked to one another and to goals for action. To put it in a slogan, *cultural models* (i.e., culturally formed cognitive schemas, Quinn and Holland 1987) *can have motivational force* because these models not only label and describe the world but also set forth goals (both conscious and unconscious) and elicit or include desires (D'Andrade 1981, 1984, 1990). (Note: cognitive schemas are learned, internalized patterns of thought-feeling that mediate both the interpretation of on-going experience and the reconstruction of memories.) This insight is the starting point for all of the papers in this volume, although some of the contributors (e.g., Shweder and Lutz) would not phrase their objections to traditional studies of motivation in quite these cognitive terms.

D'Andrade's essay makes clear that there are many advantages to thinking of motives as embedded in cultural models: we are no longer limited to a small universal set of motives; we can explain situational variation in behavior more easily; and we can study motives the same way we study other cultural models. Particularly important in D'Andrade's account is the hierarchical organization of goal-embedded schemas: at the highest level are schemas (e.g., for love or success) whose goals are easily triggered by a wide range of inputs; at lower levels are schemas (e.g., for joining a dating service or attending a job fair) that direct action only if "recruited" by higher-level goals. This hierarchy of linkages among schemas helps explain the situational variability of action and gives us a way of understanding the cognitive correlates of dominant cultural values.

Since rejection of psychobiological reductionism is not only uncontroversial in contemporary cultural theory but is practically a sacrament of the faith, I will not belabor this point. I should note, however, that while we share a commitment to understanding the cultural bases of motivation, we do not necessarily assume that there are no universal needs or drives. D'Andrade (chapter 2), for example, does not see human motivation as *determined* by psychobiological drives, but he retains a theoretical place for universal needs and drives alongside and interacting with cross-culturally variable cognitive schemas (see also D'Andrade 1981). *A fortiori* it follows that we should not reject the possibility of psychic universals of some sort or other (*pace* Shweder 1990). At the very least, the fact that a human baby born anywhere in the world can acquire language and culture anywhere else in the world, while a chimp baby cannot (or cannot in the same way humans do) indicates that all humans have a built-in receptiveness to the form human cultures take, and all human cultures probably share some bedrock commonalities because of these coevolved features of human neurophysiology and morphology.[5]

Traditional sociocultural models of motivation

In the last section I stated that to understand why people do what they do, we have to understand the cultural constructs by which they interpret the world. There are probably few cultural anthropologists who would disagree with this point, which is directed against earlier psychological rather than anthropological models of motivation. In this section I will argue that to understand why people do what they do, it is not enough to know the dominant constructs of a society; it is also necessary to study how actors internalize those constructs. This point may be more controversial.

Focusing on the ways culture is internalized is hardly new in psychological anthropology. A concern with internalization is present, as well, in some critical theorists' studies of social resistance (e.g., Martin 1987, Scott 1985, Willis 1977), for one effective way to critique overly strong theories of social reproduction is to explore the varying meanings individuals assign to the dominant values and practices of their society. The importance of internalization is also a theme in the work of such iconoclastic researchers as Barth (1975, 1982), Bloch (1985), and Sperber (1985). Yet, while this focus is not new, espousing it means rowing against two major currents of sociocultural theory. Riding on the first current are theorists who argue that studies of internalization are misguided in principle. Travelers along the second current accept the importance of internalization in principle but have failed to study it in practice.

Interpretivism is an especially powerful stream in the first current. Although it is not the only stream (French structuralism and many versions of contemporary poststructuralism have also contributed), I will focus on it here because it continues to exert a strong influence on anthropological analyses of action. Ricoeur (1979) presents a straight-forward argument for an interpretivist position: human social action is like a written text; written texts are most fruitfully analyzed without reference to the psychology of the author; therefore, human social action is most fruitfully analyzed without reference to the psychology of the actor. Ricoeur gives special attention to the first premise, making a distinction between written texts and spoken discourse. He claims that social action is more like a written text than like spoken discourse because, among other reasons, both written texts and social action are inscribed (literally or, in the second case, figuratively on the "historical record") and both have effects or meanings that escape the intentions of their authors.

These claims, central to much current work in literary criticism, require a much fuller response than I can give them here. An outline of a response would go as follows. First, Ricoeur ignores the fact that spoken discourse is also a form of action, with the same kind of metaphorical inscription on the historical record as any other action. Second, from the fact that the effects of all action escape their authors' intentions it does not follow that intentions are irrelevant to an understanding of action. Finally, a herme-neutic interpretation of action in the light of other actions only explains why people do what they do if they have consciously or unconsciously internalized whatever patterns of signification the analyst may find.

Geertz's (1973c) arguments in this vein are not as clear as Ricoeur's, but what they lack in clarity they compensate for by eloquence. Now, almost twenty years after Geertz published "Thick Description: Toward an Interpretive Theory of Culture," the criticisms presented there are still being used as a bludgeon against internalist (e.g., cognitive or psycho-analytic) analyses of action.[6] If we want to advance our understanding of human action beyond the point anthropologists reached two decades ago, we need to examine Geertz's claims in some detail (see also Ewing, in press).

Geertz's primary target is earlier cognitivists' reductions of culture to mental phenomena; he also critiques the reduction of culture to patterns of behavior. Geertz does not deny that desires and thoughts exist, or that patterned behaviors exist. What he denies is that either of those things is culture. Culture "consists of socially established structures of meaning" and "culture is public because meaning is [public]" (1973c:12). By "public" we can assume he means not only *shared* but also *open to view* – out in the world – as rituals and artifacts are, rather than hidden, as people's thoughts and feelings are. Geertz would have to mean "public" in both of these senses to argue against psychological analyses, because psychological anthropologists would agree that culture is public in the first sense of being (in varying degrees) shared, or held in common.

Geertz's contention that culture is publicly accessible rests[7] on two, by now famous, examples of "structures of meaning," Beethoven quartets and winks. This is what Geertz said about a Beethoven quartet:

> no one would, I think, identify it with its score, with the skills and knowledge needed to play it, with the understanding of it possessed by its performers or auditors, nor . . . with a particular performance of it . . . that a Beethoven quartet is a temporally developed tonal structure, a coherent sequence of modeled sound – in a word, *music* – and not anybody's knowledge of or belief about anything, including how to play it, is a proposition to which most people are, upon reflection, likely to assent. (1973c:11–12; emphasis added)

Beethoven's quartets are a sample of culture; what is true of them, therefore, Geertz supposes to be true of culture as a whole.

One way we could interpret this passage is to highlight the phrase "temporally developed tonal structure" and infer that Geertz was suggesting that culture is an abstract entity, hence not the sort of thing that could be in the head. This interpretation makes sense in light of Geertz's further examples of cultural things: "Tantrism, genetics, the progressive form of the verb, the classification of wines, the Common Law, or the notion of 'a conditional curse'" (1973c:13). It also makes sense if, as Geertz proposes elsewhere (1973a:92), culture is like a genetic code (rather than any particular string of DNA molecules). The problem with this interpretation is that abstract entities are not public (in the out-in-the-world sense); abstract entities are neither publicly accessible like artifacts[8] nor private like psychological states.

It may be, however, that Geertz did not mean that culture is an abstract entity, because he also characterized a Beethoven quartet as a "sequence of modeled sound – in a word, *music*." Sequences of sounds are concrete things and "music," according to my dictionary, is "agreeable sound," that is, sound plus a subjective reaction. What makes "a temporally developed tonal structure" *music* rather than *noise* are the internalized schemas that mediate people's responses to those sounds. A Beethoven quartet is not identical with these schemas, but it cannot be music without them.[9]

It is thus not clear what moral we should draw from the example of a Beethoven quartet. The most plausible moral is that culture as a whole is like music: it includes both the public actions, objects and symbols that make shared learning possible (D'Andrade pers. comm., Sperber 1985) and the private psychological states of knowledge and feeling without which these public things are meaningless (Spiro 1987a) and could not be recreated (Goodenough 1981; see also Colby and Colby 1981, Shore 1991). This, however, seems not to be the conclusion Geertz wants us to reach. For our present purposes it is not necessary to settle this question, because this debate concerns what *culture* is, not how we should study culturally informed *action*. We could agree that culture is either an abstract construct or a collection of concrete out-in-the-world objects and events and still contend that culturally informed action follows from private, even if shared, thought-feelings.

Geertz seems to want to cut off that possibility as well, for after having devoted the first part of his essay to the proposal that cultural analysis should aim for a "thick (i.e., meaning-laden) description" of things like winks, he goes on to argue as follows: 'Culture is public because meaning is. You can't wink . . . without knowing what counts as winking . . . But to draw from such truths the conclusion that knowing how to wink is winking . . . is to betray as deep a confusion as, taking thin descriptions for thick, to identify winking with eyelid contractions' (1973c:12).

Granted, knowing how to wink is not the same as winking. But what is publicly observable here? Not winking, in the meaning-laden "thick" sense, only eyelid contractions. What makes that eyelid contraction a wink rather than a twitch lies not in the external realm of behavior but in the internal realm of psyche: the winker's intention to deliver a message. That intention is in the winker's head, as is the winker's knowledge of what a wink means, and the knowledge that the winkee should know how to distinguish winks from twitches, and hence know which is which. This knowledge is intersubjectively shared, but it is internal to the actors involved, thus private in the sense we have been talking about here.

What holds for winking holds even more strongly for more complex and interesting forms of social behavior. Consider Beethoven's music again. Tereza, of Milan Kundera's *The Unbearable Lightness of Being*, falls in love while listening to Beethoven's music, quite unlike Alex, the antihero of Anthony Burgess's *A Clockwork Orange*, who commits mayhem while listening to Beethoven. (This is not just a result of the differences between the bleak culture of the future imagined by Burgess and the Czechoslovakia of the 1960s described by Kundera. Compare Tereza's reaction to Beethoven with Tomas's in *Unbearable Lightness* or Alex's with his mates' in *Clockwork Orange*.) To understand why someone acts the way they do it is not enough to know the discourses, objects, and events to which they have been exposed; we need to know the psychic structures that assimilate those things and render them a basis for meaningful action (Spiro 1987a).

In practice Geertz did sometimes take into account the way shared cultural assumptions are internalized: "Ritual and Social Change: A Javanese Example" (1973b) is an excellent example. That analysis is insightful precisely because it leaves the hermeneutic circle to ask questions about the meaning of cultural "texts" for their "authors," that is, for the people creating social action.

In the second major current I alluded to at the outset of this section a completely different tack is taken in denigrating the need to study how the public social world is internalized. This second tack was taken by many structural-functionalists and continues in some current versions of practice theory. For Durkheimian structural-functionalists (e.g., Durkheim himself, Radcliffe-Brown, and Parsons) psychological states play an important role but not an independent one, because social values are assumed to be transmitted unproblematically through a society's socialization mechanisms. For societies to survive they need to inculcate dominant values in their members. Whether through sacred rituals or mundane child-rearing practices, these dominant values are imparted, creating the motivational states that will lead to actions that recreate the social order. If all goes well, everyone lives happily ever after in consensual harmony (within a social group; structural-functionalists certainly recognized the presence of conflict between differently socialized groups). According to structural-functionalists, if we want to know why people do what they do, we need only look at what they have been taught.

Given that human action is certainly underdetermined, if not undetermined, by innate drives, we do indeed have to examine the cultural sources of motivation, including the social behavior people observe, the instructions they are given, and the constructed realities they bump up against. But, as every parent will recognize, transmission of values and beliefs is no straightforward matter. This is not a simple problem of "noise" in the fax line from the public social order to individuals' psyches causing imperfect copies. Transmission is more complicated than this because the social order is more complicated than this. If our cultural-ideological milieux were unchanging, unambiguous, and internally consistent, there would be no need to study how social messages are appropriated by individual minds. Early childhood experience would be consistent with adult experience, explicit messages consistent with each other and implicit messages, and the meaning of a society's messages would be clear to anyone who learned them. Yet, as we now recognize, conflicting messages, ambiguity, and change are found in all societies, even "traditional" ones. If we reject structural-functional understandings of society, it becomes all the more important to study how individuals grasp the social order (see also Whitehead 1987). This point needs to be stressed because, paradoxically, at present the very analysts who are most likely to stress ambiguity, contestation, and multiple voices in social life are also most likely to be persuaded (e.g., by Foucault 1977) that we need to "decenter" discourse and behavior away from the individual actor.

Bourdieu's theory of practice (1977, 1990) is, in many respects, an improvement over structural-functionalism (see also Giddens 1979). Bourdieu retains structural-functionalists' insight that social reproduction must be accomplished through a process by which social facts are internalized. In his model, however, the primary social facts are not social norms but rather practices of everyday life. Everyday behavior is not copied exactly in the child's 'habitus' (Bourdieu's name for the mental structures created through this process of inexplicit learning); instead, learners unconsciously extract from practice a pattern that can be flexibly and innovatively enacted in new situations. This model of the formation of the habitus is remarkable in anticipating current connectionist models of cognition, which are discussed further below.[10]

There are two serious problems with Bourdieu's practice theory, however. Although he does discuss explicit ideological learning, his focus is on inexplicit learning and the unreflective, automaton-like behavior that follows from it. (In fact, in *Distinction* Bourdieu ridicules the pretensions that keep us from agreeing with Leibniz that "'we are automatons in three-quarters of what we do'" [1984:474].) This is a useful corrective to theories that focus too exclusively on self-conscious goal-directed behavior. But Bourdieu goes too far in the other direction, ignoring social action that *is* consciously goal-directed. (Note: "consciously goal-directed" does not necessarily mean "rational" in a narrow cost-benefit [Weber's *zweckrational*] sense. For example, a religiously motivated suicide mission is consciously goal-directed.) Furthermore, Bourdieu's analysis is limited because it is not person-centered. In *Outline* he never analyzes the habitus of any particular individuals, but instead, like all too many social researchers, makes assumptions about the contents of the habitus of his Kabyle informants on the basis of social facts such as the organization of their households or the rhythms of their agricultural calendar.[11] This leads him to ignore the potential for intracultural variation and change that is built into his theory of habitus formation and to stress instead the reproduction of hegemonic relations, at least for "traditional" societies. In other words, although Bourdieu's theory takes us away from what I call "fax" models of socialization, his own practice falls back into them. (The fax analogy is used here to highlight the assumptions about both transmission and copying that are part of these models of culture.)

Not just the fax: complexities in the development of motivation

The papers in this volume suggest a different model, one that is person-centered (LeVine 1982) and takes into account three complexities of the socialization process: (1) public social messages may change, be inconsistent, or hard to read; (2) internalizing these messages does not mean copying them in any straightforward way; and (3) motivation is not automatically acquired when cultural descriptions of reality are learned. The next section will describe in greater detail the contributions the papers in the volume make towards a greater understanding of each of these points. Like the recent studies of social resistance referred to at the outset of this section, many of these papers show that social reproduction looks very different from the "bottom" (the actor's point of view) than it does from the "top" (the perspective of dominant institutions and ideologies).

The public social order is complex

The complexity of the public social order is not due simply to the many intentional worlds (e.g., surfing, curing, or performance art) there are in every society. If that were the only problem, each of these micro-worlds could be treated as a community unto itself, with a fax model of internalization working unproblematically within that world. Fax models do not work because even within an intentional world, people receive inconsistent and unclear messages.

Harkness, Super, and Keefer (chapter 7) illustrate this in their discussion of the child-rearing schemas of some middle-class adults in the greater Boston, Massachusetts area. These men and women did not come to parenthood with ready-to-apply theories of child rearing; instead, they have responded to their children's changing behaviors by drawing on memories of how their parents raised them, models provided by friends and acquaintances currently engaged in child rearing, and the advice of "experts." However, the way these parents remember being raised is often not the way their peers raise children, and the experts may suggest still another approach or disagree with one another ("Be strict!" "Be indulgent!"). There is the further problem that some cultural values are vague (e.g., independence is good); it may not be clear how to translate these values into practice. That people can sort through changing, inconsistent, and ambiguous messages like these to arrive at reasonably coherent actions, as Harkness *et al.* show they do, demonstrates one limitation of approaches that assume social facts are simply copied into internal schemas.

Another difficulty for the fax theory of internalization is that social facts take different forms. Information that is given to us as an explicit rule is internalized and acted on differently than information that is only implicit in practice. As Bourdieu (1977, 1990) recognized, skills that are built up through repeated practice have two interesting properties. On the one hand, this knowledge can be applied flexibly to meet ever-changing variations in circumstances. On the other hand, unlike explicit rules, these abilities are not likely to be recognized as encoding contestable social values. This is a further reason why the "text" metaphor for cultural action is problematic: cultural messages that are only implicit in action have neither the precise specification nor, often, the same kind of ideological force as actual texts (see Strauss 1990).

The extent to which cultural messages are explicitly verbalized is not the only factor affecting their ideological force. Mathews's discussion (chapter 6) of the Mexican *La Llorona* morality tale shows that genre is important as well. She argues that morality tales create motivation in different ways than proverbs and myths do. The special genius of the morality tale is to make horrifying outcomes seem to be the inevitable consequence of small, cumulative deviations from accepted morality. Proverbs, on the other hand, gain motivational force through economical, easy-to-remember, seemingly timeless statements of cultural wisdom (White 1987); myths draw their power by tapping unconscious fears and desires (Spiro 1987b, Hutchins 1987).

Of course, these different genres can transmit the same message, and some messages, such as the importance of encouraging independence and the usefulness of "stage" theories of development for Harkness *et al.*'s Boston-area parents or theories of emotion for Lutz's U.S. interviewees, seem to come through loud and clear, generation after generation, to nearly everyone in a society. In stressing complications in the social world I do not mean to deny that societies have dominant, persistent ideologies, only to point out that rarely, if ever, does the public realm of culture present a single, clearly defined, well-integrated reality.

The process of internalization is complicated

These complications in the public world of social facts make it clear that it is not enough to know *what* information people are exposed to; we also have to study *how* they internalize that information. Current work in the cognitive sciences has much to contribute to an understanding of this process and further undermines any fax theory of the relation between public life and private representations.

Some of the most interesting work in the cognitive sciences at present comes from new ways of thinking about the mind – approaches inspired more by the workings of the brain than by the specifications of the digital serial computer. One particularly important feature of these new "connectionist" models for our purposes is that knowledge need not be learned or retained as explicit generalizations or formulae; instead regularities in behavior reflect cognitive patterns unconsciously extracted from repeated experience (Rumelhart, McClelland, and the PDP Group 1986; McClelland, Rumelhart, and the PDP Group 1986). In connectionist models the meanings of concepts such as piety, love, or success are represented not as a symbolic string (love is a feeling state with features x, y, and z) but rather as links of different strengths among units representing co-occurring features of experience. Stated another way, in connectionist models *semantic information* (e.g., what love is) is not stored in anything like a dictionary, separate from *episodic information* (e.g., specific experiences of loving and being loved or not loved, reading and hearing about love, etc.).

If that is the case, it follows that members of a society can use the same language and share exposure to many of the same repeated social messages while differing greatly in the penumbra of associations around their shared concepts, because no two people have exactly the same experiences. Additionally, two people may share some of the same cognitive schemas but link them in different ways, with differing results for the way they act on their schemas. As an example of the latter situation, consider two North American middle-class 18-year-old women (Zoe and Chloe). Both have learned a get-married-and-have-kids schema as well as a go-to-college-and-have-a-career schema. For Zoe the two schemas are closely linked in a picture of adulthood, because she knows women who are married, have children, and have careers. For Chloe the two are not at all linked, because she knows some women who are married and have children and others with careers, but none who have combined the two.[12] These differences in patterns of cognitive organization would doubtless make a significant difference in the choices each woman made.

Given the many possibilities for individual variation in concept-experience links, it follows that ideas that, to the analyst, may seem closely associated may not be connected in an informant's belief system. Cognitive links depend not on abstract semantic similarity but rather on the concrete associations we experience in life. The order of learning can make a difference too, for regularities learned early in life set up expectations that affect the way we interpret later experience (Quinn and Strauss in press).

Some of these properties of cognitive networks are revealed in Quinn's (chapter 5) analysis of three United States women's conflicting feelings about their marriages. One interviewee, Kay, disputed her husband's claims that waiting on him was part of her "wifely duties," but still did wait on him out of a desire for a successful marriage. Quinn's fine-grained analysis shows how shared cultural models are linked to Kay's memories of significant life experiences to form a belief system that explains her otherwise difficult-to-understand behavior. Holland's analysis (chapter 4) of some Southern United States college women's participation or lack of participation in romance likewise points out the importance of understanding the way general-purpose cultural models are linked to specific life experiences and to goals for action (see also Holland 1988). Finally, my analysis (chapter 9) of the lack of congruence between some Rhode Island workingmen's talk about success and their behavior when faced with opportunities to get ahead once again stresses the need to look at the ways in which dominant social ideologies are connected (or not connected) to people's experience. In that chapter I propose ways of tracing cognitive linkages from clues in talk.

Motivation is not automatically acquired from cultural descriptions of reality

It is implicit in what has been said so far that shared cultural constructs do not automatically impart motivational force. As D'Andrade puts it below (chapter 2), it is not enough to say "action is culturally constituted," for that does not answer the question of how this happens or to what extent action is culturally determined (see also Spiro 1987a). Speaking more positively, what can we say about the reasons why some cultural constructs, but not others, acquire motivational force?

Shweder's essay (chapter 3) contends that behavior follows the curves of culturally defined realities and no other forces (of material interest or repressed needs, for example) are required to explain why we do what we do. Although in this volume he stands alone in this position, the other contributors would probably agree that this is part of the answer. It is important to investigate the types of experiences that lead people to feel (often without thinking about it much) that a certain course of action is their only reasonable alternative.

Mathews shows that morality tales are particularly effective at imparting a feeling of inevitability to certain sequences of actions. In the Zapotec-Mixtec community Mathews studied, the La Llorona tale of the horrible consequences that befall wayward wives (in men's versions of the tale) and wayward husbands (in women's versions) was used frequently in everyday conversations to inculcate values, interpret experience, and justify action. Traditional ethnographic accounts would stop with this demonstration of the cultural salience of the La Llorona tale, assuming its motivating force for individuals to follow. Mathews, however, takes the unconventional step of asking why listeners to the tale find it convincing. Part of her answer is that this tale (along with other forms of social practice) imparts cultural descriptions of emotion and gendered human nature. Learning these models in turn makes the sequence of events depicted in the tale seem inevitable and its moral convincing, a circularity that is typical in culture acquisition.

Yet, people do not act only out of a sense of what is realistic or right. (Moreover, those two need not coincide. The assumptions about human nature that form the background for the "realism" of the *La Llorona* tale are quite different from its morals about what adult women and men *ought* to do.) In every culture definitions of what is reasonable and what is right still leave a lot of room for variation in wants. How do we get from learning that x is good to being motivated to *do* x (Spiro 1987a)? To bridge this gap we need to add to the connectionist cognitive model presented above a further assumption that is implicit in connectionism's neurological inspiration, if not explicit in most connectionist formulations: life experiences are remembered along with *feelings* associated with them. Consider a different pair of young women (Gina and Tina). Both know the get-married-and-have-children schema as a norm for their culture, but they have very different feelings about it. For Gina this schema is associated with strong positive feelings because she grew up in a closely knit, loving family. For Tina, on the other hand, this schema is associated with strong negative feelings because her parents fought a great deal and treated her harshly. There is a good chance that these experiences will produce different motivational structures. Knowing the feelings that people associate with different cultural models as a result of their specific life experiences is crucial in order to understand what motivates them (see also Quinn and Strauss in press and Rosaldo 1984).

The importance of strongly affect-laden life experiences is demonstrated in Quinn's analysis of some wives' inner conflicts about their marriages. Quinn focuses on the motivating force of self-defining concepts, for the self seen as a human entitled to the same treatment as other humans, as the occupant of social roles with attendant obligations, and as the possessor of inherent personal or category-specific attributes. Self concepts are acquired slowly over the course of development as learned social ideologies about what is right and natural for people like oneself are linked to and energized by memories of powerful life experiences. Although Quinn does not say so here (but see Quinn 1987), it is possible that what makes some life experiences more powerful than others are their links to primitive universal needs. In a similar vein, my essay (chapter 9) explores the way a set of affect-laden experiences is interlinked for one of my interviewees, creating a motivational system that accounts for actions as diverse as his political outspokenness and his participation in marathons.

Holland, too, notes the importance of strong feelings, but argues that emotional involvement not only precedes but also follows from practice.

For the college women she interviewed and observed over a one-and-a-half-year period, clear, compelling images of themselves as romantic partners codeveloped with practice in and growing expertise at romantic pursuits. Holland shows that although Americans usually think of interest in romance as natural (or acquired early, through Cinderella stories and like messages), the motivating force of romance changes over time, depends on social support, and can be lost. It is not enough that romance be a widely shared, salient cultural category for it to direct individuals' action.

Finally, Lutz's analysis (chapter 8) of her U.S. interviewees' discussion of emotions steps away a metalevel to make a point not given much emphasis elsewhere in this volume: the social science interview can elicit goal-embedded cultural models but also gives rise to goals of its own as speaker and hearer interact. Lutz makes the further argument, drawing on Kenneth Gergen's (1984, 1985) analyses of psychological discourse, that our theoretical models of motivation are themselves shaped by social needs. This leads Lutz to critique the emphasis given to cognitive models by other contributors to this volume and call for greater attention to the social context of both discourse and motivation. One response to this critique is that there need be no conflict between studies of social pragmatics and studies of cognitive models. For social interaction to take place, actors need to call on their learned, internalized knowledge structures to interpret others' words and actions. On the other hand, thought-feeling structures are not learned or enacted in a vacuum, but in social life.

It should be noted that the "cognitive" model of motivation being developed here converges nicely with recent theories of action proposed by some psychoanalytic anthropologists (e.g., Paul 1990, LeVine 1982). Paul (1990), for example, refers to drives "not as quantities of hypothetical energic stuff in finite supply, but as cognitive mental images already endowed with an affective tone which renders them motivational" (p. 439). The model of cognition I described can accommodate unconscious knowledge and desires as well. Neural links can be excitatory or inhibitory. Traumatic experiences associated with painful feelings may be learned along with strongly inhibitory neural connections that keep these memories from coming to consciousness. The research presented below demonstrates that there are no clear boundaries between personality and cognition.

The primary method used by the contributors to this book is discourse analysis, applied to the transcriptions of many tape-recorded interviews conducted with a relatively small number of people. Although this is not the only way to study knowledge structures, discourse analysis based on in-depth interviews can yield subtle indicators of those structures. Of course, some feeling states can be only imperfectly conveyed by verbal description, but if we are to attempt to understand others' lives from their point of view, their words are indispensable.

Careful discourse analysis takes a long time, imposing practical constraints on the number of interviewees in a study. That, however, is not the only reason why most of these studies focus on particular individuals, rather than the people of society x as a whole. The point is not that Susan's, Kay's, or Tony's knowledge structure represents all of culture in the microcosm. Nor is it that person-centered approaches are warmer and more humanistic. Rather, social action is the result of a process by which public events are turned into private representations and acted on, thereby creating new public events (Sperber 1985), and we need a better understanding of how this happens. If the papers in this volume only begin to illumine this process, they will have achieved their purpose.

Organization of the volume

The organization of this volume reflects the theoretical issues discussed above. The importance of cultural knowledge in motivation is the focus of the programmatic essays by D'Andrade and Shweder in Part I. In Part II Holland, Quinn, Mathews, and Harkness, Super, and Keefer present detailed case studies that not only show how to integrate studies of knowledge and motivation but also shed light on how motivation is acquired. The papers in Part II make an integrated ethnographic unit as well, moving from cultural models of romance (United States), to marriage (United States and Mexico), to parenthood (United States). Lutz's paper and my paper in Part III extend these discussions, while also disputing claims made elsewhere in the volume. Finally, the Afterword by D'Andrade reviews what is accomplished in this volume and suggests directions for future research. D'Andrade's final essay returns to one of the central themes of this introduction: the importance, for studies of human action, of analyzing the interaction between the public and private realms of culture.

NOTES

1 I am grateful to Roy D'Andrade, Katherine Ewing, Byron Good, Robert LeVine, Catherine Lutz, Holly Mathews, Robert Paul, Naomi Quinn, and Lee Strauss for helpful comments on earlier drafts of this introduction. I am particularly grateful to Naomi Quinn for reading several early drafts and commenting insightfully on each one. Some of the ideas presented here owe their origins to collaboration with Dorothy Holland and Naomi Quinn on other projects. My ideas have also been shaped by discussions with Rick Shweder that have helped me clarify my own, opposing, point of view.

2 This contrast is somewhat overdrawn, for rhetorical purposes. In between the "compelling" and "hollow shell" extremes there lie, of course, many partly motivating discourses and symbols, as well as those that are motivating in some contexts but not in others (K. Ewing, pers. comm.).

3 This "new" perspective is in some ways akin to still earlier views of cultures as the products of historical accidents (Fox in press).

4 This example was taken from *Psychology today: An introduction* (1970).

5 This point was once made by Geertz, too (1973c:13).

6 Twice in recent years my discussions with anthropological colleagues about the importance of studying internalization have been met with the response, "But what about Geertz's Beethoven quartet example? Didn't he show that culture is not in the head?" – as if no further proof were necessary.

7 He also refers, in passing, to arguments by Husserl and Wittgenstein against privacy theories of meaning.

8 Abstract entities could be publicly accessible in something like a Platonic realm, but I do not think that is what Geertz had in mind.

9 I am grateful to Roy D'Andrade for comments that helped me see the ambiguities of Geertz's Beethoven quartet example.

10 The close parallels between Bourdieu's description of the habitus (1977) and connectionist networks are described in Quinn and Strauss (in press), Holland and Strauss (forthcoming). Some of the overlap between Bourdieu's theory of practice and current connectionism is attributable to his having read and been influenced by Wittgenstein's protoconnectionism in *Philosophical Investigations*.

11 *Distinction* (1984) does examine the habitus of individuals, but superficially. See McHugh (1989:76) for a discussion of the incongruence of "texts, rituals, and rules" with subjective experiences and beliefs.

12 These examples were inspired by research David Meyers conducted among Duke undergraduate women.

REFERENCES

Barth, Fredrik
    1975 *Ritual and Knowledge Among the Baktaman of New Guinea*. New Haven: Yale University Press.
    1982 *Sohar: Culture and Society in an Omani Town*. Baltimore: Johns Hopkins University Press.
Bloch, Maurice
    1985 From Cognition to Ideology. In *Power and Knowledge: Anthropological and Sociological Approaches*, Richard Fardon, ed. Edinburgh: Scottish Academic Press. Pp. 21–48.
Bock, Philip K.
    1988 *Rethinking Psychological Anthropology: Continuity and Change in the Study of Human Action*. New York: W. H. Freeman.
Bourdieu, Pierre
    1977 *Outline of a Theory of Practice*, Richard Nice, trans. Cambridge: Cambridge University Press.

1984 *Distinction: A Social Critique of the Judgement of Taste*, Richard Nice, trans. Cambridge, MA: Harvard University Press.

1990 *The Logic of Practice*, Richard Nice, trans. Stanford: Stanford University Press.

Colby, Benjamin N. and Lore M. Colby

1981 *The Daykeeper: The Life and Discourse of an Ixil Diviner*. Cambridge, MA: Harvard University Press.

CRM Books

1970 *Psychology Today: An Introduction*. Del Mar, CA: CRM Books.

D'Andrade, Roy G.

1981 The Cultural Part of Cognition. *Cognitive Science* 5:179–95.

1984 Cultural Meaning Systems. In *Culture Theory: Essays on Mind, Self, and Emotion*, R. A. Shweder and R. A. LeVine, eds. Cambridge: Cambridge University Press. Pp. 88–119.

1990 Some Propositions about the Relations between Culture and Human Cognition. In *Cultural Psychology: Essays on Comparative Human Development*, J. W. Stigler, R. A. Shweder, and G. Herdt, eds. Cambridge: Cambridge University Press. Pp. 65–129.

Ewing, Katherine P.

In press Is Psychoanalysis Relevant for Anthropology? In *The Social Life of Psyche: Debates and Directions in Psychological Anthropology*, T. Schwartz, G. White, and C. Lutz, eds. Cambridge: Cambridge University Press.

Foucault, Michel

1977 *Discipline and Punish: The Birth of the Prison*, Alan Sheridan, trans. New York: Random House.

Fox, Richard G.

In press Studying the Characters and the Plot: For a Nearly New Culture History. In *Anthropologies of the Present*, Richard G. Fox, ed. Albuquerque: University of New Mexico Press.

Geertz, Clifford

1973a Religion as a Cultural System. In *The Interpretation of Cultures*. New York: Basic Books. Pp. 87–125.

1973b Ritual and Social Change: A Javanese Example. In *The Interpretation of Cultures*. New York: Basic Books. Pp. 142–69.

1973c Thick Description: Toward an Interpretive Theory of Culture. In *The Interpretation of Cultures*. New York: Basic Books. Pp. 3–30.

Gergen, Kenneth

1984 Aggression as Discourse. In *Social Psychology of Aggression*, A. Mummendey, ed. New York: Springer-Verlag.

1985 Social Pragmatics and the Origins of Psychological Discourse. In *The Social Construction of the Person*, K. Gergen and K. Davis, eds. New York: Springer-Verlag.

Giddens, Anthony

1979 *Central Problems in Social Theory: Action, Structure and Contradiction in Social Analysis*. Berkeley: University of California Press.

Goodenough, Ward H.

1981 *Culture, Language, and Society*. Menlo Park, CA: The Benjamin/ Cummings Publishing Company.

Holland, Dorothy
  1988 In the Voice of, In the Image of: Socially Situated Presentations of
    Attractiveness. *IPrA Papers in Pragmatics* 2(1/2):106–35.
Holland, Dorothy and Claudia Strauss
  forthcoming *Mind in Society/Society in Mind: A Critical Anthropology of
    Cognition.* Boulder, Colo.: Westview Press.
Hutchins, Edwin
  1987 Myth and Experience in the Trobriand Islands. In *Cultural Models in
    Language and Thought,* D. Holland and N. Quinn, eds. Cambridge: Cam-
    bridge University Press. Pp. 269–89.
Isen, Alice M.
  1984 Toward Understanding the Role of Affect in Cognition. In *Handbook of
    Social Cognition,* Vol. III, R. S. Wyer and T. K. Srull, eds. Hillsdale, NJ:
    Lawrence Erlbaum Associates.
Lazarus, Richard S., James C. Coyne, and Susan Folkman
  1984 Cognition, Emotion and Motivation: The Doctoring of Humpty-Dumpty.
    In *Approaches to Emotion,* K. R. Scherer and P. Ekman, eds. Hillsdale, NJ:
    Lawrence Erlbaum Associates.
LeVine, Robert A.
  1982 *Culture, Behavior, and Personality: An Introduction to the Comparative
    Study of Psychosocial Adaptation.* 2nd edn. New York: Aldine.
McClelland, James L., David E. Rumelhart, and the PDP Research Group
  1986 *Parallel Distributed Processing: Explorations in the Microstructure of
    Cognition,* Vol. II: *Psychological and Biological Models.* Cambridge, MA:
    MIT Press.
McHugh, Ernestine L.
  1989 Concepts of the Person Among the Gurungs of Nepal. *American Ethnolo-
    gist* 16(1):75–86.
Martin, Emily
  1987 *The Woman in the Body: A Cultural Analysis of Reproduction.* Boston:
    Beacon Press.
Paul, Robert
  1990 What Does Anybody Want? Desire, Purpose, and the Acting Subject in the
    Study of Culture. *Cultural Anthropology* 5 (4):431–51.
Quinn, Naomi
  1987 Love and the Experiential Basis of American Marriage. University of
    Virginia Center for Advanced Studies Working Paper Series.
Quinn, Naomi and Dorothy Holland
  1987 Cognition and Culture. Introduction to *Cultural Models in Language and
    Thought,* D. Holland and N. Quinn, eds. Cambridge: Cambridge University
    Press. Pp. 3–40.
Quinn, Naomi and Claudia Strauss
  In press A Cognitive Cultural Anthropology. In *Assessing Cultural Anthropo-
    logy.* R. Borofsky, ed. New York: McGraw-Hill.
Ricoeur, Paul
  1979 The Model of the Text: Meaningful Action Considered as Text. In
    Interpretive Social Science: A Reader, P. Rabinow and W. M. Sullivan, eds.
    Berkeley: University of California Press.

Rosaldo, Michelle Z.
  1984 Toward an Anthropology of Self and Feeling. In *Culture Theory: Essays on Mind, Self, and Emotion*. R. Shweder and R. A. LeVine, eds. Cambridge: Cambridge University Press. Pp. 137–57.
Rumelhart, David E., James L. McClelland, and the PDP Research Group
  1986 *Parallel Distributed Processing: Explorations in the Microstructure of Cognition*, Vol I: *Foundations*. Cambridge, MA: MIT Press.
Scott, James
  1985 *Weapons of the Weak: Everyday Forms of Peasant Resistance*. New Haven: Yale University Press.
Shore, Bradd
  1991 Twice-Born, Once Conceived: Meaning Construction and Cultural Cognition. *American Anthropologist* 93(1):9–27.
Shweder, Richard A.
  1990 Cultural Psychology – What is It? Introduction to *Cultural Psychology: Essays on Comparative Human Development*, J. W. Stigler, R. A. Shweder, and G. Herdt, eds. Cambridge: Cambridge University Press. Pp. 1–43.
Sperber, Dan
  1985 Anthropology and Psychology: Towards an Epidemiology of Representations. *Man* 20(1):73–87.
Spiro, Melford E.
  1972 Cognition in Culture-and-Personality. In *Culture and Cognition: Rules, Maps, and Plans*, J. P. Spradley, ed. San Francisco: Chandler Publishing. Pp. 100–10.
  1987a Collective Representations and Mental Representations in Religious Symbol Systems. In *Culture and Human Nature: Theoretical Papers of Melford E. Spiro*, B. Kilborne and L. L. Langness, eds. Chicago: University of Chicago Press. Pp. 161–84.
  1987b Whatever Happened to the Id? In *Culture and Human Nature: Theoretical Papers of Melford E. Spiro*, B. Kilborne and L. L. Langness, eds. Chicago: University of Chicago Press. Pp. 250–61.
Strauss, Claudia
  1990 Who Gets Ahead? Cognitive Responses to Heteroglossia in American Political Culture. *American Ethnologist* 17(2):312–28.
White, Geoffrey M.
  1987 Proverbs and Cultural Models: An American Psychology of Problem Solving. In *Cultural Models in Language and Thought*, D. Holland and N. Quinn, eds. Cambridge: Cambridge University Press. Pp. 151–72.
Whitehead, Harriet
  1987 *Renunciation and Reformulation: A Study of Conversion in an American Sect*. Ithaca, NY: Cornell University Press.
Wikan, Unni
  1989 Managing the Heart to Brighten Face and Soul: Emotions in Balinese Morality and Health Care. *American Ethnologist* 16(2):294–312.
Willis, Paul
  1977 *Learning to Labor: How Working Class Kids Get Working Class Jobs*. New York: Columbia University Press.

Part I

Cultural models as motives

2   Schemas and motivation

Roy G. D'Andrade

In current anthropological theory there is no clear relation between *culture* and *action*. Of course, one can say "people do what they do because their culture makes them do it." The problem with this formulation is that it does not explain anything. Do people always do what their culture tells them to? If they do, why do they? If they don't, why don't they? And how does culture make them do it? Unless there is some specification of how culture "makes" people do what they do, no explanation has been given.

This explanatory gap is especially apparent when one tries to understand why people in a particular culture put much effort into doing some things rather than other things. The standard account of such phenomena is that such strivings are the result of *motivation*; what remains unclear is how culture is connected to motivational strivings. Without an account of the relation between culture and motivation we may have an intuitive sense that there are culturally based strivings, but we have no explanation of this.

The theoretical need to include motivational analysis in the study of culture and society is generally recognized. The point that motivation is necessary for the performance of cultural roles, for example, has been made with force and clarity a number of times (Fromm 1944, Spiro 1987a, Whiting 1941). But in spite of the cogency of this argument, most ethnographies do not contain accounts of the motivational life of the people being studied. Perhaps this is because most ethnographers have found that the study of motivation requires unfamiliar and uncongenial techniques of data collection and analysis. This paper is an attempt to conceptualize motivation so that it is more amenable to ethnographic description. This paper is also an attempt to relate motivation to culture on a theoretical level.

What are motives?

Subjectively, motivation is experienced as a desire or wish, followed by a feeling of satisfaction if the desire is fulfilled or a sense of frustration if it is

23

not. Observing others, one notes that people become aroused and active under certain conditions. Along with this increase in activity there is typically a striving for something – a goal directedness in behavior – followed by various emotional reactions related to the success or failure of the goal pursuit. These facts are common-sense understandings of motivation. The western folk model of the mind – of what happens inside people – contains a rich set of conceptualizations about how desires are related to thoughts, feelings, perceptions, intentions, and actions (Bilmes 1986, D'Andrade 1987).

Psychology has developed a complex body of experimental and clinical findings over the past century concerning motivation (see, for example, the recent text by D. G. Mook, *Motivation: The Organization of Action,* 1987). A major part of the scientific understanding of motivation has come from the investigation of hunger and thirst. This kind of investigation typically treats motivation as a *drive*, an internal stimulus which becomes painful if not satisfied. Hunger, thirst, sex, pain, and other physically experienced states are typically conceptualized within this framework. Aggression and even self-esteem needs, although lacking peripheral physiological sources of stimulation, can also be conceptualized as drives.

A different approach to the study of motivation begins by defining motives not with reference to internal stimuli but with reference to *goals*. By definition, a goal, to be called a motive, should have some degree of *autonomy*; if somebody strives to establish friendly relationships, for example, not because they want friends, but because they want to "sell cars," their friendship strivings would not be considered a "real" motive. However, to the extent that somebody strives to establish friendly relationships just for the sake of having friends, to that extent the friendship goal can be treated as having an autonomous power to instigate action and to that extent can be considered a motive.

Pioneer work on the goal-striving approach was carried out by Henry Murray and his associates in the thirties. Murray turned to the definition of motive as goals rather than drives out of necessity – having decided to study human personality in all its richness, he discovered that he simply could not describe the things people strive for with just the limited vocabulary of tissue needs, aggression, and sex. Human goal striving is too complex and differentiated to be encompassed by the vocabulary of drives alone.

To describe the different types of goal striving, Murray constructed an extensive category system. He called the psychological component of goal striving a *need* to distinguish it from a drive. The list below presents the major needs Murray used for personality assessment in the research reported in *Explorations in Personality* (Murray 1938).

Need Abasement: To submit passively to external force. To accept injury, punishment. To surrender. To resign to fate. To admit inferiority, error, wrong-doing. To confess and atone.

Need Achievement: To accomplish something difficult. To overcome obstacles and attain a high standard. To excel. To rival and surpass others.

Need Acquisition: To gain possessions and property. To grasp, snatch, or steal things. To work for money or goods.

Need Affiliation: To draw near and cooperate enjoyably or reciprocate with an allied other. To please and win the affections of others. To adhere and remain loyal to a friend.

Need Aggression: To overcome opposition forcefully. To fight. To revenge an injury. To attack, punish, belittle, censure, curse or ridicule maliciously others.

Need Autonomy: To get free. To resist coercion and restriction. To be independent. To be unattached, unconditioned. To defy conventions.

Need Cognizance: To explore. To ask questions. To satisfy curiosity. To look, listen, inspect. To read and seek knowledge.

Need Contrarience: To act differently from others. To be unique. To take opposite sides. To hold unconventional views.

Need Defendance: To defend the self against assault, criticism and blame. To conceal or justify a misdeed, failure or humiliation. To vindicate oneself.

Need Deference: To admire and support a superior. To praise, honor, or eulogize. To yield eagerly to the influence of allied others. To emulate an exemplar. To conform to custom.

Need Dominance: To influence or direct the behavior of others by suggestion, seduction, persuasion, or command. To dissuade, restrain, or prohibit. To get others to cooperate.

Need Exhibition: To make an impression. To be seen and heard. To excite, amaze, fascinate, entertain, shock, intrigue, amuse or entice others.

Need Harmavoidance: To avoid pain, physical injury, illness and death. To escape from a dangerous situation. To take precautionary measures.

Need Infavoidance: To avoid humiliation. To quit embarrassing situations or to avoid conditions which may lead to belittlement.

Need Nurturance: To give sympathy and gratify the needs of a helpless other. To assist others in danger. To feed, help, support, console, protect, comfort, nurse, heal.

Need Order: To put things in order. To achieve cleanliness, arrangement, oganization, balance, neatness, tidiness and precision.

Need Play: To act for "fun," to take a playful attitude. To devote time to various forms of amusement.

Need Rejection: To separate onself from negatively regarded others. To exclude, abandon, expel, or remain indifferent to inferior others. To snub or jilt others.

Need Retention: To retain possession of things. To refuse to give or lend. To hoard. To be frugal, economical and miserly.

Need Sentience: To seek and enjoy sensuous impressions.

Need Sex: To form and further an erotic relationship. To have intercourse.

Need Succorance: To have one's needs gratified by the sympathetic aid of allied others. To be nursed, supported, sustained, protected, loved, advised, guided, indulged, forgiven, consoled.

There is no necessary conflict between *drive* and *goal* approaches. Food, for example, is a goal that people strive to obtain for its own sake (although people often eat food for reasons besides just the food itself), and food is directly connected to relief from the drive of hunger. One can imagine that, for any one person, there is a complex network of learned connections between the drives and various goals. The various goals, in such an analysis, function as *canalizations* of the drives. In the psychological literature, both drives and general goals of the kind listed by Murray are called motives, although some theorists prefer to restrict the list of "true" motives to biologically based drives, and to call the sorts of goals that Murray formulated "secondary" or "learned" motives.

Problems in the analysis of motivation

While theoretically satisfying, a number of empirical problems were encountered with this formulation of the relation between motives and behavior. First, it is difficult to determine how many *kinds* of drives or goals there are. Theorists of motivation have different lists of motives, of which Murray's list is just one example. This is disconcerting because one cannot determine which behaviors are related to which motives without a clear idea of the kinds of motives that exist.

Second, the literature on motivation has been filled with complaints concerning the reliability and validity of the operational measures for the assessment of motives. It has been argued that fantasy measures of motivation, such as the TAT, are low in reliability and have only small correlations with predicted outcome variables. From the perspective of an outsider, these complaints seem somewhat exaggerated; it surely is impressive that short written responses to a set of drawings can predict occupational success and interpersonal adjustment achieved more than ten years after testing (Winter, McClelland, and Stewart 1981). However, it should be pointed out that what is being measured by the TAT and similar techniques is a general state of the person, not the motivation for specific acts; someone who has a low degree of power needs, for example, might very well perform specific actions motivated by the need for power.

Third, it has been found repeatedly that humans display a great amount of "situational variance" in behavior. A very "hostile" person, for example, as assessed by whatever measure, may prove to be quite aggreeable and non-hostile in certain situations, say when talking to his boss, but quite hostile when drinking in bars. Another person, assessed as equally hostile, may act in just the reverse fashion, and be quite hostile when talking to his boss but quite friendly when drinking in bars. Given that the variability in behavior across settings is much greater than the variability between persons, one needs a theory that will account both for differences in behavior between persons and differences in behavior across settings.

All these indeterminacies add up to more than a theory can bear without basic change. Mischel's book, *Personality and Assessment,* published in 1968, was a summary of these problems, and is widely recognized as marking the end of an era of a certain type of motivational research. It was not that the research on motivation was bad; everyone agreed many fine pieces of work had been done. However, to go beyond the initial research findings of Murray, McClelland, and others, improvements in conceptualization and method were needed.

For most anthropologists, the major problem encountered in trying to do motivational research was the difficulty in determining what motives people had. One could use the TAT, or some other fantasy measure, and say something about the kinds of imagery that characterize some group, but how that imagery could be related to various cultural practices was unclear. When a child goes to the cookie jar and gets a cookie and eats it, it is perhaps not too difficult to identify the drive and the goal. But when a Trobriander spends much time and effort piling up yams in a yam house, how can one tell which drives and goals are really involved? Are the regnant drives hunger, or aggression, or self-esteem? Are the general goals exhibition, or infavoidance, or retention, or affiliation, or achievement, or acquisition, or conformity, or a special goal called "brotherism"? For most anthropologists it was not apparent what field methods could be invoked to answer such questions.

Current cultural research in anthropology, while informative about things like categorization and symbolization, has not thrown much light on the questions that the motivational theorists were trying to answer: that is, how does the great variability in human goal striving come about, and how is such goal striving related to culture? These questions have not gone away. To answer such questions, concepts and methods which make is possible to identify motivational goals need to be developed. It is therefore relevant that recent work in cognitive anthropology and cognitive psychology indicates that the techniques used to identify cognitive schemas can be used to identify motivational goals (Gallistel 1985, Mandler 1984). The basic idea is that some cognitive schemas function as goals, and so have motivational force.

Motives and schemas

The concept of a schema is of central importance in much work in cognitive anthropology (Casson 1983, Holland and Quinn 1987), cognitive psychology (Mandler 1984, Rumelhart *et al.* 1986), and cognitive linguistics (Lakoff 1987, Langacker 1987). A schema is a conceptual structure which makes possible the identification of objects and events. Imagine that one wanted to construct a computer program that could recognize a particular face from the pattern of light and dark pixels on a television screen which receives images from a video camera. Suppose the program had to be able to distinguish this one face from many other faces, and do so whatever the angle of viewing or the background. One would have to build an interpretive system which could both pattern search and simplify drastically. The program would have to simplify because it would be impossible to build a program which recognized every possible combination of light and dark pixels which that face might produce – there are many billion potential patterns. The program would have to recognize the upper-level patterning created by the face – the particular patterned relations of nose to eyes to mouth, etc. Basically, a schema is this sort of program: a procedure by which objects or events can be identified on the basis of simplified pattern recognition.

A considerable body of literature exists documenting the various properties of schemas (for a review of the literature relevant to human motivation, see Singer and Salovey 1991, and Stinson and Palmer 1991). Cognitive psychologists have recently developed simulations of schema processing based on multilayered networks of neuron-like elements which display remarkably human capacities (Rumelhart *et al.* 1986). These capacities include content addressable memory, priming effects, graceful degradation under injury, completion of partial information, the formation of prototypes, and systematic distortion in memory. These multilayered networks of neuron-like elements are called parallel distributed processing (PDP) models because each of the elements can be considered to be a small, simple computer linked in parallel to thousands of similar computers, making it possible to carry out thousands of tiny computations simultaneously.

The physical realization of PDP models makes vivid the fact that schemas are processes, not objects, and that specific interpretations, represented by particular patterns of activated elements, vary in degree of schematicity. To say that something is a "schema" is a shorthand way of saying that a distinct and strongly interconnected pattern of interpretive elements can be activated by minimal inputs. A schema is an interpretation which is frequent, well organized, memorable, which can be made from minimal cues, contains one or more prototypic instantiations, is resistant to change, etc. While it would be more accurate to speak always of *interpretations with such and such a degree of schematicity*, the convention of calling highly schematic interpretations schemas remains in effect in the cognitive literature.

Another important property of schemas is that they have the potential of instigating action – that is, they can function as goals. Consider the example of the schema for achievement. For many Americans such a schema is more than just a recognition process by which an achievement can be identified when it occurs; it has the potential of instigating action; that is, for some people it *is* a goal. Of course, the strength of instigation depends at any one point on the important particulars involved in each interpretive instance – what can be achieved, the difficulties and rewards involved, how that kind of achievement is related to ones own situation and abilities, etc.

There are large differences among schemas in the degree to which they function as autonomous goals. Some schemas are partial goals, in that they become goals only if other goal-schemas are also activated. Consider the ordinary "get-in-line" schema. Except for certain brain-damaged people, the goal of getting-in-line is not triggered *just* by seeing a line of people. The "getting-in-line" goal becomes salient only under conditions in which other interpretations, provided by other schemas, recruit "getting-in-line" as a sub-goal – for example, if the line is in a bank from which one wants to draw money which one has on deposit, etc.

However, some goal-schemas are much more autonomous than the "getting-in-line" schema. Consider again the schema for achievement. There is a large body of research that shows that people differ in the degree to which achievement acts as a motive – that is, the degree to which just the recognition that something can be achieved is likely to trigger doing something to bring about the achievement (Rosen 1962). People who have a strong need for achievement, as measured by the amount of achievement imagery produced in response to TAT cards, are more likely to do the sorts of things that bring achievement about, such as setting high but attainable standards for their own performance and putting more effort into reaching these standards, even when no extrinsic reward is involved (McClelland *et al.* 1953).

Another property of schemas, hierarchical organization, is also of importance for understanding motivation. They are hierarchical in the sense that interpretations provided by one schema are "passed on" to higher-level schemas in order to make more and more general interpretations. One recognizes some chair as part of the "finding a seat" schema, which is part of the "attending a lecture" schema, which is part of the "finding out what's going on" schema, which may be for some people part of the "doing anthropology" schema, or perhaps a "meeting friends" schema, or whatever. This type of means–ends goal linkage is one principle of schema hierarchy. There are other hierarchical principles, for example the part/whole relation – one recognizes a music chord as part of a musical phrase, which in turn is part of an identifiable movement of a particular symphony. Implicational relations also give rise to hierarchical relations – one recognizes the sidewalk is wet and this leads to the inferential interpretation that it has been raining, and from the inferential interpretation that it has been raining to the inferential interpretation that one's car, which was left with open windows, is likely to be wet inside, etc.

While there are many possible kinds of linkage through which one schema passes its interpretation to another, it is the topmost level of interpretation which is typically linked to the actions by which an organism operates in its environment. That is, the top-level schemas tend to be goals. This is, of course, not a hard and fast rule – sometimes one makes a very general interpretation just to understand what is going on, as in watching a play and trying to understand why one character is acting in a certain way. However, since we assume that the major function of top-level schemas is to guide action, it is our hypothesis that *a person's most general interpretations of what is going on will function as important goals for that person.*

As a rough approximation, one can divide schemas into three groups on the basis of their position in the hierarchy. At the top of the interpretive system are those which function as a person's most general goals. These might be called master motives – for things like love and work, which instigate action with no more ultimate goal in sight. Further down the hierarchy are schemas for things like marriage, my job, surfing, etc., which one might call middle-level motives. Such schemas generally require the presence of other goal-schemas to instigate action, but may on occasion instigate certain actions (see Quinn, this volume). Near the bottom of the hierarchy would be schemas for things like memos, birthdays, and water glasses. These are schemas that instigate almost no actions except when other higher-level ones interact with them, as in Shweder's example (this volume) of the relation between danger and water glasses.

Not all schemas function as goals, but all goals are schemas. The reason for this is that for something to serve as goal, the person must have some cognitive structure which is activated and which instigates action. The person does not have to be conscious of the interpretation which instigates the action, but some interpretation – whether accurately or inaccurately made from the point of view of an outside observer – must occur for the action to have an instigation.

In summary, the argument here is that to understand people one needs to understand what leads them to act as they do, and to understand what leads them to act as they do one needs to know their goals, and to understand their goals one must understand their overall interpretive system, part of which constitutes and interrelates these goals, and to understand their interpretive system – their schemas – one must understand something about the hierarchical relations among these schemas.

The role of drives in this process is complex. Theoretically, drives are a source of strong activation of schemas (affects, external stimulation, and other schemas can also independently activate schemas). Hunger, for example, typically activates those for identifying the location of obtainable food and plans for obtaining this food. Ideally, in every case one would want to be able to retrace the causal nexus from action to goal-schema to drive. Unfortunately for such an enterprise, it is an undisputed fact about humans that the network of connections between goals and drives is extremely complex, involving "many-to-many" mappings; these relations are so intricate that they can rarely be empirically determined. Perhaps it is this indeterminacy in drive–goal linkage which led Freud to group a number of potentially distinguishable drives together into one great reservoir, the libido. That humans are like this – that is, have such complex many-to-many relations between drives and goals that it is very difficult to determine which goals are activated by which specific drives – seems to be the product of a general evolutionary process in which, as intelligence increases, the connections between instinct and action become more and more complex, indirect, and modifiable.

Despite the fact that it is difficult to identify the drives that activate or "energize" particular goals, it is a task which psychotherapists routinely undertake. Two academics, for example, may both be described as having the goal of maintaining high standards, but have different configurations of drives which are importantly satisfied by this goal. For one academic this goal may be importantly connected to a narcissistic self-esteem drive – high standards need to be maintained to keep the high prestige of a department from which this person derives great satisfaction; while for the other, academic high standards may be maintained as a way of satisfying aggressive, competitive, and punitive desires involved in keeping out and beating down various unworthy candidates for degrees, appointments, or promotions. However, it is often the case that it takes considerable insight and knowledge about the individual to discover such connections. Furthermore, it is rarely the case that some goal like high standards will be connected to just one drive. It is interesting that the result of successful psychotherapy in which there is a real shift in drive configurations does not usually change things like an individual's goal of maintaining high standards, but rather makes the pursuit of such a goal more flexible, less a matter of anxiety, anger, and distress than formerly. The general point is that the basic drives, in so far as we understand them, pervade many goals in a complex fashion, and do not by themselves explain why one goal rather than another is "cathected." To explain this, one needs to know not only the history of the individual, but also the kinds of cultural and personal goal schemas to which the person has been exposed.

At first glance, it may appear that treating goal-schemas as motives (or, more precisely, as "having motivational force") is simply putting new labels on old wine bottles. But this is not the case; using the notion that goal-schemas have motivational force makes it possible to resolve a number of problems that previously undermined attempts at motivational analysis. First, the problem of determining which motives are related to which behaviors can be treated by analyzing means–ends linkages. That is, if one knows that somebody has a particular schema, determining if this serves as a goal for that person should be a relatively straightforward task. Strauss (this volume), for example, is able to determine on the basis of ethnographic interviews and observation that while her sample of working-class Rhode Islanders have learned the American "ethic of success" schema, this does not function as a strong goal, and is only weakly connected to sub-goals and action. The "breadwinner" schema, on the other hand, she finds functions as a powerful goal, with a rich variety of sub-goals and clear connections to individual actions.

Second, the problem of developing a list of motives is resolved in the sense that it becomes clear that there is no one list of human motives – that there are at least as many kinds of motives as there are kinds of goal-schemas. Murray's list of motives is highly culture bound (Suarez-Orozco 1989). An important implication of this point is that it becomes possible to use the techniques which have been developed for identifying schemas as a first step in determining motives. For example, Quinn (this volume), in her investigation of the American model of marriage, finds that the schema for marriage functions, for her informants, as a goal with enough autonomy for her to treat the model of marriage as having a motivational force which can give rise to painful conflicts with other motives.

Third, situational variance becomes explicable: schemas are context-dependent interpretive devices; situations which look the same to the observer may be quite different to the actor. The man who was aggressive with his boss but not his drinking companions, for example, may have a high-level goal-schema about bad authority and the protection of self which triggers boss-attack sub-goals, while the man who was not aggressive with his boss but was aggressive with his companions may have a high-level goal-schema about competition, macho-ness, and self-esteem which triggers bar-room attack sub-goals.

Thus treating motives as goal-schemas results in a different type of description – on both the cultural or the individual level – from the usual treatment of motives as vectors. Basically a vector is something which has both a direction (to get food, to help others, to make money) and an amount – a scale to measure the strength of a drive as indicated by frequency, persistence, emotionality, or fantasy. One might characterize someone with the vector model of motivation by saying that he is high on the need for aggression. This is quite different than saying that someone has a top-level schema in which this person sees himself as threatened by bad authority which will destroy his autonomy. And to say something about the nature of the situations which most strongly activate this interpretation, and more specific sub-goals that are activated whenever this interpretation is regnant, presents a picture of a kind of organized complexity which outlines the way in which various goals are organized and activated. One of the important potentials of treating motivation as schemas with embedded goals is that such an account not only connects cognition to behavior, it also shows how goals are patterned or organized.

The central idea being presented here is that the identification of motives proceeds through the identification of schemas. The theoretical argument goes as follows: (1) schemas, which form the reality-defining system of the human, provide information about what states of the world can and should be pursued; (2) because of the centrality of schemas in determining appropriate action, top-level schemas tend to function as goals; (3) drives, affects, and other kinds of instigations to action function by activating goal-schemas, not by instigating behavior directly, since for humans appropriate action depends on role and setting contexts which require elaborate cognitive interpretation prior to action.

It should be noted that these ideas are not new. McClelland, in his *Personality* (1951) treated schemas – including cultural ones – as a major component of personality, and hypothesized that motives were strongly associated with self-relevant schemas. Schank and Abelson (1977) have considered the ways in which scripts can generate goals. Gallistel (1985) and Mandler (1984) have discussed the ways in which action hierarchies are connected to hierarchies of cognitive schemas. Simon (1967) has looked at the way goals and emotions can be integrated in a general information processing system. Roberts has carried out studies of expressive models of culture (e.g., games of various sorts, sports, institutions such as riddling and jewelry wearing, etc.), pointing out that these models can become deeply motivating (see Roberts 1987 for a general review of these studies).

Motives and culture

At this point, the reader may object that all this theorizing has nothing to do with culture. The response to this objection goes as follows: of the huge number of schemas every human learns, a very important subset are cultural. These cultural schemas range from highly concrete and specific constructs for things like spoons and left-turns to high-level schemas for things like love, success, authority, pollution, and the like.

Since the 1970s cognitive anthropologists have developed a variety of methods for the description of cultural schemas, or cultural models as they are called by Holland and Quinn (1987). Generally, the basic elements of a cultural model will be lexically encoded and used frequently by people in ordinary conversation. Such models have normative properties; inappropriate use is sanctioned. Typically, for most aspects of the model, an investigator can ask direct questions about it and argue with informants using various kinds of counter-examples. While informants usually cannot fully describe such cultural models, they usually can give judgments about the kinds of events and contingencies which are acceptable within the model, and they usually can give explanations which articulate specific workings of the model (see Quinn and Holland 1987 for a review of the methodological issues involved in the identification of culturally based schemas).

My current interest in the relation between motives and schemas came from the finding, as part of a research project on American person perception, that some American cultural models are remarkably similar to some of the needs in the Murray need list. Using a variety of cognitive tasks, including similarity sorting, restricted word associations, ratings of personal characteristics, and free listing of various kinds of personal concerns, it was found for a sample of middle-class American respondents that people were evaluated with respect to three general domains: interpersonal relationships, the world of work, and the world of self. Each of the three domains was found to be subdivided: using factor analytic methods for restricted associations, interpersonal relationships were divided into terms relating to

1. family and home (parents, security, love, support, dependency, etc.)
2. friends and popularity (fun, togetherness, loyalty, openness, acceptance, etc.)
3. spouse and marriage (romance, commitment, sex, children, happiness, etc.)

The domain of work divided into terms clustered around

1. career and money (success, job, work drive, accomplishment, etc.)
2. education and intelligence (knowledge, ability, school, skill, effort, etc.)
3. power and competition (wealth, authority, control, rivals, drive, etc.)

The domain of self was divided into terms clustered about

1. recognition and self-esteem (respect, power, self-confidence, conceit, inferiority, etc.)
2. personal growth and independence (freedom, responsibility, maturity, learning, etc.)
3. comfort and relaxation (luxury, possessions, security, leisure, fun, sports, etc.)

As I began to work on the organization of the propositional networks based on informants' statements about each of these topics, the correspondence between the Murray needs such as affiliation, achievement, and autonomy, and what informants said about friends and jobs and their own selves was obvious. Further, from what has been said about Americans (e.g. Gorer 1964, Inkeles *et al.* 1961) there was good reason to expect that these cultural models did in fact have correspondences to what other investigators had found to be salient American characteristics.

The correspondence between cultural models and Murray needs is especially notable in the case of achievement. Achievement is not a brute fact; an achievement is a culturally constructed object which exists only because some group of humans have developed the notion of "achievement" and agreed that certain things will count as an achievement (D'Andrade 1984). Typically, something counts as an achievement when certain actions, evaluated by some kind of standard of excellence, are judged to be exceptional or outstanding. Standards of excellence are things which people construct, they are not things in the world. Achievement is a culturally constructed object *par excellence*.

These correspondences led to an obvious question: was I carrying out an investigation of needs or of cultural models? An obvious answer was that I was doing both. My first conceptualization of this correspondence used the concepts developed by Austin, Searle, and other speech act theorists. The basic idea was that the statements generated by a cultural model could be considered to have both locutionary (propositional) and illocutionary force (Austin 1962). According to Searle (1975) a statement can have four major kinds of illocutionary force: representative (a speech act which represents how things are in the world, e.g. "The cat is outside"); declarative (a speech act which creates some event or relation which then is taken to be real, e.g. "You're hired"); expressive (a speech act which expresses the speaker's feelings about something, e.g. "Damn cat!") and directive (a speech act which directs the hearer to do something, e.g. "Put out the cat"). Thus it could be said that the statements generated by cultural models had directive force for some people, that is, had a force which made people feel obligated to do what the statement said.

However, the term "directive force" refers to a specific kind of motivation – the moral or quasi-moral sort, where one feels obligation. That was the way I first thought of the connection between schemas and action. But upon reflection it became clear that "sense of obligation" was a special case of the more general phenomenon of motivation, and that schemas were equally central to things people wanted directly – love, friendship, success, etc. And even more complexly, some of these schemas turn out to have their own obligations as well as their direct and indirect rewards, as Quinn points out in her paper in this volume on the conflicts generated by the marriage relationship.

Once formulated in this manner, the relation between the motivational force of cultural models and Spiro's concept of internalization became apparent. Spiro has pointed out that all parts of a culture are not held by people in the same way; that cultural propositions vary in the degree to which they are internalized (1987b). At the first level of internalization, a person is acquainted with at least some part of the cultural system without "assenting to its descriptive or normative claims." Essentially, the person is indifferent to, or may even reject, the beliefs so that the cultural system has no directive force.

At the second level of internalization, cultural beliefs are acquired as clichés – the person "honors" the directive force of the model "more in the breach than the observance." Thus, to use Spiro's example, many Americans say they believe that Jesus died for their sins, and that one ought to care for the poor, but actually have little sense of sin and negligible concern for the poor. "When a cultural system is acquired at this level, it is, as Edward Sapir (1924) put it, 'spurious'." (Spiro n.d. 38)

Continuing from Spiro:

It is only when it is acquired by the actors as a personal belief system – the third level of acquisition – that a cultural system may be said to be *internalized*. When, for example, the propositions that Jesus died for man's sins, and that one ought to care for the poor, are acquired by the actors at this level, they themselves evince a sense of sin and they are generous in their assistance to the poor. Since, at this level, cultural systems are not only external to the actors (they are not only represented in external symbols and other signs), but are internal to them (they engage their minds and influence their action), they are, as Sapir...put it, "genuine."

At the fourth (and final) level of acquisition, the cultural system is not only internalized, but it is highly *salient*. That is, the actors hold it with especially strong conviction because it engages not only their minds, but also their emotions. Thus, believing that Jesus died for man's sins, the actors are preoccupied with their own sins; and believing that one ought to care for the poor, their assistance to the poor represents a personal sacrifice.

Spiro's term "cultural system" is directly comparable to the concept of a cultural model. The concept of "internalization" appears to include in a different metaphor the notion presented above – that certain schemas come to function as positive or negative goals.

Various issues concerning the motivational properties of schemas

One issue that arises in many of the papers is the issue of how goal-schemas are learned. Why does one person have a salient goal-schema for surfing, for example, while someone else does not? Obviously, one must first learn the surfing schema to learn the goals associated with it, but not everybody who learns to surf becomes a surfer. As Holland (this volume) points out, the process of learning itself is complex and interacts with other factors. Holland finds that the learning of the romance model is affected by the degree to which the person gets involved with and feels successful in carrying out romantic activities, and that initial involvement seems to depend on how well the new goals and meanings of the new schema fit the person's already existing self schema.

The learning of motives has long been investigated by anthropologists interested in the relation between culture and personality. The general thesis has been that the learning of motives is a result of the experience of the infant and child as shaped by socialization and parental identifications (Whiting 1961). Roberts has argued that involvement with different kinds of games is affected by previously learned motivational conflicts. Using cross-cultural ratings he has found that games of physical skill go with conflicts about achievement and mastery; games of strategy with conflicts about command and obedience; and games of chance with conflicts about responsibility (Roberts 1987).

The child's experience sometimes preadapts – to use Spiro's term (n.d.:43) – the child to internalize certain cultural propositions. For example, according to Spiro, various experiences of the Burmese infant preadapt Burmese men to internalize at a highly salient level the culturally elaborated schema of women as dangerous creatures – oversexed, polluting, dishonest, unintelligent, and low born. Spiro traces out the behavior and affective consequences of this schema – the sub-goals embedded in this schema such as taboos surrounding women, varieties of avoidances of sexual behavior, along with male maintenance of a sense of superiority and domination by means of culturally constituted fantasies (n.d.).

There are other hypotheses about how schemas acquire motivational properties besides early socialization. Strauss (this volume) finds that life conditions are related to the degree to which schemas can realistically function as goals. She speculates that her sample of Rhode Island working-class men are not strongly motivated by the American success model because their social situation limits their chances for social mobility. For only one man in her sample were the usual goals implicit in the success model actually salient. Strauss notes, however, that the success model does have enough moral force for these men to engage in defensive rationalizations about their own success.

Another point made by Strauss is that some schemas are experienced not as models of reality, but as reality itself. Hutchins has used the term "transparency" to describe the way in which people sometimes see the world through schemas without seeing the schemas themselves (1980). The very transparency of some schemas helps give them motivational force because although the person sees the world a particular way, it is experienced as an undeniable reality. For Strauss's informants, being a breadwinner is a fact of life.

The way in which cultural representations aid in teaching both schemas and the importance of using certain schemas as goals is exemplified by the Llorona folk tale discussed by Mathews in this volume. Hearing such representations teaches people about the appropriate evaluations and goals associated with one's gender, sensitizing the hearer to these linkages and reinforcing those evaluations of sub-goals which are already linked to gender schemas.

Preadaptive socialization experiences, mutually supporting interrelations among cultural schemas, fit between cultural schemas and self schemas, opportunities for pursuing appropriate goals, cultural representations about how schemas should serve as goals, etc., can combine together to create cultural schemas that motivate the individual with great power. Added to these intrinsic motivations, the extrinsic forces of conformity and external reinforcements, including positive and negative sanctions, can combine to form extremely powerful instigations to action. Most sociocultural systems appear to contain a small number of these highly elaborated motivational complexes, or "master motives." In such complexes, the central schema tends to have a number of sub-schemas, each of which contains a variety of sub-goals.

It should be mentioned that only some of any person's schemas with motivational force are formed by cultural models. Many motivationally powerful schemas are learned as part of the direct social experience of the child. Schemas for universal social conditions of the child–parent relationship, such as dependency, nurturance, autonomy, etc., are learned as part of the socialization of every child. How salient such schemas will be, and how strongly they will function as goals, is thought to depend on the child's experience of the affective consequences of these conditions. Sometimes such socially learned schemas will correspond more or less directly to particular cultural models, thereby preadapting the child to those cultural models. However, certain socially learned motivational schemas may not correspond directly to any specific cultural model, although they may be linked indirectly to various cultural models. In her paper in this volume Strauss points out that a number of personal schemas with various degrees of motivational force, linked in complex ways to cultural models, can be identified in an analysis of interview materials (see D'Andrade 1991 for a related analysis of the problems of identifying personal schemas from psychotherapy transcripts).

Implications

Given this account of the motivational properties of schemas, what are its implications for doing ethnographic research? One point, made by Holland, is that much ethnographic work is slanted toward the expert's culture. That is, an ethnographic account of the romantic life of American undergraduate women would probably correspond more to the understandings of those women who are experts in romance than to those who are novices. As Holland puts it,

If expertise, salience, and identification do co-develop in an interrelated process, as argued in this paper, then our descriptions of cultural content – by implication – become even more complicated than we had thought. The manner of formulating the content – as rules and maxims or gestalts (in the way of an expert) – implies a level of expertise, a level of salience, and a level of identification that may in fact be appropriate only for describing a small subset of the people studied. The description may falsely imply a homogeneity of expertise, salience and identification, as well as a homogeneity of content. (This volume: 85)

Some recently developed techniques for describing and analyzing intracultural variation have been presented in a special edition of *Behavioral Science,* edited by James Boster (1987). In accord with Holland's remarks, it is probably a good practice in ethnographic work to estimate how widely expertise in particular cultural models is distributed. For example, Dogon cosmology, as described, is the expert's model. It would be useful to have some estimate of how many of the Dogon control this level of expertise if we are to understand how this model is related to action.

A major implication of the papers in this volume is that the analysis of the motivational properties of cultural models is not esoteric; it can be done as part of any normal ethnographic investigation. The work reported in this volume takes a cognitive approach to the study of culture, but whatever approach is taken – cognitive, interpretive, structural, processual, Marxist, etc. – at some point every ethnographer will describe a variety of interrelated cultural beliefs and understandings. Whether these complexes are called schemas, cultural models, ideology, structures, or whatever, is unimportant. Given a particular culturally based complex of understandings and beliefs about some aspect of the world, ethnographic questions can be asked about the degree to which this complex serves as a goal. Those upper-level models of the world with strong motivational force should be easy to identify because of their relatively direct connection to observable goal striving.

Many ethnographies contain at least some information of this sort; Evans-Pritchard, for example, presents graphic descriptions of the way in which the complex Nuer model of cattle gives rise to strong feelings and goal strivings concerning cattle such as the raiding of cattle. Vogt's ethnography, *Modern Homesteaders,* which is the study of values of a small New Mexican farming community in the early 1950s, describes how certain cultural models common to many American farming commu nities (e.g. mastery of nature, individual autonomy, group superiority, emphasis on future achievement, etc.), function not only as powerful sources of value, but also as master motives. There is a special theoretical interest in the case of these homesteaders because they live in a physical environment which continuously frustrates the accomplishment of many of the goals invoked by these cultural models. Despite great difficulties, the homesteaders pursued persistently these goal-schemas and resisted governmental, economic, and practical pressures to change. Once internalized, it appears that cultural schemas are difficult to abandon or even modulate.

However, in most ethnographic reports, information about the motivational aspects of cultural models is unsystematically presented. One use of the ideas presented here is to initiate the building of an explicit conceptual framework for what is often a neglected part of ethnography. With further conceptual development it should be possible to orientate an entire ethnography around the description of the motivational properties of central cultural models.

Concluding

The general argument of this paper is that motivation forms one link between culture and action. A hoped-for by-product of this argument is to highlight the irrelevance of theoretical conceptions of culture which have no psychological reality and cannot be related to either action or feeling. Psychological reductionism has been a great fear of a large number of social and cultural anthropologists. Perhaps if it is seen that psychological constructs, such as schema and motive, offer real understanding of the part culture plays in shaping action, some of this fear will dissolve – at least for those who have not already strongly internalized a psychophobic schema of culture.

This general "pro-psychology" position involves a related point, the need for a theoretical specification of exactly how culture is related to action. It will not do to simply say "action is culturally constituted" or "the self is culturally consituted" or "emotion is culturally constituted." Such a position is wrong for a number of reasons. First, it postulates a causal link ("x constitutes y") without specifying any kind of mechanism or process by which x and y might be connected. At best this kind of talk is a huge oversight, at worst it is word magic. Second, it ignores the salient fact that not all of any culture is internalized in anybody. Much of any culture remains at the "cliché" level – sometimes called "ideal culture" – and does not influence action. Third, different individuals internalize different parts of the same culture in different ways, so that the statement "action is culturally constituted" deeply misrepresents the degree of individual and group variation within a culture. Fourth, as most anthropologists in moments of intellectual sobriety recognize, action, the self, emotion, etc., are influenced by many things besides culture – the way the human body is constructed, the way the brain works, social factors of many kinds, economic considerations, individual interests, etc. To trace out the process by which culture influences action requires a theoretical multi-causal vocabulary which can encompass variation and similarity; the argument here is that motivational and cognitive concepts form an important part of such a vocabulary.

REFERENCES

Austin J. L.
1962 *How to Do Things with Words*. Oxford: Oxford University Press.

Bilmes, Jack
    1986 *Discourse and Behavior*. New York: Plenum Press.
Boster, James
    1987 Intracultural Variation. *American Behavioral Scientist* 31(2):150–52.
Casson, Ronald W.
    1983 Schemata in Cognitive Anthropology. In *Annual Review of Anthropology*.
        Pp. 429–62.
Chase, W. G. and H. A. Simon
    1973 Perception in Chess. *Cognitive Psychology* 4:55–81.
D'Andrade, Roy G.
    1981 The Cultural Part of Cognition. *Cognitive Science* 5:179–95.
    1984 Cultural Meaning Systems. In *Culture Theory: Essays on the Social Origins
        of Mind, Self, and Emotion*, R. A. Shweder and R. LeVine, eds. Chicago:
        University of Chicago Press. Pp 88–123.
    1987 A Folk Model of the Mind. In *Cultural Models in Language and Thought*,
        D. Holland and N. Quinn, eds. New York: Cambridge University Press.
        Pp. 112–48.
    1991 The Identification of Schemas in Naturalistic Data. In *Person Schemas and
        Maladaptive Interpersonal Behavior Patterns*, M. Horowitz, ed. Chicago:
        University of Chicago Press. Pp. 279–310.
Fromm, Eric
    1944 Individual and Social Origins of Neurosis. *American Sociological Review*
        9:380–4.
Gallistel, Charles R.
    1985 Motivation, Intention, and Emotion: Goal Directed Behavior from a
        Cognitive-Neuroethological Perspective. In *Goal Directed Behavior: The
        Concept of Action in Psychology*, M. Frese and J. Sabini, eds. Hillsdale, NJ:
        Lawrence Erlbaum. Pp. 48–65.
Gorer, Geoffrey
    1964 *The American People: A Study in National Character*. Revised ed. New
        York: W. W. Norton.
Holland, Dorothy and Naomi Quinn
    1987 *Cultural Models in Language and Thought*. New York: Cambridge
        University Press.
Hutchins, Edwin
    1980 *Culture and Inference: A Trobriand Case Study*. Cambridge, MA: Harvard
        University Press.
Inkeles, Alex, E. Hanfmann, and H. Beier
    1961 Modal Personality and Adjustment of the Soviet Socio-Political System. In
        Studying Personality Cross-Culturally, B. Kaplan, ed. Evanston, IL: Row,
        Peterson. Pp. 201–24.
Lakoff, George
    1987 *Women, Fire, and Dangerous Things*. Chicago: University of Chicago Press.
Landauer, Thomas K.
    1986 How Much Do People Remember? Some Estimates of the Quantity of
        Learned Information in Long Term Memory. *Cognitive Science* 10:477-93.
Langacker, Ronald
    1987 *Foundations of Cognitive Grammar*. Stanford: Stanford University Press.

McClelland, David C.
1951 *Personality*. New York: William Sloane.
McClelland, David C., John W. Atkinson, R. Clark, and E. Lowell
1953 *The Achievement Motive*. New York: Appleton-Century-Crofts.
Mandler, George
1984 *Mind and Body*. New York: W. W. Norton.
Mischel, Walter
1968 *Personality and Assessment*. New York: Wiley.
Mook, Douglas G.
1987 *Motivation: The Organization of Action*. New York: W. W. Norton.
Murphy, G.
1947 *Personality: A Biosocial Approach to Origins and Structure*. New York: Harper.
Murray, Henry A.
1938 *Explorations in Personality*. New York: Oxford University Press.
Quinn, Naomi and Dorothy Holland
1987 Introduction. In *Cultural Models in Language and Thought*, D. Holland and N. Quinn, eds. New York: Cambridge University Press. Pp. 3–40
Roberts, John M.
1987 Within Culture Variation. *American Behavioral Scientist* 31:266-79.
Rosen, Bernard C.
1962 Socialization and Achievement Motivation in Brazil. *American Sociological Review* 27:612–24.
Rumelhart, D., J. McClelland, and the PDP Research Group
1986 *Parallel Distributed Processing*, Vol. I: *Foundations*. Cambridge, MA: MIT Press.
Sapir, Edward
1924 Culture: Genuine and Spurious. *American Journal of Sociology* 24:401–29.
Schank, Roger C. and Robert Abelson
1977 *Scripts, Plans, Goals, and Understanding*. Hillsdale, NJ: Lawrence Erlbaum.
Searle, J. R.
1975 A Taxonomy of Illocutionary Acts. In *Language, Mind, and Knowledge*, K. Gunderson, ed. Minneapolis: University of Minnesota Press.
Simon, Herbert A.
1967 Motivational and Emotional Controls of Cognition. *Psychological Review* 74:29–39.
Singer, Jerome and Peter Salovey
1991 Organized Knowledge Structures and Personality: Person Schemas, Self-Schemas, Prototypes, and Scripts. In *Person Schemas and Maladaptive Interpersonal Behavior Patterns*, M. Horowitz, ed. Chicago: University of Chicago Press. Pp. 33–79.
Spiro, Melford E.
1987a Social Systems, Personality, and Functional Analysis. In *Culture and Human Nature: Theoretical Papers of Melford E. Spiro*, B. Kilborne and L. L. Langness, eds. Chicago: University of Chicago Press. Pp. 109–44.
1987b Collective Representations and Mental Representations in Religious Symbol Systems. In *Culture and Human Nature: Theoretical Papers of*

Melford E. Spiro. B. Kilborne and L. L. Langness, eds. Chicago: University of Chicago Press. Pp. 161–84.

n.d. Cultural Ideology and Social Reality: An Essay on Cultural Internalization. Manuscript.

Stinson, Charles and Stephen Palmer
1991 Parallel Distributed Processing Models, Person Schemas and Psychopathologies. In *Person Schemas and Maladaptive Interpersonal Behavior Patterns*, M. Horowitz, ed. Chicago: University of Chicago Press. Pp. 339–77.

Suarez-Orozco, M. M.
1989 Psychological Aspects of Achievement Motivation among Recent Hispanic Immigrants. In *Anthropological Perspectives on Dropping Out*, H. Trueba, G. Spindler, and L. Spindler, eds. London: Falmer Press. Pp. 99–116

Vogt, Evon Z.
1955 *Modern Homesteaders: The Life of a Twentieth-Century Frontier Community*. Cambridge, MA: Harvard University Press.

Whiting, John W. M.
1941 *Becoming a Kwoma*. New Haven: Yale University Press.
1961 Socialization Process and Personality. In *Psychological Anthropology: Approaches to Culture and Personality*, F. L. K. Hsu, ed. Homewood, IL: The Dorsey Press. Pp. 355–80.

Winter, David G., David C. McClelland, and Abigail J. Stewart
1981 *A New Case for the Liberal Arts*. San Francisco: Jossey-Bass.

3   Ghost busters in anthropology[1]

Richard A. Shweder

Friedrich Nietzsche is not an acknowledged founding father of cultural anthropology, yet, far more than is realized, his way of thinking propagated and took over in modern anthropology. Some time in the 1880s Nietzsche thought he had the answer to the central question I shall address, which concerns the experience of felt obligation.

That central question is this: how are we to represent the directive content of a culture and how are we to explain and/or justify its directive or motivational force? That is, what are the directives of a culture and why in the world do people feel bound or compelled to obey their commands? Nietzsche's answer to the question is given in one of his famous aphorisms: "being moral means being highly accessible to fear." Most contemporary anthropologists seem to think he was right, at least in one crucial respect.

Nietzsche's aphorism neatly and radically divides into two isolated or independent parts our central question. On the one hand there is the question: how are we to represent the directive content of a culture? That directive content, the "moral" order, includes, for Nietzsche, not only the specific obligations of a tradition – bury the dead – but also the various demand-generating principles – God, sin, justice, rights, duty – that support them. On the other hand there is the question: how are we to explain and/or justify its directive or motivational force. It should be noted that Nietzsche explains rather than justifies the directive force of culture; for he believes there is no justification for a fear-driven feeling of boundedness to the received injunctions of one's tradition.

It is that radical division of explanatory labor that has appealed to so many contemporary anthropologists and social theorists. Indeed, the very first step in most analyses of society as a moral order is to partition the "content" and "force" aspects of obligation into separate boxes. In one box, sometimes labeled "culture," gets put the doctrines, symbols, discourse, maxims and "information" definitive of the injunctions of a tradition – eat with a fork not with your hands, do not make love to your sister, widows may not remarry, all "swarming things" are prohibited food, except crickets and grasshoppers, etc. In a second box, sometimes labeled "personality," gets put the motives, desires, needs and "energy" which explain feelings of commitment to those injunctions.

The idioms used for describing those feelings of commitment may vary across cultures, yet an experiential core is recognizable: the feeling of being under the command of God or bound by some force greater than the self; the experience of guilt or dread or loss of sanctity; the experience of a compulsion or constraint superior to the ego; Freud's super-ego, Durkheim's collective conscience, Kant's categorical imperative.

Not everyone agrees with Nietzsche that it is fear *per se* that explains the force behind the directive content of culture. Some argue that the force has its source in a universal desire to produce agreeable feelings in high-status members of your ingroup, or that it is a by-product of defensive identification and the resolution of the Oedipus conflict. Many other external "energy" sources have been proposed to account for the directive force that gets attached to the directive content of a cultural tradition.

Not everyone labels the two boxes in the same way. Some have two boxes with names like "primary" (adaptive institutions) and "secondary" (cultural institutions) on them. Others have boxes with names like "ideology" and "disguised interests" on them. Whatever the names on the boxes, however, most social theorists follow Nietzsche in having two of them, and in having the directive force of culture as something external to, or outside of, or a supplement to, the directive content of culture. The directive force of culture, according to that widespread view, is not something that can be accounted for simply by reference to the directive content of a tradition. Information, it is argued, cannot supply its own energy.

D'Andrade (1981:192–3) makes a very similar observation about theories in anthropology when he notes that "many social scientists break cultural representations into two components – 'affective' and 'ideational'." D'Andrade views the analytic distinction as abnormal. It is abnormal in the sense that the ordinary language expressions of a culture seem quite able to fuse together and to represent simultaneously, within a unitary description (such as "John is a crook"), a proposition about a state of the "external" world ("Joe took funds in a manner that could be prosecuted by law") conjoined with a proposition about our "internal" reactions to it ("this has made me angry and I want him punished.") The great challenge for culture theory, as I see it, is to find a way to defend and justify this commonplace ordinary language practice of merging or conflating things that so many analysts have felt compelled, by their theory of culture, to separate.

That challenge is to develop a theory of culture and human motivation in which the directive force of culture can be understood in terms of its directive content. This will require a major break with received wisdom, and success is by no means guaranteed. For it is by no means obvious that the "external" world of nature, independent of human involvement with it and reactions to it, contains something called a "crook"; and if it is merely a factual description of the world that "Joe took some funds in a manner which could be prosecuted by law" then that is all it is, a factual description with no "logical" or "rational" force to impel the reaction "I am angry and want him punished."

Indeed, it is precisely because the ordinary language expression "Joe is a crook" does lend itself to analysis into separate components, the "ideational" and the "affective," that once those components have been separated out and laid bare, the hard work begins: to justify fusing them back together by showing how the force of the reaction (anger) "logically" or "rationally" follows from the description of the act. The goal is to fuse, through a theory of culture, the directive force of culture to its directive content, without the assistance of a supplementary irrational or extra-rational or extrinsic energy source. That is not going to be easy, and the stakes are high.

Historically the radical separation of the directive content of culture from its directive force has been justified by an appeal to two very powerful arguments. To overturn those arguments would be tantamount to a revolutionary (or perhaps, counter-revolutionary, that is, premodern) rethinking of the relationship between culture and nature, subjectivity and objectivity.

The first argument is Nietzsche's null-reference ("God is dead") argument. One very terse version goes like this: from the point of view of a "scientific" description of the directly observable world, the "things" (for example, God, sin, natural rights) do not objectively exist with respect to which most people feel bound. Thus, since there are no such things as Gods, sin, or "natural" rights, etc., the experience of their directive force (for example, guilt following transgression) is irrational and illusory, and must have its source in something other than a rational respect for objective reality itself.

Nietzsche's null-reference argument can be more fully explicated by considering his answer to one of anthropology's most provocative questions, the "witch" question: cross-culturally and historically, why have so many accused witches been positively convinced of their own guilt? One conceivable answer to that question is this: because they were witches.

I happen to think that something like that is the kind of answer that will have to be defended if the directive content of culture (for example, the idea of being a "witch") is going to be put to work as an explanation for the directive force of culture (for example, guilt leading to confession), without having to appeal to an extrinsic energy source.

Nietzsche's answer is quite different and, not surprisingly, it sits comfortably with the modern ways of thinking of which it was an expression, and to which it gave rise. Says Nietzsche: "Although the most acute judges of the witches, and even the witches themselves, were convinced of the guilt of witchery, the guilt nevertheless was non-existent." He goes on to say, shockingly, "It is thus with all guilt."

Nietzsche gives a null-reference answer to the witch question. Then he generalizes the null-reference argument to each and every case where the following two conditions hold: (1) a supposed objective-external yet invisible entity is invoked (e.g., God, witches, natural rights); (2) with respect to that unseen thing the self is supposed to be subordinate, bound or guilty.

As you can see, Nietzsche not only suspected that God was dead. Under the influence of an empiricist or positivist philosophy of science, with which he flirted at various times in his career, Nietzsche had doubts about the objective existence of all unseen things, including God, witches, souls, sin, necessity, rights, values, and moral obligations.

Positivism is empiricism in its purest form. Its central doctrine is that only seeing is believing, while any other claim to knowledge is either tautology or metaphysical nonsense. According to the positivists, only the senses can get you to reality. In his work *Human, All Too Human* (1982 : 481) Nietzsche put it this way:

And what magnificent instruments of observation we possess in our senses...Today we possess science precisely to the extent to which we have decided to *accept* the testimony of the senses – to the extent to which we sharpen them further, arm them, and have learned to think them through. The rest is miscarriage and not-yet-science – in other words, metaphysics, theology, psychology, epistemology – or formal science, a doctrine of signs such as logic and that applied logic which is called mathematics. In them reality is not encountered at all, not even as a problem...

That is the same Nietzsche who, moved by a positivistic impulse, described Asia as a "dreamy" place where they still do "not know how to distinguish between truth and poetry."

The gist of a null-reference argument goes like this: when it comes to God, sin, morality, obligation, necessity, and witchery there is nothing real "out there" in the nature of things to be guilty of, or to be bound by. Thus, there is no objective basis for the experience of being commanded by God; or for a feeling of sin; or for a pang of conscience; or for a perception of inevitability and necessity; or for the conviction that one is a witch; or for the directive "force" of culture. Such experiences, feelings, pangs, perceptions, convictions, and compulsions tell us nothing about the external world but much about phantoms that haunt the human mind.

Nietzsche reasons on. Moral obligations are phantoms, not objective facts out there waiting to be discovered through positive inquiry. Belief in the God-phantom, sin-phantom, conscience-phantom, and witch-phantom is little more than slavish susceptibility to custom, suggestion, indoctrination, conformity, reward or social pressure – extrinsic compulsions which explain our subordination to the directives of our culture. We certainly do not feel bound by our obligations because they are true, for there is nothing out there for them to be true of.

God (that is, objective reality) has been long dead for contemporary anthropologists. The major measure of his fate is that almost all theory in contemporary anthropology designed to explain the origin and function of other peoples' ideas (e.g., sin, ancestral spirit attack) and practices (fasting, pilgrimage, confession, self-flagellation) is made possible by a Nietzschian null-reference assumption. Nietzsche's answer to the "witch question" (they don't exist) has become the "conventional" wisdom. This is quite ironical since it was Nietzsche who advised: part from your cause as soon as it triumphs; hold suspect all "received wisdom" and cross-examine it as a prejudice from the past.

Despite Nietzsche's admonition, his null-reference reasoning has become the conventional form of reasoning in anthropology. Prominent theorists of culture who are in dispute about almost everything else share with each other the Nietzschean assumption that tradition-based beliefs are phantoms of mind. In general, so-called "super"-natural entities, feelings of moral obligation (the directive force of culture), and society itself are presumed to have standing only as internal mental representations or as collective subjectivity projected into or reified as a symbolic form. Out of anthropological theory comes the resounding judgment that the native has confused his or her own mental constructs with external reality, and that the world in which he or she lives is a kind of fantasy or delusion or false consciousness.

Murdock (1980:89), with characteristic directness, gives clear expression to this anthropological judgment, although cognate formulations could be cited from theorists as diverse as Schneider, Spiro and Foucault (indeed, we are all prone to the fashion). Thus, while reflecting upon the category of "sin" among the Semang (the Semang seem to believe it is a sin to comb your hair during a thunderstorm, or to tell a joke to your mother-in-law), Murdock asserts that the ethical doctrines of other peoples are often arbitrary and devoid of objective justification. Nietzsche-like, he argues that, among the Semang, feelings of obligation have their origin in fear of the sanctioning power of a phantom called God

– a learning process by which one phantom (God) begets another phantom (sin).

Most contemporary anthropologists are modern, without assuming much responsibility for it. Being modern they are Nietzschean individualists, and being Nietzschean individualists and anthropologists they spend their time analyzing other people's ideas about reality, constraint, and obligation as though "reality," "constraint," and "obligation" ought to be put in quotation marks. They see a culture's view of "things" and "obligations" as meanings imposed or projected by human beings onto an inchoate world, imposed meanings first dignified by each generation as so-called "objective knowledge" about the world and then passed off as "received wisdom" from one generation to the next. Under the influence of Nietzschean null-reference reasoning (all those things people bow down before do not exist) a central problematic for anthropological theory is the question of how to explain the purported fact that so many phantom-like, delusionary, or arbitrary ideas have got themselves lodged and stuck inside people's heads.

Accordingly, under the influence of Nietzschean assumptions, culture theorists seem to sort themselves out into two major Nietzschean roles: the "ghost busters" and the "psyche-analysts."

The "ghost busters" engage in the revelatory unmasking of other people's pious beliefs about reality and obligation, dramatically exposed by the anthropologist as phantom culture. The goal is to promote free individualism (rebellion and liberation) through the criticism of cultural beliefs and social practices. Numerous phantoms (in addition to God, sin, and witches) have been added to the Nietzschean list of things that do not exist, except in the self-deceiving mind of its beholder: childhood, kinship, authority, sacredness, even ethnographic writing itself – all now listed as figments of a compliant imagination held hostage to the sway of convention.

Then there are the "psyche-analysts." These try to understand the origin and function of all those notorious ideas about reality and obligation that seem to haunt the human mind. The "psyche-analysts" try to develop a positive science and/or an interpretive discipline for the study of other-than-rational and less-than-rational processes to help account for the perplexing worldwide distribution of what appears to them as a slavish susceptibility to custom and tradition. Thus, when it comes to explaining the origin and function of the directive force behind cultural obligations – that feeling of being under the command of something greater than the self – the literature on conscience and super-ego formation is rich in postulated irrational processes. Some theorists point to fear, others point to hostility meant for the father directed against oneself, still others to defensive identification, etc.

Whichever the anthropologist's preferred calling – ghost buster or psyche-analyst – we end up with those two neatly separated analytic boxes. On the one hand, there is the "directive content" of a culture, which makes claims to authority over the mind of the native by reference to things that, according to Nietzscheans, do not exist. On the other hand, there is the "directive force" behind culture, which is real enough as a force in experience, but which, according to the ghost busters and psyche-analysts, certainly cannot derive its force, as that force is experienced, from things that are unreal. And, of course they are right, if those things are unreal.

So, why have so many accused witches been positively convinced of their own guilt? "Because they were witches" is something like the kind of answer that will have to be defended if the directive force of culture (e.g., feeling guilty and confessing to witchcraft) is to be derived from its directive content (e.g., witchcraft exists, and it is evil and should not be practiced), and if it is to be done without the postulation of irrational or extrarational states of mind.

That kind of answer will not be easy to defend, of course. Yet speaking on behalf of the defense it seems to me it is a noble challenge. The challenge is to restore realism and reference to cultural concepts; it is to show how cultural meanings can work to illuminate aspects of reality, rather than to fantasize or hallucinate or mystify them.

The second argument standing as a hurdle before a rationalist or realist view of the directive force of culture is the so-called "naturalistic fallacy," the argument that it is logically impossible to derive a moral or directive conclusion from a premise consisting merely of a factual description of the objective world. Thus, for example, in the orthodox Hindu community where I do research on moral argumentation (Shweder and Miller 1985; Shweder, Mahapatra and Miller 1987; Shweder and Much 1987) the apparently factual premise "she is a widow" is often used to support an evaluative or directive conclusion to the effect "it is bad, wrong, improper and inadvisable for her to eat fish, meat, garlic, onions and all other foods classified as 'hot' foods, and she should be stopped from doing it."

According to the "naturalistic fallacy" argument, since nothing about the object world *per se* (e.g., the fact that such-and-such a person is dead) lends logical support to any particular normative conclusion, the subjective feeling that the facts impel you to do this and not to do that is, once again, illusory and irrational, and must have its source in something other than a rational respect for reality.

Notice, quite crucially, the concept of reality presupposed by the argument. Reality, it is presupposed, consists solely of observable events or directly measurable states of the world as they exist independently of human involvement with them or reactions to them. As the argument goes, there is nothing you can observe about exterior states of the object world that logically impels you to one type of evaluative attitude ("this is right and good") versus some other ("this is wrong and bad").

The main point of the "naturalistic fallacy" argument, if I understand it, reduces to a very simple and undefeatable truism: if the exterior, object world is described in a value-free way, then those descriptions carry no implications for values.

A major implication of the argument is that the logical gap cannot be crossed between the objective world of events and objects and the subjective world of evaluative attitudes to them. The only way across the logical gap between statements of fact ("the female next door whose husband died last year just ate some fish") and assertions of evaluative attitude ("I want to banish her from the community") is through the brute force of some irrational or extrarational projection.

In ordinary language and folk culture, of course, the gap is crossed all the time. But, according to those who prefer to keep things in two boxes, ordinary language and folk culture do it by brute force. That is why (so the argument goes) we have a vast literature on conformity, rich in postulated irrational or extrarational processes for explaining obedience to traditional obligations or obedience to the so-called mystifications built into the conventions of ordinary language. There is fear of disapproval, and dread of sanctions, and imitation and modeling, and so forth.

Those two arguments (the Nietzschean null-reference argument and the naturalistic fallacy argument) are formidable obstacles to any attempt to link through rational processes or reality-testing the directive content of culture to its directive force. The two arguments, if accepted without revision, virtually guarantee that the directive content of culture, the things "out there" to which cultural notions refer, cannot explain its directive force, and that something else (an irrational or extrarational energy source) must be added to do that explanatory work. Let me reiterate by means of an example from Orissa, India.

Orthodox Hindu Brahman men tell me they must never address their father by his first name, because their father is a "moving God" and they are his "devotee." Orthodox Hindu Brahman women tell me that they must never ask their husband to massage their legs, because their husband is a "moving God" and they are his "devotee."

The problem I face as an ethnographer trying to understand and make sense of those assertions is the following: if Gods do not exist, and if your father or your husband is not a God, and if the description "he is my father" or "he is my husband" logically or rationally implies nothing about your evaluative attitude towards him or how he ought to be treated or behave (as a God), then whatever you feel impelled to do (address him with a term of respect; keep your distance) or not do (address him with a first name; ask for a massage) must have its origins in an extra-logical or illogical source – such as fear, indoctrination, cultural conditioning, conformity, etc.

Now try to imagine for a moment that Gods exist, and that fathers and husbands are Gods. Imagine that somewhere within your conception of what the world is like ("he is a moving God; I am his devotee") there is contained the idea of the proper ends or levels of excellence, the *telos*, that things in the world might realize if, through cultivation and enlightenment, those things were to realize their potential.

If you can imagine those things then you can see that in that world there would be no difficulty establishing an "internal" (one-box) connection between the directive content of culture and its directive force. In such a world the state-of-the-world description "as a son I am the devotee of my father, the moving God" would illuminate some aspect of reality. The idea of "reality" would include, or contain within itself, the proper end or level of excellence that a thing might obtain. The "good" devotee as well as the "worthless" devotee would be objective facts of the world; and the really real world would consist of the level of fulfillment that things might obtain when functioning at maximum potential.

What I am presenting here is, of course, a skeletal version of the ancient teleological vision of reality. In such a teleological world, nature itself is perceived to be striving for, or at least capable of, the attainment of some natural state of genuine excellence (the "good" for that thing). A major theoretical advantage of a teleological view of reality is that the idea of the "good" is contained within the idea of reality; thus the feeling that one is obliged or bound to do this or that can, in a straightforward way, be derived from that one pervasive, characteristically human motive that sometimes goes by the name "the reality principle."

That motive, the reality principle, simply states: have a decent level of respect for the objective constraints of reality, be in touch with what is real, strive to eliminate error and contradiction from your thinking, and let there be a proportionate fit between the real nature of an object or situation and your subjective response to it.

The reality principle defines an ideal form for a one-boxed approach to the analysis of culture and motivation. The aim of such an analysis is to portray, by means of the reality principle, the internal ("logical," "rational") connection between reality and a culture's conceptions of it and reactions to it.

I have described one way to derive the directive force of culture from the directive content, without having to appeal to any motive other than the reality principle. That way is to adopt the ancient and very widespread teleological view of reality, where contained within the objective world is the idea of the "good" and the standards of maturity or excellence that objects can achieve. I recognize (with some regret) that the proposal is probably too much to stomach for modern sensibilities. But, even if that is the case, take comfort, for there is an alternative way to derive the directive force of culture from the directive content, without having to appeal to supplementary motives other than the reality principle.

That alternative is to stop trying to represent the world independently of the human experience of it and human involvement with it. While it remains a debatable and open issue whether this is an advisable strategy for comprehending the non-artifactual physical world, there is much to recommend it for the comprehension of social reality and the directive force of culture.

The basic idea, which I take to be D'Andrade's central point (1981, this volume), is that social reality is built up out of concepts and terms (so-called intentional concepts) that already contain within their semantic meaning propositions about our needs, motives, and desires and the way we respond to the world.

Our "natural" language supplies us with many examples of concepts whose very meaning depends on reference to our needs, desires, purposes, and responses to the world: functional concepts and terms (for example, for tools, body parts, and, quite crucially, social roles), concepts and terms for so-called "institutional facts" (for example, promising), and concepts and terms for objects of art or artifice (e.g. a "weed").

What, for example, is a "weed"? A "weed," one might propose, is something you do not want growing in your garden; hence a rose in your vegetable patch might be plucked out as a weed. There is no third-person, "scientific," botanical, independent-of-human-response, anatomical, genetic, or chemical definition of plants that can specify which objects count as "weeds." "Weeds" are not (so-called) "natural kinds," yet "weeds" are as real as raindrops, even though we, and our responses to them, are directly implicated in their existence.

And what is a "chair"? It is something that a person can sit on. And what is a "mother"? Certainly what a mother is for, for us, is part of its meaning; and if you have the chance to be a mother you are not a good one unless you recognize your obligation to strive to live up to the standard of excellence defined by her social function.

When it comes to intentional concepts, the force of the concept is "internal" to its content. That content has already taken account of our needs, desires, motives, and purposes, and the force internal to that content becomes activated as soon as it is drawn out and properly understood. Thus it is not a violation of the naturalistic fallacy to say "She is his mother; therefore she ought to care about her child's strep infection."

It is not a violation of the naturalistic fallacy because the factual premise ("She is his mother") is not a description of the world independent of our involvement with it. The factual premise already contains within its proper meaning our beliefs about the importance of the obligations associated with protection and nurturing of the vulnerable. The evaluative and directive conclusion ("Therefore she ought to care about her child's strep infection") simply draws out the logical implications of a factual description of a world built up out of intentional concepts, concepts that are designated "intentional" precisely because they portray a world indissociable from our desires towards it, reactions to it, and beliefs about it.

Here is another example of the way factual descriptions are used with directive force in a real world built up out of intentional concepts. The example comes from Shweder and Much (1987), and it consists of a brief verbal exchange between a teacher (Mrs. Swift) and a 4-year-old child (Alice) in an American preschool classroom.

Alice is seated at a table. She has a glass full of water. Mrs. Swift the teacher approaches and addresses Alice. The verbal exchange contains three utterances:

1. Mrs. Swift: That is not a paper cup.
2. Alice: I want to put it down (broken, whimpering voice).
3. Mrs. Swift (taking the glass away from Alice): No, that's just for snack time when the teacher is at the table.

Now one can imagine a two-boxed approach to the analysis of this episode, where one tries hard to keep analytically distinct the directive content of the episode from its directive force. The teacher, a powerful and high-status member of the child's social world imposes upon the child an arbitrary and convention-based directive (children must use paper cups and not glasses, except at snack time with the teacher's supervision), which bears no logical or rational relationship to the factual descriptive premise "That is not a paper cup" (which from a factual descriptive point of view is true of almost every object in the classroom!). The logical or rational gap between the factual premise ("That is not a paper cup") and the directive conclusion ("Put it down!") is bridged by the brute force of the teachers "weight" as an object of fear or identification, or what have you, and the child whimpering with anxiety is motivated by "extrinsic" forces to associate the commanded evaluative attitude (avoidance) with the factual object (the glass).

An alternative, one-boxed analysis, in which there is no logical or rational gap between the factual premise and the directive conclusion, might look something like this. The terms and concepts we use to describe the world take account of our needs and desires. Thus the state-of-the-world description, "That is not a paper cup," used in that context (an adult approaching a 4-year-old who is holding in her hand a drinking vessel made of glass), already contains within itself the directive conclusion, "Put it down!"

The factual premise "That is not a paper cup" is a category contrast, meaning "That is not a paper cup, it is a glass." It refers the meaning of the event to what is assumed to be known about the relevant differences between paper cups and glasses (a potential for harm through breakage), focusing the meaning of the event on the issue of harm, and thus encoding within the factual premise the issue of potential harm and the human motivation of harm avoidance. Although the teacher never explicitly mentions the issue of harm, the child seems to understand it, as she shows by her offer to "put it [the glass] down" (so that she would be less likely to break it?).

The teacher's utterance ("That is not a paper cup") leaves a lot unsaid. Indeed, no one has actually stated that paper cups are different from glasses because glasses break, or that glasses are dangerous when broken, or that young children (you Alice) are insufficiently competent or conscientious to be trusted with the unsupervised use of fragile and potentially harmful materials. Nor has anyone mentioned the directive proposition lurking behind all this: that teachers (adults?) should take responsiblity for protecting young children from classroom activities in which they are at risk of injuring themselves. All that factual and directive content remains implicit in what was said, yet all of it is necessary for an understanding of what was said. And anyone who understood what was said would have no difficulty understanding why the teacher was highly motivated to get Alice to use a paper cup instead of a glass, and why Alice, if she understood what was said, might be motivated by the force of reason and the reality principle to do what the teacher implicitly directed her to do: put it down!

Please note that I am not saying that the "weight" of the teacher's authority position (she is the highest-status member of the local in-group, and it is her classroom) added nothing to the force of her directive. Her "weight" may well have got the child to attend to the message or to treat it as an important communication. But I would argue that the main force of the message comes from the "inner" or "internal" logic of its directive content, which is already sufficiently well adapted to the needs and desires of the child that it may appeal to her reason. The teacher's "weight" is merely status in the service of reality testing; and as long as hierarchy and power are used in defense of truth, beauty and goodness, why should anyone complain?

NOTES

1 One part of this essay is a condensation of a more extensive treatment of Nietzchean reasoning, which can be found in Shweder (1991, chapter 1).

REFERENCES

D'Andrade, R.G.
1981 The Cultural Part of Cognition. *Cognitive Science* 5:179–95.
Murdock, G.P.
1980 *Theories of Illness*. Pittsburgh: University of Pittsburgh Press.
Nietzsche, Friedrich
1982 *The Portable Nietzsche*, Walter Kaufmann, ed. and trans. New York: Penguin Books.
Shweder, R. A.
1991 *Thinking Through Cultures: Expeditions in Cultural Psychology*. Cambridge, Mass: Harvard University Press.
Shweder, R.A., M. Mahapatra, and J.G. Miller
1987 Culture and Moral Development. In *The Emergence of Morality in Young Children*, J. Kagan and S. Lamb, eds. Chicago: University of Chicago Press. Reprinted in J. Stigler, R. A. Shweder, and G. Herdt, Eds. *Cultural Psychology*. New York: Cambridge University Press.
Shweder, R.A. and J.G. Miller
1985 The Social Construction of the Person: How Is It Possible? In *Social Construction of the Person*, K. Gergen and K. Davis, eds. New York: Springer Verlag. Reprinted in Shweder, 1991.
Shweder, R.A. and N.C. Much
1987 Determinations of Meanings: Discourse and Moral Socialization. In *Moral Development Through Social Interaction*, W. Kurtines and J. Gerwirtz, eds. New York: John Wiley. Reprinted in Shweder, 1991.

Part II

How do cultural models become motives?

4 How cultural systems become desire: a case study of American romance

Dorothy C. Holland

> ... she took him to the prom ... he was about 26 ... he was with a whole lot of girls, it wasn't like he was just talking to her ... she really didn't know what she was getting into ...

Americans speak of romance as though it were a "natural" activity which most find intrinsically motivating and which most, by the time they reach a certain age, engage in at a reasonable level of competence. In the quote, Cylene, a woman in the study to be described, alludes to a much less frequently encountered conception, namely that "affairs of the heart" are an area of expertise. This chapter addresses the infrequent recognition that expertise in romantic pursuits is learned and that the motivating force of romance – as culturally constructed in the United States – may not come about automatically, but rather is formed in the learning process. The larger issue concerns the ways in which cultural models come to have "directive force."[1]

In the study, we followed Cylene – the woman quoted above – and twenty-two other women for a year and a half, through three semesters of college. The study was designed to investigate how women's peer groups affected their choice of career. As it turned out, much of the women's time and energy, much of what they said in their interviews, and much of what we observed in participating in their peer activities, had to do with romantic relationships. Because the women were interviewed again and again over the time period, it was possible to follow their developing ideas and skills with the conduct of romantic affairs. Because we were participating in some of their peer activities, it also was possible to describe the social interactional context in which these ideas were developing. This paper describes the women's process of learning about romance as that process is discernible from the interviews and participant observation. It relates their developing expertise and involvement with romance to Spiro's (1982) levels of cognitive salience of cultural systems and to Dreyfus's (1984) stages of the development of expert knowledge. The cultural model of romance acquired motivating force as the women developed mastery of it and their mastery, in turn, depended upon their development of a concept of themselves as actors in the world of romance. Although American culture tells us that the urge to romance is "natural" – that the directive force is supplied by nature – the study suggests that the desire for romance is formed during the learning process and that this process occurs in the context of social interaction.

Processes of internalization and the directive force of cultural meaning systems

The larger issue of the chapter is a perennial one for the social sciences: how is it that meaning systems "become a desire" or, more mundanely put, that a cultural system directs or motivates people to action? This question is central because it lies at the interface between the collective and the individual and is implicated in any theory which purports to explain important processes such as social reproduction. Parsons alludes to the importance of the issue in an essay he published in 1961. In his opinion, the question of the relations of "social structure" and "personality" had been solved by a convergence between Freud's account of the ego, superego, and id and Durkheim, Cooley, and G.H. Mead's accounts of society. His excitement was evident: "This convergence is one of the few truly momentous developments of modern social science . . ."

Parsons's enthusiastic assessment notwithstanding, there was, and continues to be, serious contention within the social sciences and within anthropology in particular as to the proper conceptualization of the relationship between society, behavior and the "presocial" nature of humans. In anthropological accounts the issue is phrased in terms of culture. To what extent does culture determine behavior? Is culture – defined as collective interpretations of social and material experience – but an after-the-fact labeling of deep-seated human needs and concerns stemming, say, from psychodynamic forces or perhaps from inbuilt materialist orientations? Or, taking the opposing view, are cultural meaning systems influential to the point that they profoundly shape and define human needs (Henriques *et al.* 1984:11–25, Spiro 1982:47–51)? As Spiro points out, these assumptions determine one's interpretation of the problem of the directive force of cultural systems.

If culture is assumed to define and determine individual human needs, then the challenge is to explicate the form and nature of the cultural model and so its power to dictate action. The directive force is supplied by the cultural model itself. Most cognitive anthropologists take culture to be profoundly important in determining human motivation and thus adopt this first approach.

If, on the other hand, culture is conceived as a surface labeling of deep-seated human needs, then questions about the directive force of cultural systems become questions about how the cultural system – the surface form – is harnessed to and so derives its power from underlying psychodynamic forces. This second approach can be found in the cognitive anthropology literature as well. The cognitivist position does not exclude the possibility that cross-culturally variable meaning systems are but gilt upon a more fundamental psychodynamic, materialist, or even structuralist substrate (see Quinn 1987 and Hutchins 1987 for examples of connections between cognitivist approaches and psychodynamic analyses). A third approach – one that emphasizes the formation of motivation during development – is less familiar in the cognitive anthropology literature. This third position is the one that is taken here (see also Harkness *et al.*, Quinn, and Strauss, this volume).

In the neo-Vygotskian developmental approach that informs the present paper, thought and feelings, will and motivation, are *formed* as the individual develops. In the context of social interaction, the individual comes to internalize cultural resources, such as cultural models, language, and symbols, as means to organize and control her thoughts and emotions. To use Vygotsky's terms, these internalized cultural devices enable and become part and parcel of the person's "higher mental functions." Becker's (1963) analysis of the use of marijuana provides an example of the kind of study and conclusions implied by Vygotskian theory.[2] Although Becker does not refer to Vygotsky's concepts, his study of how people become inveterate pot smokers indicates that the motivation to smoke pot is developed in the learning process. Becker's findings challenged the then prevalent ideas that either personality traits or the physiological effects of the drug itself motivated use. He found that the full measure of the motivation to smoke was not brought by the individual to the activity of pot smoking, nor was the individual fully compelled to continue smoking by the nature of the drug. Rather the compelling nature of activity developed and was maintained in the context of interaction with others. The neophyte not only learned how to use the drug from others, he also learned how to attend to and value the experience from others. Similarly, although one may not wish to draw any sort of parallels between using drugs and being involved in romance, the present research suggests that the compelling nature of romantic pursuits comes about, or is constructed, *in the process* of learning the cultural system.

The study

The study was originally designed to investigate college women's decisions about their future careers and the relationship of those decisions to their peer activities. A three-semester period, from near the beginning of the informants' freshman year to the middle of their sophomore year, was chosen for intensive study. Over the course of the study, researchers conducted monthly interviews with the women and participated with them in various of their campus activities. The interviews – "talking diary" interviews – were open-ended and designed to encourage respondents to discuss their experiences and concerns in their own terms. A second type of interview, the "life history" interview, was conducted near the end of the study, in the middle of the women's sophomore year. Details of the ethnographic study and of the survey study that followed it are presented in Holland and Eisenhart (1981, 1990).[3]

The following is a close analysis of approximately half of the cases. The 200 or so pages transcribed from each woman's "talking diary" and life history interviews were combed for passages about male/female relationships, as were the notes from the peer activities that we observed. The remaining cases have been reviewed, but not as systematically. Although "American" is sometimes used to designate the group that supplied the material analyzed here, it should be kept in mind that the sample is both small and from the southeast. There were subcultural differences between the black and white women's interpretations of romantic relationships, but those differences are not relevant to the argument here. Descriptions and analyses of these differences can be found in Holland and Eisenhart (1988a, 1989, 1990).

The next section briefly describes the context in which the women were learning about and carrying out romantic relationships. The discussion then turns to an analysis of the ways in which the individual women differed in their engagement with and knowledge of the world of romance. The findings of the research, summarized in a phrase, are that romantic expertise, identification of self as a romantic type, and the compelling force of the cultural system co-develop as part of a socially assisted, interrelated process.

The social and cultural importance of romance at the two schools

At both Bradford and SU, social activities usually involved or related to the conduct of romantic encounters and relationships. Going out with, or seeing, friends of the opposite sex ranked high on the list of valued activities, and places where one might meet new men and women, such as parties, mixers, or the local bars, were favored locations. The women and their friends also spent a lot of time talking about potential romantic partners and their own and others' cross-gender relationships. Attractiveness – as validated by attention from a man or men – contributed in a major way to a woman's status in the peer system (Holland and Eisenhart 1988b, 1990: chapter 7).

The romantic sphere of life was especially important to the women of SU. Those who experienced less success at coursework than they had expected began to emphasize romantic relationships even more than they had. Relationships with women were subordinated to relationships with men. At both Bradford and SU, although in different ways, romantic relationships often interfered with relationships with other women (Holland and Eisenhart 1989).

The themes of male/female relationships also dominated a vocabulary that the students used to talk about one another. Women knew literally hundreds of words for types of men: "jerks," "jocks," "cowboys," "frattybaggers," "brains," "pricks," etc. and vice versa (Holland and Skinner 1983, 1987). And romance figured in the semiotics of clothes and personal adornment.

The cultural model of romance

An earlier study at SU of the meaning of the gender-marked terms and of the descriptions of male/female encounters and relationships had suggested that student discourse about romantic and close cross-gender friendships presupposed a "cultural model" of how such relationships develop. To understand the students' talk one had to know what the students considered unremarkable or took for granted about these relationships (Holland and Skinner 1987). Since their ideas about the world of romance are important background information for the analysis to follow, the results of the earlier project are briefly summarized here.

As with other cultural models, the cultural models of romance that we inferred posited a simplified world populated by a set of agents (e.g., attractive women, boyfriends, lovers, fiancés) who engage in a limited range of important acts or state changes (e.g., flirting with, falling in love with, dumping, having sex with) as moved by a specific set of forces (e.g., attractiveness, love).[4]

Holland and Skinner (1987) concluded that when the young adults talked about their acquaintances, friends, and (potential) romantic partners in terms of gender-marked types such as "hunks," "jerks," "Susie sororities," or "dumb broads," they were assuming that the talk would be understood in relation to a simplified world of cross-gender relationships. In the simplified world posited by the cultural model, cross-gender relationships progress in a typical way:

> An attractive man ("guy") and an attractive woman ("girl") are drawn to one another.
>
> The man learns and appreciates the woman's qualities and uniqueness as a person.
>
> Sensitive to her desires, he shows his affection by treating her well, e.g., he buys things for her, takes her places she likes, and shows that he appreciates her and appreciates her uniqueness as a person.
>
> She in turn shows her affection and interest and allows the relationship to become more intimate.

The model also describes the motives or purposes of such relationships:

> The relationship provides intimacy for both the man and the woman.
>
> The relationship validates the attractiveness of both the man and the woman.

And the model accounts for some exceptions:

> In some cases, the attractiveness or prestige of the man is less than that of the woman. He compensates for his lower prestige by treating her especially well.
>
> If the woman's attractiveness is the lower of the two, she compensates by being satisfied with less good treatment from the man.

The hundreds of gender-marked names that the young adults in our study used, as it turned out, designated, for the most part, "problematic" types of males and females – problematic in relation to the taken-for-granted progress of male/female relations posited by the cultural model. They cause such relations to go awry. "Jerk" provides an example: "jerks" are lowly, negatively evaluated types. In the definitions given by our informants, "jerks" were described as "insensitive" and "stupid." But the definitions did not fully spell out why a "jerk" was considered to be such a negative type or why women found them disgusting and irritating. The reason became clear when a "jerk" was considered as a relevant character in the world posited by the cultural model. A "jerk" is a type who is neither attractive *nor* sensitive to women. He cannot compensate for his low prestige by treating the women especially well. He's too stupid or too "out-of-it" to discern her special qualities and anticipate her desires. He cannot figure out the things that he could do to make her feel well treated. He may be so insensitive, in fact, that he cannot even tell that she dislikes him. Because he cannot "take the hint," he will not leave her alone and thus he becomes more and more irritating as time goes by.[5]

Not only were the women in our study expected to know the cultural model of romantic relationships and these many types who populated the world of romance, they also were constantly exposed to model-based interpretations of their own behavior.

In short, life among women students at both universities was dominated in large part – both socially and culturally – by romance. Social activities and relationships – including relationships between women – often revolved around romantic encounters or around talk about romantic relationships. Status was interpreted, especially for women, in relation to attractiveness. The students shared ways of communicating about and conventions for interpreting romantic relationships. And one's goals, intentions, and qualities were likely to be interpreted according to these ideas about romance.

Differences in romantic expertise and involvement

In the peer situation just described, with its emphasis on romance, with its constant enactments of, and talk about, romantic relationships, individual differences in expertise and involvement were obscured or masked. Knowledgeability about the types of men and the ways romantic relationships work was more-or-less assumed. Further, in as much as romance was assumed to be a natural activity, a basic level of competence in the conduct of relationships was presumed.[6]

American culture does not generally treat romantic relationships as an area of expertise. The women did not usually talk about romance and romantic relationships as something at which one is good or bad, expert or inexpert. Love and romance were more often talked about fatalistically, as something which happened to one, not something that one affected. Unsuccessful relationships were more often attributed to character flaws, to the luck of the people involved, or mismatches in interests rather than to a lack of skill or expertise.

Nonetheless, despite all the alternative ways of talking about romance, there was some talk that turned upon questions of expertise and competence. The women did sometimes see themselves or others as having made mistakes. They had a sense of romantic situations that were "challenges" or situations that they were too inexperienced or "too young" to handle. They sometimes assessed themselves and others as more or less proficient at romantic activities and the world of romance.

Judging from the women in the study, this latter, infrequently articulated idea, of differing levels of expertise, seemed to be the more accurate view. The more common taken-for-granted notions of similar levels of competence and involvement with romance did not hold up. A close look at the women as individuals revealed that some were quite ambivalent about romance American style and had less than compelling images of themselves in romantic relationships. Further the women differed in their facility with romantic situations. The next section describes those differences in their "involvement" with the world of romance; the section following, their different levels of expertise in conceiving and responding to romantic situations.

Involvement in the world of romance

For some of the women, romance was much more "salient" or present in their thoughts. Apart from, but related to, the "salience" of romance, there was another aspect of involvement: identification of self in the world of romance. These two aspects of involvement are discussed in turn.

The salience or directive force of the American cultural system of romance

Spiro (1982:48) describes five levels of "cognitive salience" of cultural systems. At the next to highest level of salience, a cultural system *guides* action. At the very highest level, it *instigates* action. For some of the women, everyday life was translated into, or seen through the lens of, the cultural model of romance. Judging from the observations of the women's peer activities and from their interviews, romantic involvements – actual or hoped for – occupied a lot of their time and thoughts. They spent much of their time being with boyfriends, talking about boyfriends, looking for boyfriends, adjusting their plans and activities to boyfriends than did others. For others romance was less salient; they spent time instead on other things such as classes, clubs or committees, friends or family relationships.

For several of the women, the salience of romance changed over the course of the study. In some cases, romantic activities became more important; in others, less. As will be developed in more detail in later sections of the paper, these cases helped to tease out not only the concomitant aspects of increasing and decreasing salience, but also the various factors that affected the rise and fall of salience.

Experiences in non-romantic pursuits sometimes occasioned changes in a woman's emphasis on romance. Holland and Eisenhart (1988b) describe several of the women who came to college proud of having done well in high school and then grew upset when their university grades were not as good. As time went by, they gradually became less involved with their school work and instead switched their attention and time to romantic pursuits. Romance became an even more salient system for them.

Friends were another impetus to romance. Peers generally encouraged the pursuit of romance as in the case of Susan which is described in a later section of the paper. Sometimes, however, they stimulated opposition to the cultural system and for one woman, Sandy, may have figured in her eventual loss of interest. For her, the decrease in salience was dramatic.

At the beginning of the study, Sandy seemed interested, along with her dorm-mates, in finding a male romantic partner ("You can have the blondes, I get the dark-haired ... cute ones"). But, as time went by, she had trouble establishing the kind of relationships that she wanted with men at college. During this period, she also learned that a potential boyfriend back home did not feel similarly attracted to her and, later, she learned that he was involved with another woman. Her friends all seemed to be having similarly unhappy romantic experiences as well. At the same time, Sandy began to feel that she did not fit in with the other students at SU. "In my hometown, I was pretty much respected in the community and accepted for what I am, or was, in that community. [I was] basically your nonconformist, and I dressed to suit me. But when I came down here I ... got the impression that here I was a sloppy little girl and I didn't have any class or I didn't have any style ..." She came to stress friendships even more than she had before and to concern herself about helping her friends. "Friendships were ... and probably still are one of the most important things to me. They were important to me not so very much socially. They were important to me as a person ... I pride myself in my friendships." As the study progressed, she came to develop a very special friendship with one woman, Leslie. Despite the jealousy of her other friends and the admonitions of her parents who felt that she was not availing herself of all her options at college, Sandy felt it important to pursue her friendship with Leslie. "Our friendship is terrific ... I just would like to spend more time ... [so far] it's all been crammed into one semester ... there's probably not gonna be another time in my life when I can just sit down and just be friends."

Eventually Sandy came to spend all her time with Leslie. She had begun her freshman year with an emphasis upon romantic relationships with men, but for the various reasons discussed dropped those interests altogether. For her, such romantic attachments became markedly less salient and her identity as an attractive woman in the world of romance, as culturally construed, became unimportant to her.

Identification with the world of romance

Aside from the importance or quantity of time devoted to romance, the nature of the woman's relationship to romance varied. Some of the women seemed to have an idea of themselves as participants in the world of male/female relationships – as beings in the romantic world – and to accept their romantic selves as real parts of themselves. Others either had an unclear image or sensed a discrepancy between themselves and the role(s) they were acting out. Of the cases reviewed in depth (roughly half of the twenty-three), at least one woman, Susan, explicitly contested the way romance was conceived and enacted in the student culture. Another – Natalie – had more or less explicitly devalued some aspects of the taken-for-granted ideas of romance and marriage as important to her.

The women's process of identifying with the romantic world took place in the context of constant social input. Their peers, and sometimes their professors, cast them as romantic actors. Although she was not pleased by her professor's typing of her as a romantic/sexual character, Della's account provides a graphic example of such casting. One day she had gone to class dressed in a skirt and blouse.

And I sits in front . . . of the class, and my teachers says, "What's this? What's this? Della, where's she at?" And I just sat there looking at him cause he looked dumb looking around me. . . . and he said, "Oh, there's Della." He looked my legs up and down, up and down, and the whole class [was] looking at him. He said, "Oh, oh, I see. I see, Della, I see. Oh, oh." . . . I was so embarrassed; the whole class was looking at me.[7]

In another case, Karla told about a seduction attempt by a former teacher. The events took place during the study and were described over several interviews. Karla's story consisted of the following episodes. She ran into a former teacher of hers from high school. He was a teacher she had liked and respected and she continued to value his opinions highly. He gave her a book to read – a book by Freud – and they made plans to discuss it later. She read the book and went to meet him ready to have an intellectual discussion. Instead she found out that he wanted to be her lover. She deflected his advances. Because he had a family, she had not thought of having a romantic relationship with him and she disapproved of his invitation. He persisted. When she finally made her reluctance clear he became angry and told her that "intellectuals" were not concerned about whether their lovers were married or not.

These attempts to interpret or identify the women in certain sorts of romantic or sexually related male/female relationships were fairly explicit and direct. In addition to many such cases we also observed an abundance of cases in which the attributions were more indirect. Even comments such as "Oh, you're wearing your add-a-beads," could be an abbreviated reference to a romantic type. At the time of the study, "add-a-beads" were popular among sorority women. Such a comment on clothing, or even a look, was sufficient to communicate an interpretation – in the "add-a-bead" case, that one was acting out a certain femininity and style of carrying out romantic relationships.

Sometimes the women accepted these frequent interpretations of self as a romantic type, sometimes explicitly rejected them, and sometimes ignored them. It was clear in the interview, for example, that Della – quoted above – rejected her professor's casting of her in a sexual role. In Karla's discussion of her experience with the high-school teacher, she ignored the teacher's claim that intellectuals really did have different moral codes when it came to extramarital affairs and that if she wanted to be an intellectual she had better change her ideas about romantic relationships. In another case, however, Cylene seemed to be entertaining the possibility that a characterization of her as a romantic type was true. Her father had told her that she wanted so many things – a house, a car, a boat – that she was going to "kill" her man. The gist of her father's comment was that she expected her boyfriend to treat her too well – to supply her with too many material possessions. She did not dispute his characterization and, in fact, went on to consider his statement as a possibly valid interpretation.

The women seemed to winnow the possible interpretations and accept some parts while rejecting others. Natalie, for example, talked explicitly about a vision of herself that she had formed as a young child and had since given up at least in part. " 'Marrying rich' is just a term for marrying the whole ideal guy ... that's just a thing that most everybody thinks about ... a good-looking rich man who loves me very much and won't let me cook ... and lives in a big house." By the time she participated in the study Natalie said she had discarded a piece of this vision of herself as a married woman. For various reasons, including her sister's experiences with a husband who could not hold a job, Natalie had decided to prepare herself to earn money so that she would not have to depend upon her future husband for economic support. She said that she no longer envisioned being financially supported.

Despite the fact that the women were frequently supplied with images of themselves in the world of romance, and despite the fact that many of their peers seemed to have sorted through various interpretations and arrived at a fairly stable view of themselves as participants in the romantic world, some had failed to form such an identity. They had no clear idea of a possible "romantic" self that engaged them – either as a self to avoid or a self to realize.[8] Susan, for example, had an extremely unsettled and ambivalent identification with romance.

Susan's ambivalence surfaced in many ways. At one point, for example, she spoke of her trip out West and what a beautiful place it was for a romance, but said that she had not got involved with anyone because it was "too much trouble." Her boyfriend, as will be described below, seemed more of an accommodation to peer demands than a reality. Further, she was openly critical of one of the motives, summarized above, for romantic relationships: the idea that boyfriends should be a source of prestige. She took the researcher to her dorm precisely to show her the way in which the girls brought their boyfriends to the lounge to "show them off." In Susan's opinion boyfriends were not for showing off.

During most of the study, Susan spent a lot of time thinking about the sort of lifestyle she wanted to have. Her dilemma seemed to be a choice between becoming what she considered a "socialite" or becoming a "hippie." By the time of the study she was inclined to reject the upwardly mobile, upper-middle-class lifestyle that she felt pressured – perhaps by her family – to embrace. This struggle, which occupied a lot of her time and efforts, related both to her ambivalence about her studies and, of direct relevance to this paper, to her ambivalence about romantic relationships. Reliance upon boyfriends as a source of prestige as emphasized in the student culture seemed to remind her of socialite women in her hometown. These women, in Susan's mind, were typified by their frequent attendance at the country club where they talked on and on about their rich husbands. Her feelings about socialites – and her distate when she thought about herself as one – made it difficult for her to identify with the world of romance at SU.

In addition to the case of Susan's explicit reluctance and overt criticisms of the idea of romance as construed on campus, there also were cases in which the women – including Susan – participated in relationships without their hearts being totally in them, so to speak. These women had or were participating in romantic relationships according to the accepted cultural notions but they told us of a distance between their true feelings and the ways they were acting. Cylene, for example, talked about how she had had a steady boyfriend in high school, but that, looking back, she probably had had him as a steady not because she was particularly attached to him and did not want to date other men, but because she was worried about people "talking."[9]

The person who was most straightforward about the felt distance between her actions and her true feelings was again Susan. Although some of the others also had absentee boyfriends who primarily seemed to be useful excuses for not going out with other men, Susan's way of talking about Howard, her boyfriend, clearly revealed her limited involvement in the relationship. She talked explicitly in the interviews about their awkwardness with one another when they did get together. She also made statements about Howard that were in a stereotyped tone of voice that indicated she was not serious. For example, in describing her feelings about Howard's decision to attend a university more than half way across the country from her university, she said: "I don't know exactly when he's going but, um, I'm sure I'll see him sometime. So . . . heartbreak, sob and everything like that!" In another instance when an "older" man from a nearby city tried to persuade her to go out with him, she told the interviewer: "But 30 years old, that's old. I mean I'm 18 years old. I don't want to go out with someone who's 30. It's not that bad but – shucks, I don't want to go out with anybody but Howard. He's worth the wait."

Although she was not as ambivalent as Susan, Natalie also seemed to participate only half-heartedly in activities where one might meet potential romantic partners. Natalie did attend many parties and mixers but seemingly only for appearance's sake. As she presented herself in the interviews, Natalie was actually much less involved in romantic endeavors than most other women in the study, and had much more of herself invested in her schoolwork. She constantly talked in the interviews not about boyfriends but about her schoolwork and her interactions with her family. She appeared to be not much identified with the world of romance. As she described it, her earlier childhood vision of herself as a romantic partner (described above) had largely disintegrated as she watched her sister's marital troubles. She spoke in positive terms of becoming romantically involved with a man in the future, but, at least as she spoke of her vision of this future relationship in the interview, the vision was vague and without detail.

What these cases and the previous ones suggest is that although they were constantly cast as romantic actors in the world and treated as though they were seriously involved with (potential) romantic relationships, the women's involvement with romantic pursuits varied. Some resisted being identified as romantic participants, some opposed pieces or parts of the views of romance that they associated with their peers, some had strategies for avoiding or circumscribing their romantic experiences, and many indicated a recognition that the way they felt was at odds with the way they were acting out a relationship.

The women's involvement varied along two interrelated dimensions: salience and identification. About half of the women defined themselves in large part as (potential) romantic partners and devoted a great deal of time and energy to romantic pursuits. Others like Susan had an unclear or contested identification and some like Natalie and Cylene (as she described herself in high school) had a sense of distance between their actions and their identifications. They devoted less time and energy to romantic activities and their identifications were of a different quality from those of persons who defined themselves in large part as romantic types. For Sandy, her identification with the world of romance – one in which she perhaps saw herself as a hurt or rejected admirer – was not sufficiently compelling or salient to keep her involved in the pursuit of a boyfriend. Over the period of the study she lost what interest she had had.

To reiterate, the general point is that the women in the study were not all equally involved with the world of romance and that the components of involvement – salience and identification – proved to be interrelated. Talk about men, focus on men, orientation toward romantic relationships with men – as noted in the observations and as came through in the interviews – seemed to be positively correlated with the degree to which the women talked about and acted toward themselves as actors in the world of romance. Those such as Cylene, Natalie, and Susan, all in their different ways, seemed less personally involved in their romantic relationships and activities than many of the other women. Although they participated in these relationships and activities, their comments conveyed a sense of distance, a lack of emotional involvement. Correspondingly, their degree of talk and concern about romance in the interviews was less than for the women such as Karla who did identify with the world of romance and for whom such relationships and activities were salient.[10]

Expertise in formulating and responding to romantic situations

In addition to degrees of involvement with the world of romance, the women in the study also seemed more or less expert at the conduct of romantic relationships. They differed in the extent that they relied upon the directions and motivations of others and in ways that they formulated and responded to problematic situations. The women who gave the impression of being less knowledgeable or less expert were those who closely copied and took directions from others, who attended to relatively circumscribed parts or aspects of relationships, and who had trouble generating possible responses to romantic situations.

Adopting the words and directives of others

The women's ways of talking about men and relationships with men conveyed different degrees of facility with the cultural ideas. One woman, for example, had sufficient knowledge of campus types to be able to extract the essences of the types and put them together in a skit. She and some of the other women also were facile in talking about their own strategies for handling relationships. Karen, for example, talked about "keeping the upper hand," in a relationship and Rosalind about "putting one man up front." While Karen and Rosalind may not have invented these strategies – described below – they seemed to be fully at ease with describing and putting them into action. Susan, on the other hand, as will be described below, seemed to be constrained to repeating and attempting to carry out the directives of others.

In the case of "getting the upper hand," Karen was describing her behavior toward Hal, a man that she had just met. She was trying to convince him that she was attractive – possibly more attractive than he was. A woman who is less attractive than a man she goes out with – according to the cultural model – compensates for her relative lack of attractiveness by settling for less good treatment and by allowing the relationship to become intimate faster than she might wish. On the other hand, if she is more attractive than the man, he compensates for his relative lack of attractiveness by being especially sensitive to and attentive to her. Karen tried to get the upper hand by giving Hal the idea that other men were interested in her. She did this by giving him the impression that she was going out with other men, that she had a boyfriend back home and that she had a fuller social calendar than he did.

In the case of "putting one man up front" Rosalind – a woman at Bradford – intended to play up her involvement with only one man. At Bradford, romantic relationships were complicated by one's having to maintain integrity and self control. A way to lose control was by having information about one's emotional investments become known to those who might use it to try to manipulate one or to interfere in one's relationships (Holland and Eisenhart 1989). Rosalind's idea was to emphasize one man as the person that she was primarily interested in, thereby deflecting attention from the others.

Both the idea of "getting the upper hand" and "keeping one man up front" were strategies for achieving the valued outcomes of romantic involvements while avoiding bad outcomes. These strategies seemed to be ones that the women themselves had decided to use and could describe without too much trouble. Susan, on the other hand, gave the impression of repeating and trying to act upon what others had said.

During the first year and a half of her college career, Susan talked about gender relations in a variety of ways – ways that for the most part could be traced to her friends. During this period she was searching for a group of friends. She cast about and struck up friendships with a variety of women having different lifestyles and orientations and different ways of talking about men and gender relations. In the interviews she sometimes talked about her friends' relationships in terms that we knew from the observations were terms her friends used. Lee, a friend of Susan's, was having to fend off sexual advances from the owners of the restaurant where she worked. In describing Lee's troubles with her employers, Susan said that a guy at the café had "pinched Lee on the buns and told her to loosen up." In another description of the same incident, Susan said that a "Greek was messing with her [Lee]." Words such as "buns" and "messing with her" were not the types of words that Susan used in other interviews to describe somewhat similar situations.

Susan described another friend's, Patricia's, relationships as being "open" or "not open," "serious" or "not serious." Speaking of one of Patricia's relationships she says: "It seems really good, the relationship they have, because they talk a whole lot, and its a lot more open [than the] relationship that she had with George, as far as saying what she wants and feels." The "openness" of Lee's (the other friend's) relationships was not something Susan talked about, presumably because Lee did not talk about them in those terms.

Susan used euphemisms to talk about a topic – the sexual aspects of gender relations – that she seemed not to discuss with her friends. For example, she told the interviewer that she had learned that a potential boyfriend was "homosexual" and that she was relieved: "[I'm] glad not to have to worry about that [sex] with him anymore." Knowing Patricia and some of Susan's other friends, one doubts that any of them would have referred to sex as "that."

Susan also seemed willing to adopt the arguments of others regarding herself. In one interview, for example, Susan described a situation (referred to above) in which an "older" man was trying to get her to go out with him. The man originally had called Susan's dorm in search of a woman who had previously lived there. Susan answered the phone. They began to talk and he asked her out. She put him off by saying that she had homework and eventually told him she had a boyfriend back home – Howard. The man was not so easily put off. She admitted to going out with someone else besides Howard. The man argued that if she went out with other people in the area then she should go out with him. He almost had her persuaded. In the next interview, although she eventually returned to her boyfriend-back-home position, Susan debated about going out with the man. She said, "But I guess I should meet him, you know, he seems like a pretty interesting person to meet."

By the end of the study Susan had settled more or less upon one group as her primary set of friends and her talk about men and gender relations had begun to conform to the way her group talked about such relationships.

It could be suggested that, in Susan's case, the motivation to participate in romance, as well as the words, were initially supplied by her friends. She did not find the culturally defined motives for romantic relationships – prestige and intimacy – sufficiently attractive to overcome her discomfort with romantic encounters. And, as pointed out, she even disputed one of the motives – prestige – as a proper motive for relationships.[11]

Nonetheless, in her sophomore year, Susan began to look for a boyfriend in earnest. It appeared that her efforts were spurred by her desire to participate in the same activities and talk that her friends did. She needed to find a boyfriend in order to be like her group of friends. Indications of the difficulty she had in making these attempts and of the support supplied by her friends in the activity are clear in the following passage. She had just told the interviewer that she would like to find a boyfriend and the interviewer had asked her how one goes about finding one. "You just scope out the crowd first . . . see I found this guy that I'm interested in . . . But I never see this guy so that makes it difficult . . . I get all nervous and paranoid so I can't ever talk to him. It's pretty funny, all my friends are like: Go talk to the guy, Susan. Let's go talk to him. *I just can't.*" In the follow-up interviews, especially the one conducted in 1987, Susan evidenced more positive associations with romantic experiences, but in 1980 her motivation seemed to be supplied by her friends.

Scope or overview of romantic situations

Besides their facility with ways of talking – and presumably thinking – about relationships, the women seemed to vary in the scope or overview that they had of romantic relationships. Susan, for example, answered the interviewer's question about finding a boyfriend in terms of small-scale, step-by-step procedures that one could follow at a mixer or a party. In contrast, Karen and Rosalind with their strategies of getting the upper hand and keeping one man up front seem to be paying attention to a larger chunk or bigger-scale view of the relationship.

Another comparison of the women's different levels of analysis or overview is presented by the following. Paula, a woman at SU, became annoyed at starting relationships with men she was meeting at parties only to find that they were also going out with her friends. Following several similar experiences, she decided that meeting men at parties did not work. In contrast, a woman at Bradford similarly was having trouble with the men she was meeting. She, however, thought that the men behaved as they did because the women outnumbered the men at Bradford. Because they were in demand, the men, she thought, were unjustifiably arrogant and expected more from the women than they were entitled to.

At this school, it's about six girls to one guy . . . so the ugly [guys] . . . think they look like heaven and will try to [talk to you] all the time. It's really sick . . . Some of these guys have the cutest girlfriends, and I don't know how they got them . . . He must have the money. That's the reason why an ugly guy could get a fairly decent-looking girl. He has one of two things: a car or he's got money . . . And most of the guys here that look good, they're real dumb and . . . as far as holding a conversation, just forget it; I'd rather talk to a wall . . . But with so many girls to one guy, he gonna get somebody regardless of how he act.

This latter woman seemed to have a fairly broad overview of the relationship between men and women at Bradford while the former woman at SU seemed to have learned from trial and error that the relationships started at parties did not work out the way she wanted them to.

Generating responses to romantic situations

Besides the differences in the overview or scope of analysis of romantic situations and problems, the women also seemed to vary in how rapidly they came up with responses. In the case of Della and the teacher who embarrassed her in class, according to her interview, she was stymied and could not think of any sort of response. The only way she could think of to stop him from making further such remarks was to avoid him.

Susan's processes of responding to the romantic situations described above seem different from the ones that Karla described in her interviews. Recall Susan's process of thinking about her move regarding the man who called her dorm and asked her out. At least in terms of how she talked about the situation in the interview, Susan did not seem to have any overview of the situation or hypothesis about what he was doing. She consciously thought through the calls, the man's arguments and her various reactions, such as her feeling that he was old. She eventually fell back upon the absentee boyfriend to make up her mind and it was not clear at all how she might put off the man should he call her back. He already had argued against her "Howard" excuse. Karla's story about the former teacher's attempt to seduce her – at least in the way she told it – revealed a different sort of process. Karla seemed to form a hypothesis about the situation and the man and then to have devised – more or less at once – a response. She had to change her hypothesis several times when things did not go as expected. Each time, however, she seemed to form a new hypothesis and a new response without having to work through the situation piecemeal as Susan did. As an aside, she was finally successful when she had a friend of hers – a very large football player – call up the high-school teacher and tell him that he better leave her alone or else. After the telephone call, the teacher left Karla alone.

Discussion

Although the women in the study all participated in student society at the two universities and so were exposed constantly to social activities organized around romantic relationships and to shared interpretations of romance, they varied in their identifications with the culturally constructed world of romance. Not all of them found it compelling or salient. Further they also varied in their apparent expertise with the conduct of romantic relationships. The less expert women seemed to repeat the words and follow the directions of others. They also seemed to have less of an overview of romantic relationships and to have to work harder to come up with responses to romantic situations. Perhaps it comes as no surprise that those who were less identified with the world of romance and for whom it was less salient also were the ones who were less expert with the relationships. Those who were resisting, avoiding, lacking in interest, and enacting romance without having their hearts in it were the ones who were less expert.

The research suggests, in other words, that involvement – the salience of and identification with the cultural system of romance – co-developed along with expertise. If the woman had not developed a clear identification of herself in the world of romance – an image of herself that mattered to her – then romance was not likely to be very salient for her and she was not likely to be very expert in conducting romantic relationships. Similarly, if for some reason she had not been able to develop expertise then she was unlikely to have formed much of a romantic identification. Salience, identification, and expertise appear to develop together as an interrelated process – a process that was continually supported and shaped in the context of social interaction.

The research findings on the interrelations of expertise, identification, and salience are corroborated and informed by theoreticians such as Spiro (1982) and Dreyfus (1983, 1984). As shall be discussed, each is concerned explicitly with only one dimension – Spiro with cognitive salience, Dreyfus with expert knowledge. Nonetheless, references to the other dimensions – including, I will argue, identification – are present in both analyses.

Spiro (1982) describes the varying intensities of the directive force of cultural symbols and explains why these symbols are more or less motivating for different individuals. His scheme (p. 48) depicts five levels of the "cognitive salience" of cultural systems that can be summarized as follows: (1) the actors *learn about* the doctrines; (2) the actors come to *understand* the meanings of the doctrines as they are interpreted by specialists; (3) the actors, in addition, *believe* that the doctrines are true, correct, or right; (4) the doctrines come to structure the actors' perceptual worlds and *guide* their actions; and (5) the doctrines further come to *instigate* their actions.

Spiro is especially concerned to point out that cultural systems may or may not reach a very high level of cognitive salience and so may or may not have anything to do with instigating or even guiding an individual's behavior. Although he was primarily interested in discussing religious systems in his article, his differentiation of different levels of cognitive salience certainly applies to the present findings regarding the culturally constructed activity of romance. There were women in the study for whom romance – American style – was more or less cognitively salient. Also of relevance to the research reported here is that Spiro found it necessary to refer to knowledgeability. His first two stages are devoted to the individual's developing knowledge of the system. The individual, his scheme implies, must develop at least a certain mastery of or expertise with the cultural system, before he or she will find it motivating. In the present study, salience appeared to co-develop with expertise.

Dreyfus (1983, 1984), in contrast to Spiro, is interested in the development of expert knowledge. He too proposes five stages: (1) novice stage; (2) advanced beginner stage; (3) competency stage; (4) proficiency stage; and (5) expertise stage. Since he opposes the more traditional conception of expert knowledge, it is necessary briefly to describe his stages. Dreyfus denies the usual idea that expertise develops through the formulation of more and more sophisticated rules or propositions from which inferences are more and more rapidly drawn. Dreyfus argues that it is primarily novices and advanced beginners – not experts – who rely upon rules. Those who are more advanced have a more comprehensive, "three-dimensional" understanding of the system, be it a game such as chess, a sensorimotor skill such as driving, or a contentionalized or culturally-interpreted system of relationships such as romance.

In the novice and advanced beginner stages, the individual's knowledge is organized into rules and maxims. These rules, which the learner has probably heard from others, address single elements or aspects of the situation. They are like steps in step-by-step recipes for winning the game, driving the car, or finding a boyfriend. Susan's rules about scoping out the crowd come to mind.

With competency, the various elements of the situation become organized into a gestalt. The individual learns to think in terms of broader elements or chunks of the overall situation. Karen's concept of getting "the upper hand" in her relationship with Hal is an example of such a chunk.

At the competency stage, one must work consciously to arrive at possible responses and assessments of those responses. At the more advanced stages of proficiency and expertise, the experience of arriving at a response changes. The generation and assessment of responses becomes less conscious. Susan's process of thinking about her response to the man who called her dorm and asked her out exemplifies a less proficient stage than that represented in Karla's account of her response to her former teacher's attempt to seduce her.

Dreyfus's stages seem plausibly represented in the present research, but it also seems telling that just as Spiro did not restrict his levels of salience to salience alone, Dreyfus does not restrict his scheme to expertise alone. In order to describe the changes from advanced beginner and competency to more advanced stages, Dreyfus finds it necessary to speak of emotional involvement and sense of responsibility in the system.

The shift between the advanced beginner stage and the later stages of competency, proficiency, and expertise is marked, wrote Dreyfus, by a qualitative change in the relationship between the individual and the system. The individual comes to experience herself not as following rules or maxims taught by others but as devising her own moves. Dreyfus (1984:30) described this change as obtaining a sense of responsibility in the system. Perhaps a better phrasing would be to say that the individual gains a sense of being in the system – as understanding him or herself in terms of the activity. She identifies herself in the world as described by the cultural system:

The novice and the advanced beginner applying rules and maxims feel little or no responsibility for the outcome of their acts. If they have made no mistakes, an unfortunate outcome is viewed as the result of inadequately specified elements or rules. The competent performer, on the other hand, after wrestling with the question of a choice of perspective or goal, feels responsible for, and thus emotionally involved in, the result of his choice.

In play, as described by Vygotsky (1978), the child suspends other possible interpretations of things in the environment and becomes caught up in a pretend world. Her desires become related to "a fictitious 'I,' to her role in the game and its rules" (p. 100). Her motives become defined by the motives of the game. Here, as described by Dreyfus, the individual gets caught up in a particular game or cultural system and sees himself or herself as an agent in it. As with play, the overall activity is emotionally engaging. Dreyfus also argues this sort of participation is necessary for further mastery:

An outcome that is clearly successful is deeply satisfying and leaves a vivid memory of the situation encountered as seen from the goal or perspective finally chosen. Disasters, likewise, are not easily forgotten.

With competency the situation becomes "three dimensional" and the individual is "gripped" by it:

> The competent performer, gripped by the situation that his decision has produced, experiences and therefore remembers the situation not only as foreground and background elements but also as senses of opportunity, risk, expectation, threat, etc. These gripping holistic memories cannot guide the competent performer since he fails to include them when he reflects on problematic situations as a detached observer. As we shall see, however, these memories become the basis of the competent performer's next advance in skill (1984:30).

Notice that the emotional involvement or identification comes only after a certain degree of competence is reached and that this degree of emotional involvement is necessary for further mastery. Phrasing this same point in a different way, Dreyfus (1983), in a talk about the acquisition of expert knowledge in the game of chess, says:

> It seems you can't acquire these skills [of having a complex view of the situation] unless you're taking the game very seriously; it won't help to just be reading book games. There's the story that Bobby Fisher, whenever he plays even a book game, says: "Pow, got him, killed him that time!" even though there's nobody [no live opponent] there.

If Dreyfus's notions of the development of expertise are accurate, then identifying oneself as an agent in the system – an actor in the world as defined by the game, is a necessary precursor to mastering the system beyond a certain level. One has to develop a concept of oneself in the activity and want either to realize that self or avoid it.

Interweaving the two schemes

Although explicitly focused on their separate concerns, Spiro's and Dreyfus's schemes interrelate. Dreyfus is describing expert knowledge; however, he writes that emotional involvement is necessary for the achievement of his fourth stage of proficiency and fifth stage of expertise. Emotional involvement is also important in Spiro's account of the motivating force or cognitive salience of a cultural system. And, in turn, Spiro's scheme implicates knowledgeability. His first two levels explicitly refer to the knowledge that the individual has of the system. Put together, the two schemes begin to describe an integrated process of the development of expertise and cognitive salience. I would also argue that both schemes predicate what I have interpreted as "identification" with the cultural system.

Dreyfus vaguely describes a sense of responsibility as necessary for the development of expertise. He argues that one cannot go to the more advanced stages of proficiency and expertise without conceiving of oneself as devising one's own moves rather than relying upon the rules and maxims learned from others. Spiro (p. 48) describes the corresponding stage as the stage of believing – one comes to think of the system as being "true, correct, or right." His article is devoted to explaining why a patently impossible – to a western scientific mind – world of the super-natural could seem true.

I would argue that the key development that occurs around the third stage in both schemes is best phrased as "identification" – the formation of a concept of self as an actor in the culturally devised system. Spiro suggests that belief is crucial for advancement to higher levels of salience. Belief probably is relevant, but it may not be sufficient. An assessment that a world – a culturally interpreted world – lacks validity, truth, correctness, or rightness may indeed affect whether an individual can conceptualize or personalize the system as relevant to him or herself. Even in the case of romantic relationships which may not strain scientific credulity as do the religious systems Spiro considers, Susan, for example, had trouble seeing herself in the world of romance as interpreted by her peers. She had trouble because she disagreed with the association between boyfriends and prestige. The world did not seem right to her. However, there may be other reasons besides credulity that one does not form a valued identity in a cultural system. Sandy apparently continued to "believe" that the world of romantic male/female relationships existed. She did not come to doubt the world, rather her concept of herself in such a relationship was uninspiring and became even less so in comparison to her valued conceptions of herself in her other close relationships.

Identification – as the more inclusive process – seems to describe better the point or phase in internalization where the system that one has been socially interacting, according to the instructions and directions of others, becomes a system that one uses to understand and organize aspects of oneself and at least some of one's own feelings and thoughts (see also Quinn and Holland 1987:12–13).

Summary and conclusions

This paper has presented a case study of young college women's internali-zation of the cultural system of romance. The interviews and observations of twenty-three women followed over a year-and-a-half period revealed processes through which romance – as culturally constructed in the southeastern U.S. – becomes (or fails to become) compelling. The larger issue at hand is the directive force of cultural systems and what the process of learning a cultural system reveals about its movitating force.

The women in the study belied Americans' commonsense notions that romance is naturally compelling, naturally salient, and an area of competence that automatically appears when one reaches a certain age. The commonsense notions imply a homogeneity of interest and competence that was not found in the present research. The women were more or less expert with romantic relationships and more or less compelled to pursue romantic activities. Further, the commonsense notions underplay the pivotal significance of social intercourse in the formation of romantic interests and skills.

A close look at the women's developing involvement and expertise suggests that expertise, salience, and identification with romance co-develops as part of an interrelated process and that this process is integrally connected to social context. In accord with D'Andrade's (1986a) point that cultural models generate rather than provide a means to satisfy pre-existing goals, the present study suggests that relative beginners may neither know nor find the rumored motives for romantic activity – prestige and intimacy – especially enticing. Further, their knowledge of the conduct of romantic relationships may be rather piecemeal, their overviews of romantic situations rather vague, their responses to romantic situations rather labored, and they may not have developed any engaging visions of themselves as a participant in the world described by the cultural system.

For the women in the study, the cultural interpretation of romance became salient and compelling as their expertise with romantic relationships increased and as they came to form an engaging interpretation of themselves in the world of romance. Women who were vague and unclear or resistant to seeing themselves in the world of romance were the ones who were less expert and who found romance relatively unimportant in their lives. Women who were more expert were those who clearly identified with the world and for whom romance was highly salient.

The research was not originally conducted to study the internalization of cultural models of romance and so much be regarded as tentative and incomplete. However, Spiro's (1982) scheme depicting the five levels of cognitive salience of a cultural system and Dreyfus's (1984) five stages of the development of expertise both corroborate and inform the research findings. A beginning attempt was made to interweave schemes of cognitive salience and expertise by showing their interrelationships and by suggesting, in the case of the Spiro and Dreyfus schemes, certain reformulations. Specifically, it was suggested that "identification" with the culturally theorized world be substituted for Spiro's concern with belief and Dreyfus's emphasis on a feeling of responsibility for generating one's own moves.

Ethnographic case studies of internalization, such as this one and that of Becker (1963), for example, make it very clear that the social interactional context of learning must be taken into account. The relationship of the social interactional context of learning romance to the development of expertise, salience, and identification was not the focus of the present paper; nonetheless, the ubiquitous presence of peers as participants in romantic relationships and talk about romantic relationships, as coaches and "motivators" and as targets of opposition, was alluded to at many points. Although the women were not all expert enough or self-engaged enough in the system of romance to find it compelling in and of itself, they all were certainly propelled into the activities by the urgings of others. Further, those that resisted, rebelled and failed to form identifications with the romantic world did so in part in reaction to their peers.

If expertise, salience, and identification do co-develop in an interrelated process, as argued in this paper, then our descriptions of cultural content – by implication – become even more complicated than we had thought. The manner of formulating the content – as rules and maxims or gestalts (in the way of an expert) – implies a level of expertise, a level of salience, and a level of identification that may in fact be appropriate for describing only a small subset of the people studied. The description may falsely imply a homogeneity of expertise, salience, and identification, as well as homogeneity of content.

Randall (1976) and others argued that ethnoscience's formulation of cultural knowledge in terms of referential function and taxonomic organization falsely presupposed that cultural knowledge is organized for "scientific analytic" purposes as opposed to, say, more practical tasks. If the conclusions drawn here are correct, then the way an anthropologist describes a cultural system also may (falsely) presuppose that the system is known by most at a particular level of expertise, with a particular level of identification, and a particular level of salience.

What may already have been perceived now becomes more clear. There is the strong possibility that we have been describing cultural systems whose content has been mastered by, and whose directive force is compelling for, only a subset of the population.

And what are the characteristics of that subset and the relationship of that subset to the remainder of the population? Unexamined assumptions of homogeneity are a problem not so much because they may be unjustified according to the canons of scientific sampling and generalization, but because they permit inattention to the social distribution of cultural knowledge and its role in the reproduction of power relations. Assumptions of homogeneity deflect attention from the important processes of social conflict, the social symbolism of knowledge, and the processes and consequences of individual resistance that are important, even in the present research on an everyday and common activity. Expertise with romance, the salience of romantic activities, and the formation of one's view of oneself in the world of romance co-develop as part of an interrelated process that occurs within, and is sensitive to, the social-interactional context. Thus, the directive force of romance – the compelling nature of romance – integrally depends upon social as well as cultural forces.

NOTES

1 The research reported here was done with Margaret Eisenhart. She and several others, including William Lachicotte, Laurie Price, Melford Spiro, and Claudia Strauss, and two anonymous reviewers made helpful suggestions and comments on earlier drafts of the paper. Roy D'Andrade first alerted me to Spiro's stages of cognitive salience. D'Andrade's ideas and the papers and comments of the other panel members at the time of the A.A.A. symposium have affected the paper as well. I also would like to thank the women who participated in the study.

2 For a general discussion of Vygotsky and references to his work see Wertsch 1986. Elaboration of Vygotskian concepts pertinent to this paper can be found in Holland and Valsiner 1988. For one of the few translated papers of Vygotsky's directly addressed to motivation, see Vygotsky 1987.

3 The study participants were drawn from two universities – twelve of the women were attending Bradford University (Bradford), a historically black school, and eleven were attending Southern University (SU), a historically white school. Both universities are located in the southern United States. Bradford, the smaller and less well funded of the two universities, draws students of predominantly black, lower-middle-class backgrounds while SU draws students of predominantly white, middle-class backgrounds. In some other respects the two schools are similar. Both are state universities. At both schools the ratio of women to men is about the same (60:40). The original study was carried out in 1979–81.

The names of the universities and all personal names are pseudonyms. Inconsequential but potentially identifying details in the quotes have been changed.

4 Cultural models are shared, conventional ideas about how the world works that individuals learn by talking and acting with their fellows. Defined cognitively, cultural models consist of "schemas" that guide attention to, drawing inferences about, and evaluation of, experience. These schemas also provide a framework for organizing and reconstructing memories of experience (Quinn and Holland 1987).

5 The research that produced the cultural model was conducted at SU in the late 1970s and included an analysis of some of the interviews that are the basis of the study described here. Because only a few men were interviewed in the latter study we describe the model as one held by women. Women at Bradford used similar sorts of terms and, in their descriptions of romantic relationships, seemed to rely upon similar ideas about attractiveness and the respective roles of the male and the female. For them, however, there was an emphasis on self-determination and self-protection that entered into their interpretation of male/female relationships. Further details are given by Holland and Eisenhart (1989, 1990) along with a discussion of the possible historical roots of the differences between the black and white women's interpretations of male/female relationships.

6 Kessler and McKenna (1978) discuss a similar process in the case of gender attributions and interpretations. Even inexperienced transsexuals in the U.S. find that it is not difficult to be convincing as a member of the opposite sex. Once an attribution of gender is made, most make efforts to interpret a person's deportment as gender-appropriate. Although the corresponding studies have not been conducted, it is probably the case that a basic level of romantic expertise is assumed to be a natural correlate of attaining a certain age.

7 Both Della and Karla, in the cases that follow, were embarrassed and offended by being cast into the world of gender relations in what they considered to be inappropriate situations by men they considered inappropriate partners. While most of the interpretations of themselves as potential romantic/sexual partners were not taken amiss, these were. The women in the study were learning of their vulnerability to romantic/sexual typing regardless of their wishes to be so typed (see Holland and Eisenhart 1990, chapters 7 through 10).

8 Markus and Nurius's (1987) article "Possible Selves: The Interface between Motivation and the Self-Concept" is relevant to the research here. From their review of the social psychological research, they argue, among other points, that individuals form personalized images of themselves in various situations – e.g., visions of oneself receiving a Nobel Prize. These visions motivate actions to realize these possible selves. There also is evidence that some images of possible selves are negatively evaluated so that one works to avoid the realization of such an image.

9 As mentioned above and as described more fully elsewhere (Holland and Eisenhard 1989, 1990), the black women at Bradford were concerned about maintaining self-direction and self-control. Since knowledge about one's behavior and feelings can be used by others to manipulate one, having a steady boyfriend – as opposed to going out with a number of boyfriends – becomes a way to control information.

10 As the study progressed, Cylene and especially Susan became more involved with romantic relationships. Examples of women who were greatly involved with romance and identified themselves as such are given below. More extensive examples and discussion can be found in Holland and Eisenhart (1990, chapters 9 and 10).

11 Susan's process of learning is a good example of the internalization of social discourse (Vygotsky 1987, Wertsch 1986).

REFERENCES

Becker, Howard S.
  1963 *Outsiders: Studies in the Sociology of Deviance*. New York: The Free Press.
D'Andrade, Roy
  1986a Cognitive Anthropology. Paper presented at the 1986 American Anthropological Association meetings in the symposium, Psychological Anthropology: Appraisal and Prospectus, Philadelphia, PA.
  1986b Cultural Schemas as Motives. Paper presented at the 1986 American Anthropological Association meetings in the symposium, The Directive Force of Cultural Models, Philadelphia, PA.
Dreyfus, Hubert L.
  1983 Telling What We Know: The Making of Expert Systems. Talk presented to the conference, The Brain and the Mind. Available from National Public Radio, N1 – 831207.01/02-c. Washington, DC.
  1984 What Expert Systems Can't Do. *Raritan* 3(4):22–36.
Henriques, Julian, Wendy Holloway, Cathy Urwin, Couze Venn, and Valerie Walkerdine
  1984 *Changing the Subject: Psychology, Social Regulation and Subjectivity*. London: Methuen.
Holland, Dorothy and Margaret Eisenhart
  1981 *Women's Peer Groups and Choice of Career*. Final Report. Washington, DC: National Institute of Education.
  1988a Moments of Discontent: University Women and the Gender Status Quo. *Anthropology and Education Quarterly* 19(2):115–38.
  1988b Women's Ways of Going to School: Cultural Reproduction of Women's Identities as Workers. In *Class, Race and Gender in U.S. Education*, Lois Weis, ed. Buffalo: SUNY Press. Pp. 266–301.
  1989 On the Absence of Women's Gangs in Two Southern Universities. In *Women in the South*, Holly Mathews, ed. Athens: University of Georgia Press. Pp. 27–46.
  1990 *Educated in Romance: Women, Achievement and College Culture*. Chicago: University of Chicago Press.
Holland, Dorothy and Debra Skinner
  1983 Themes in American Folk Models of Gender. *Social Science Newsletter* 68(3):49–60.
  1987 Prestige and Intimacy: The Cultural Models Behind Americans' Talk about Gender Types. In *Cultural Models in Language and Thought*, Dorothy Holland and Naomi Quinn, eds. Cambridge: Cambridge University Press. Pp. 78–11.
Holland, Dorothy and Jaan Valsiner
  1988 Symbols, Cognition and Vygotsky's Developmental Psychology. *Ethos* 16(3):247–72.
Hutchins, Edwin
  1987 Myth and Experience in the Trobriand Islands. In *Cultural Models in Language and Thought*, Dorothy Holland and Naomi Quinn, eds. Cambridge: Cambridge University Press. Pp. 269–89.
Kessler, Suzanne J. and Wendy McKenna
  1978 *Gender: An Ethnomethodological Approach*. New York: John Wiley.

Markus, Hazel and Paul Nurius
1987 Possible Selves: The Interface between Motivation and the Self-Concept. In *Self and Identity: Psychosocial Perspectives*, Krysia Yardley and Terry Honess, eds. Chichester: John Wiley. Pp. 157–72.
Parsons, Talcot
1961 *Social Structure and the Development of Personality. Studying Personality Cross-Culturally*, B. Kaplan, ed. Evanston, IL: Row, Peterson. Pp. 165–200.
Quinn, Naomi
1987 Love and the Experiential Basis of American Marriage. University of Virginia Center for Advanced Studies Working Paper Series.
Quinn, Naomi and Dorothy Holland
1987 Culture and Cognition. In *Cultural Models in Language and Thought*, Dorothy Holland and Naomi Quinn, eds. Cambridge: Cambridge University Press. Pp. 3–40.
Randall, Robert
1976 How Tall is a Taxonomic Tree? Some Evidence for Dwarfism. *American Ethnologist* 3(3):543–53.
Spiro, Melford E.
1982 Collective Representations and Mental Representations in Religious Symbol Systems. In *On Symbols in Anthropology: Essays in Honor of Harry Hoijer*, J. Maquet, ed. Malibu: Udena Publications. Pp. 45–72.
Vygotsky, Lev S.
1978 The Role of Play in Development. In *Mind in Society: The Development of Higher Psychological Processes*, M. Cole, V. John-Steiner, S. Scribner, and E. Souberman, eds. Cambridge, MA: Harvard University Press. Pp. 92–104.
1987 The Problem of Will and Its Development in Childhood. In *The Collected Works of L.S. Vygotsky*, Vol. I: *Problems of General Psychology*, Norris Minick, trans. New York: Plenum Press. Pp. 351–8.
Wertsch, James V.
1986 *Vygotsky and the Social Formation of Mind*. Cambridge, MA: Harvard University Press.

5   The motivational force of self-understanding: evidence from wives' inner conflicts

Naomi Quinn

This paper takes as its departure point Roy D'Andrade's discussion (1990: 157–9; this volume) of the way in which cultural schemas structure individual goals. D'Andrade observes that the structuring of goals is perhaps the most significant role that schemas play in individual functioning, and that one important way they do so is by defining means–end relationships, linking certain high-level goals to other, low-level, goals. Such goal-schemas as those for love and work, by his example, can be thought of as "master motives" that "instigate action relatively autonomously." Other schemas such as those for marriage and "my job" are middle-level motives that, while they "may on occasion instigate certain actions," typically "require the presence of other goal-schemas to instigate action" (this volume: 30–1). Thus, presumably, the marriage schema might instigate some actions only in interaction with the love schema, as "job" might instigate other actions only in interaction with work. Still lower-level schemas are those that themselves instigate almost no actions except when other, higher-level schemas are present. An instance might be a schema for sandwich making. It is easy to imagine how this schema might be instigated by hunger. Equally plausibly, it might be instigated in the presence of a marriage schema, part of which has to do with a wife's duty to prepare food and serve it to her husband. The latter schema in turn might be instigated in interaction with still higher-level schemas, performance of a wife's duty being a token of love, perhaps, or essential to a successful marriage. This last illustration will shortly take on real-life dimensions.

Since the major function of top-level schemas is to guide action, D'Andrade hypothesizes that *"a person's most general interpretations of what is going on will function as important goals for that person"* (this volume: 30). Elaborating on this point elsewhere, he observed that "schemata which are at the very top of the interpretive system, since they are the most general source of 'guidance,' 'orientation,' and 'direction' in the system, form the most general, permanent, and stable goals in the system" (1990:159).

A question that arises is *how* given schemas, including cultural ones, come to be the most general and stable goals an individual has. D'Andrade's important contribution to this volume argues persuasively that goal-schemas offer a host of conceptual and empirical improvements over the innate human drives that older theories posited at the top of all goal hierarchies. However, his formulation does not address the question it raises as to how some goal-schemas come to occupy the place of drives at the top of goal hierarchies.

In particular, how do cultural schemas come to act as important goals for individuals? The schemas used as illustration in the first paragraph of this paper are largely culturally constituted; that is, like another of D'Andrade's examples of a high-level goal-schema, achieve-ment, they exist "only because some group of humans have developed the notion of 'achievement' and agreed that certain things will count as an achievement" (this volume: 35), or an instance of love or work, or a marriage[1] or a job or a sandwich. One important way cultural schemas like achievement or love or work or marriage become high-level goal-schemas in individuals' goal hierarchies, I want to say, is by supplying us with our understandings of ourselves. The high achiever of D'Andrade's example is motivated not out of some abstract belief in the merits of achievement, but out of an abiding inner sense that he would be less of the person he wants to be should he not attain the high standards he has set himself, or at least make every effort to do so.[2] For other Americans, Strauss's (this volume) working men among them, achieving is not important to sense of self in the way that adequate breadwinning is. In what follows I will introduce some American women whose sense of themselves as good wives in successful marriages is very close to the core of their being.[3] I will try to introduce some uniformity into my discussion by referring to these "senses" as (cultural or otherwise) self-under-standings.

If "self-understandings" are more than a semantic gloss for "general goal-schemas," then the substitution must hold some new implication. I believe that it does. We are now led to ask, what is it about self-understanding that is so compelling to us that it defines our most general goals? The answer lies in the way we come to understand ourselves. The process by which cultural schemas are incorporated into a sense of "self," thereby entering into the definition of an individual's existential concerns and life ambitions, is life-long and causally complex. Most of us would agree that crucial stages of this process of self-definition occur in child-hood and adolescence; however, traumatic or otherwise compelling exper-iences at any age can inspire redefinition of the self or elaboration of prior self-understandings. The material to follow will suggest how goals, far from being inherent in self-understandings, become linked to them, in the course of experience, by the way in which such understandings are typically learned. Adopting a slightly less awkward terminology to talk about the goal-providing potentiality of schemas, we can speak of their motivational force. Motivational force, then, is not built into cultural understandings of self; rather, these understandings acquire force as they are implicated in an individual's ongoing experience and interpretation of the world.

Self-understandings are prone to acquire motivational force and they do so in interaction with experience, particularly early experience. But how this happens is not obvious. A third and final point to emerge is that the motivational force that self-understandings acquire depends crucially upon the seeming naturalness and rightness that these understandings are granted in the course of socialization. Motivational or "directive force,"[4] D'Andrade comments, "is experienced by the person as needs or obligations to do something" (1984:97). Schemas that organize our stable understandings of ourselves and our relations to the world, including other people, comprise one very important class of schemas ordinarily experienced as needs and obligations to do something. Needs are inherent either in human nature or in the particular nature of the individual; accordingly, their fulfillment is natural and necessary. Obligations are ordained by the moral order; their fulfillment is right and necessary.

Self-understandings not only fit D'Andrade's general characterization of directive force in terms of "needs or obligations to do something"; they give specification to this definition as well. The material to follow illustrates three such schemas for self-understanding, each with potential force. One kind of schema defines the self as a human being among other such beings who observe some standard of equitable relations with one another ("how I should be treated and treat others"); another defines the self as the occupant of social roles with obligations attached to them ("what someone in my position ought to do"); and a last defines the self as possessor of inherent attributes or traits ("what I am like"). In the case to be presented, these inherent attributes are attributes of gender. The case material will show how, far from being woven together into seamless identities, these different kinds of schemas accommodate self-understandings that may be radically different, and that may compete in the interpretation of a given situation, creating internal conflict over which self-understanding will direct behavior.

Before turning to this case material, I will briefly touch on several issues that arise out of the discussion so far, in the hopes of anticipating and laying to rest some obvious questions and objections. One disclaimer to be made is that the schemas for equitable human relations, for social role enactment, and for self-attribution are hardly limited in their application to this directive or motivational function; they are also "situation defining" (D'Andrade 1990:157). That is, they are used more generally to interpret behavior, one's own as well as that of others. Thus they are correctly characterized not as understandings of the self alone, but more broadly as elements in our culturally constructed understanding of personhood and interpersonal relations. It is this dual function of personhood schemas – to interpret and to motivate – which allows us to divine the goals of others from knowledge of their "roles," their "personalities," and their "relationships," and which also allows us to step back from ourselves and analyze our own motives and behavior in the same way we interpret the motives and behavior of others. Nevertheless, a key function of such understandings about personhood is to perform as understandings about the self, and in so doing to convert knowledge about people into general goals to be pursued by oneself.

It may appear from my list of schemas for personhood – the person as human being, as social role occupant, and as possessor of attributes – that what I am proposing is nothing more than a grand amalgam of exchange theory, role theory, and personality theory drawn from various quarters of psychology. Quite to the contrary it is my contention that these different academic psychologies themselves have captured, and reified into analytic constructs, three different classes of schemas for personhood that figure in western ethnopsychology. Because they are part of our ethnopsychology, these schemas for personhood play a part, not only in our social-scientific theories, but also in the everyday thinking of the wives to be described in this paper and other ordinary people.

It is entirely possible that these three classes of schemas for equitable human relations, social roles and their obligations, and gendered and other inherent attributes will be found to recur cross-culturally. If this should prove so then the academic theories which have borrowed their insights from ethnopsychology are not to be dismissed on account of this borrowing. Some evidence on this question comes from the finding of Shweder and Bourne (1982) that both the Americans and the Indians they studied interpreted others' behavior in terms of stable personality traits and role obligations – although the Americans were much more inclined to rely upon the former class of interpretations, the Indians the latter. Inasmuch as individuals in all societies face similar existential problems of self-definition and social interpretation, it would not be surprising to find these three kinds of schemas for personhood resurfacing in widely different societies cross-culturally. At present, however, I would want to make no claim for the inclusiveness or translatability of my typology. The specific content of these schemas for human relations, role enactment, and self-attribution are ordinarily drawn from a wide array of available cultural knowledge about personhood, and this cultural content may differ widely from society to society.

The method of this paper, suited to its exploratory nature, will be to present a body of rich case material with which to speculate. The cases I will use to think about the motivational force of self-understanding have to do with the concerns of American wives about their marriages.[5] Each wife describes an inner conflict over an issue in her marriage. Talk about inner conflict, like occasions for the expression of interpersonal conflict that have been analyzed by other cognitive anthropologists (e.g., Hutchins 1980, Lutz 1986, White 1985), provides a culturally defined occasion for the self-conscious examination and verbal articulation of the conflicting understandings. This opportunity is exploited here to reveal something about the nature of these understandings of self so powerful as to create the inner conflict.

The cases will illustrate three types of self-understanding that appear to be sources of importance and enduring goals for the individual women described. These cases will suggest how such understandings may have gained motivational force in the course of these women's earlier experience. In tracing the origins of this motivational force, the cases will also point to the critical part played by the seeming naturalness and rightness that experience has granted to these understandings of self. Moreover, the cases will reveal something about the way in which these differing and often opposed beliefs about what is right and what is natural do ideological work. The ideological contest reflected in this material collected ten years ago is the ongoing one in our society between conceptions of women's innate qualities and their role obligations on the one hand, and demands for women's rights on the other. While not all of the wives in my study appeared to experience inner conflict around these contested ideas, it does not surprise us to learn that none of their husbands did so (though husbands certainly experienced the consequences of these conflicts for their wives). The contest is played out here in the complexities of these three individual women's thoughts and in the particularities of their three marriages. For the wives' cases will illustrate, finally, how cultural understandings woven into individual experience result in stories that are unique and unpredictable but at the same time readily recognizable to us all.

The material I will discuss is excerpted from the first nine hours of interviews with three wives, part of a larger study of eleven married couples in which husband and wife were interviewed separately. I will provide a detailed examination of the first wife's conflict, followed by a slightly briefer description of the other two cases. Within the framework provided by these interviews about people's marriages, this first wife is somewhat unusual among interviewees, in the extent to which she introspects about the childhood origin of some of her views and attitudes about marriage. Thus, as will be seen, her story is particularly useful for thinking about self-understandings and their basis in socialization.

"I'm a human being"

This wife, Kay,[6] has been married for a year and a half and is engaged with her husband Bobby in a classic struggle over the housework. She resists his traditional definition of her household duties in no uncertain terms:[7]

1W–2: I don't like to be told – I'll tell you what really gets me more than anything else is this: he told me a couple of times, "It's your wifely duty." To me that's a crock.

She explicitly rejects such a definition of the division of domestic labor in favor of a "partnership" model, a concept which she illustrates with a scenario from the eventual time when they have children and she expects him to go out shopping for their shoes with her:

I: Do you expect Bobby to help, then?
1W–2: Yes. Fifty percent at least. I feel that – you might want to call it a partnership but I feel like everything should be fifty percent.
I: By everything – what do you mean by everything?
W: I feel like that if I give enough time – okay say we have three kids. If I give, you know, as much as I can to a child I feel Bobby should give as much as he can. I don't feel like he should just say, "Well Kay look. You're the mother. You take him to do this. You take him to go buy clothes and do their shopping." You know. I don't want him to sit here and watch TV while I takes the kids out to buy their shoes. I feel like he ought to go too.

When Bobby tries to rationalize his view of her domestic duties by claims about his own superior contributions as a breadwinner, she is neither convinced nor cowed, but counters assertively with her own clear perception of their equally taxing jobs (he is a butcher and she an apartment manager) and their equal contributions to the household income. These exchanges might have come right out of Pat Mainardi's *The Politics of Housework* (1970):

1W–2: But he tells me, he says, "You sit up there on your butt all day and you do nothing." And I said, "I do nothing? If I have to listen to somebody make three complaints in one day that's something to me." You know whether I sit there and stare at the wall I get bored to death sometimes. So I come home and I'm mentally tired from boredom. But he doesn't understand that. Because he does physical work.

1W–2: But he told me one time, he said, "Well that's your job." And I said, "Job? I don't get paid for it." He said, "What do you think that weekly allowance I give you is for?" And I looked at him and I said, "Hey wait one minute. We make equal salaries just about." I mean, you know, he makes at the most a couple thousand more a year than I do but now I'm including my apartment with it. It's not actual cash flow but it's income.
I: You know exactly how much that costs.
W: And I told him I said, you know, "I make almost just as much as you do so I don't want your telling me it's my job. I don't get paid and my allowance, whatever I get a week – big deal." You know, "I can take it out whenever I want it. It's my money too."

She does not think that the division of household labor is fair, and she tells him so in no uncertain terms. The texts of these comments convey the fervor with which Kay defends her position on different occasions as well as the ethic of fairness on which this position is founded. In one interview she says:

1W–2: There have been times when I felt like it was very unfair. I mean I've sat him down and said, "You're being very unfair about this, I might not work just as hard physically but I work too. And I'm a human being and I deserve time to myself and I just don't feel like you're being fair about money or being fair about housework or whatever." I've told him flat out. Before we got our washer and dryer we had so many arguments over the laundromat. I mean that was one of our biggest problems believe it or not. Because he didn't want to go do laundry with me. I don't know if I told you before . . .
I: Yeah.
W: . . . I left his laundry and I took mine. I said, "You wash your own. If you can't go with me to help me do it then you can wash your own." And that changed right away.

1W–3: I wouldn't ask him to do anything I wouldn't do. That makes me feel like I'm right. You know when I told him about the vacuuming I said, "I do everything around this house." I said, "I do all the clothes, I wash all the dishes. I do everything." The next day he told me, he said, "You're right. I don't do anything." And I said, "You really don't." But when I got mad I said, "Okay, if you're not going to vacuum," I said, "I'm telling you right now, you can wash your clothes from now on. You can cook your meals. You can do everything for yourself from now on."
I: You said that, eh?
W: I resigned from doing my – well this is what I told him Friday night. He asked me – Saturday night – he said, "Where have you been all day when I called?" He said, "What time did you leave here? Eight o'clock in the morning to go shopping?" And I said, "No. As a matter of fact I did my wifely duties, as you put them." I said, "I washed the clothes and I cleaned up." I didn't wake him up when I cleaned up. I dusted. I picked up. I said, "I did the things I was supposed to do."

You know and I told him I said, "Do you think – you come home from work and you lay around and do the things you want to do. Do you think I enjoy coming home and having to clean up?"

1W–3: Like I said I don't like – I can't stand this thing where it's your duty to do it, your wifely duty or your job. That just irritates me. Because I don't think of it as a job. I think of it as something that needs to be done. It's a job in a sense but I consider it my job where I get paid. You know I don't get paid for this. And I just don't think it's fair for me to come home and have to start washing clothes and doing this and doing that and doing things that I don't really enjoy doing all the time. And then him saying something to me about it.

And still again, in a subsequent interview:

1W–5: I have feelings and I don't feel like coming home and cleaning up after somebody else. You know? That's what it was with washing clothes. I wasn't going to wash clothes for two people unless he was going to help.

1W–5: I do, I run the household. I take care of the bills, I take care of keeping it clean and I am in what they would – everybody would say was a wifely role, a wife's job.
I: And you claim to like it.
W: I don't like the thought of being told that that's what I've got to do. I think that's what I don't like. I don't like the idea of having a role where somebody's going to tell me that it's my duty to do it. I don't mind doing it but if you tell me it's my duty, that really gets to me. And Bobby has said that before. Made a comment that – something about, "That's your wifely duty." I'm not getting paid for it. I said I'd do it 'cause half of it consists of me too. I mean, you know, I make half the mess here at home. I'm doing my half too. But I get tired of it. Really and truly think like, "Please. Why won't you help me do such-and-such?"

When she says, "I'm a human being and I deserve time to myself and I just don't feel like you're being fair," and again when she argues, "I have feelings and I don't feel like coming home and cleaning up after somebody else," Kay is invoking their common humanity as a basis for equal treatment of her husband and herself. Summarizing this presumption of their equality as it applies to their contributions to the housework, she declares, "I wouldn't ask him to do anything I wouldn't do," and "If I've got to do it why shouldn't he?"

Yet Kay backs down. When it is pointed out to her that she ends up doing the housework, she says,

1W–3: But I do it because I know if I don't do it, it won't get done. I'm a fanatic on cleanliness. Everything has to be clean.

Below this differential standard for cleanliness lies a deep ambivalence.

1W–2: I think he feels like now, that I don't mind doing it. And I don't really mind doing it, it's just that some days I just don't feel like doing it, you know. It's like I told him I said, you know, "What makes you think I want to come home and cook dinner or I want to come home and vacuum?" And he'll go out some nights with one of his friends and he'll say, "Well I'm going to play golf." And I'll say, "Okay. Well what am I supposed to do." He says, "Well why don't you wash clothes or something." And I'll say, "Do you think I enjoy doing that? I mean what makes you think I...?" Or he'll say, "Well um I do need some clothes ironed." And I'll say, "Well learn to iron it yourself. If you want it done that bad that soon. Do it yourself." You know, he's not helpless. And I feel like that, you know, I've just never had to wait on anybody else. And I still have not quite adjusted to it. I eventually will but I haven't quite made up my mind...

I: But you say two things. You say you're going to adjust to it and then you say when the kids come it's going to be fifty/fifty.

W: Yeah. I tell you, it won't be fifty/fifty, it never'll be fifty/fifty. But, I don't want him handing me the child every time it's got a dirty diaper and say, "Here you change it, I'm not touching it." I mean I expect him to be able to show a little bit of responsibility and do it himself. You know, Mary's husband doesn't do that, and I say, "Gah, I'd kill Bobby if he wouldn't even change a dirty diaper." What's the – you know, if I've got to do it why shouldn't he? It's his job too. Whereas now I guess – I come in with, "It's your mess too. You should help." But he doesn't and I just say, "Well," rather than cause an argument, "Just stay over there and do your thing." But I feel like if he doesn't help once we have children it will cause problems. Because – I don't know if it's because I'll have – I'll feel like I have more on me or what. Now I just come home and do it. I don't like to be told – I'll tell you what really gets me more than anything else is this: he told me this a couple of times, "It's your wifely duty." To me that's a crock.

Iterating her objection, Kay relates an incident which reveals, in the end, why she gives in:

1W–5: But I'm saying I can't stand for somebody to say "It's your wifely duty" or "It's a wife's duty to do such-and-such." You know, last night for instance, Bobby comes in from playing basketball. I'd been out, I'd gone to ceramics and I'd come home. I was tired too. And he comes in he says, "What's for dinner?" And I said, "You weren't home for dinner, I didn't make anything." He said, "Well make me a sandwich." And I said, "Make your own sandwich." You know, "You've got two hands yourself, I'm ironing clothes."

I: You were ironing and he had...

W: Yeah I was ironing his clothes and he says, "Make me a sandwich." And I said, "Make your own sandwich." And it really just kind of irritated me and I was standing here and I said, "Do you think I enjoy standing here ironing? I don't want to do this. You come over here and iron your own clothes." He says, "Okay, forget it, I'll make my own sandwich." I said, "Okay, fine." And then he laughed he says, "Aw come on Kay, make me a sandwich." And he was joking. He thought it was funny. So I just made a sandwich. I brought it in I said, "Here. Do you want me to eat it too?" And he says, "Aw, come on." And I said, "I've got to go finish ironing."

I: So you made it for him.

W: Yeah.

I: Why did you do that?
W: I don't know. It was just as easy to slap the mayonnaise on the bread and put the meat between it and hand it to him as it was to have to listen to him say, "Aw come on. Make it." I just, you know, I just did it and I handed it to him. I guess sometimes I feel like he's a child. You know they act like children.
I: They?
W: Husbands. He'll come in and he'll act like a child sometimes and you just feel like you have to treat him like a child. I feel like I – you know when you have to iron their clothes and you do this and you do that. On Saturdays I'm here cleaning up the house, I feel like my mother used to do with us. You know she always had to clean up and do the things. And I guess I feel like that too. I feel like – like I said, wifely duties. I feel like sometimes it's my duty to do it. But then I don't like that, yet I'll do it.
I: You'll do it.
W: I'm totally against having certain roles.

Husbands are like children because wives have to attend to their physical upkeep in the same way mothers do the upkeep of their children. Wifely duties are a mother's care.

Kay returns shortly to the key symbolic issue of ironing:

1W–5: It's like okay I was in there ironing all those clothes and I hated it. I thought I'd rather do anything than stay here ironing all these clothes. But he sure wasn't going in there to iron them.
I: Well how did that start that you iron his clothes? Was that the day you got married? Or was it before?
W: Mmm hmmm. The day we got married. I didn't do it – I didn't do his laundry and ironing, I didn't do nothing for him before we got married, because he lived at home, I didn't have to. But now I've always ironed all my clothes. I just have. But again, I tell you something else, here it goes again on approval. I have seen so many men, or women I guess, coming in [to her office] that look like dogs. Their clothes look horrible. They look dirty or something and I think, "God, whoever's doing their laundry isn't doing it worth a toot," you know. Husbands for instance. I think how their wife doesn't care about their appearance or something, you know? Again one of Bobby's friends comes in here and talks about how his wife doesn't keep house. That it's just filthy and grungy and dirty and that she didn't even know what an iron was. And I thought, "Gah, poor . . ." you know, "I wouldn't want Bobby to feel that way." There – you know, there's a – I wouldn't want him to feel that way, I want to please him. So I iron his clothes and stuff because I feel like they look better if they're ironed. He couldn't care less.
I: And you knew the moment you were married, you knew you would do that? That was your – forgive me, your role?
W: I knew that was – exactly.
I: You never dicussed it?
W: Nope. Mm mm.
I: You just start – you just came home and . . .
W: I just started ironing his clothes and one day I looked at him and I said, "I'm sick and tired of ironing shirts." He said, "Kay you don't have to iron my shirts." I

said, "I know I don't have to," but if I don't I feel like I sent him – that he – "Sending him to work" it's like sending your child to school with dirty clothes. It's like I sent him to work with a wrinkled shirt. And somebody at work's going to say, "God, his wife must not care about his clothes." Because people naturally assume that the wife does these things. And that's approval again – it comes right back to where I don't want people to feel that . . .

I: You want to be the kind of wife who . . .

W: Cares or looks like she cares or I don't know how to say it. It sounds like all I want is approval from everybody on my marriage but that's not true. What I really – it's just I want – I just don't want Bobby to feel like that he isn't getting what he's used to, I guess. His mother ironed all his clothes so I just naturally assumed . . . [tape changeover]

I: You wanted to live up to what?

W: I wanted to live up to her expectations through Bobby. I mean – you know, it's like – if we're going to his parents for dinner I'm going to make sure that his clothes are spotless and that, you know, he's – you know what I mean. I just don't want them to think I'm not doing what I should. Again it's doing my wifely duties. And I don't believe in them but everybody expects it from you so you end up doing it anyway.

I: You do it but you don't believe in it.

W: But you don't – but how do I correct it? I mean he's not going to do it. He's too lazy.

If we ask why Kay gives in and makes the sandwich, then, it appears that she does so because of a goal hierarchy leading back to her desire for a good marriage, one that people will approve of. Kay is caught between wanting approval for her marriage – which requires that she perform the wifely duties of keeping her house clean and her husband presentable and happy – and believing in an equal division of this domestic work – which she is in a weak position to demand from a husband who does not have the same investment in its performance as she does.

The analogy of husbands to children is one to which she returns later in the same interview:

1W–5: I guess 'cause my mother was always correcting me on grammar and things so then I think, "My mother did that to me and I'm doing it to him. I sound like my mother." So that's childish to me. I feel like he's a child when I say something like that. 'Cause my mother was constantly correcting me on grammar. And I guess I think of myself thinking, "God I'm just like my mom." And I'm like his mom correcting him.

I: Is that the main time when you feel like that, correcting grammar?

W: That and picking up after him. If I have to pick up or say, "Bobby don't do that. That's stupid. Don't you realize that you don't throw something on the floor and just leave it there for days?" Or, "You don't do this, throw a wet towel in with the clothes and they sour." You know.

I: So in general, you . . .

W: But I don't think he's a child in any other way. I don't think of him as a child except physical things around the house. Physical actions.

The analogy is one that neatly accommodates the unequal division of labor to the goal of having a good marriage. If husbands are like children, then it is up to women to be good wives as well as good mothers.

The theme of approval for her marriage, like that of equal division of the housework, is sounded again and again in Kay's interviews. The major dimension along which their marital squabbles fall, next to the housework issue, has to do with the amount of time Kay and Bobby spend together and the way they spend that time. While he would like to be free to spend most of his time away from home with his male friends, she is always trying to get him to go places with her. When he repeatedly pleads off going with her to visit an out-of-town friend, and people at her friend's house ask her "Where's your husband?" she thinks, "God I really do have one, you know."

In a characteristic passage, she explains why it is so important to her that Bobby and she be seen together in public:

1W–4: And like I said, doing things together. I just wanted to be a pair.
I: A pair?
W: Yeah I guess that's it, you know. We just did things together. We just went places together. We would just enjoy things. And of course you see it as a perfect marriage and everybody says, "They're going to have this," and "They're going to have that." You know and that "Their marriage is going to be so great." "They're not going to do this." "They make out." You know.

Elsewhere she says,

1W–4: I'm making people proud of me which is what I want to do. I want people to be proud of me.
I: Everybody does.
W: I want my family to feel like, "Hey," I've succeeded somewhere, "Kay's doing good even though the rest of the family isn't worth a shit. Kay's doing good." I don't mean that. I just mean my brother's gone through his second marriage and, you know.

When others ask her how she and Bobby are, her extravagant responses prompt her best friend to warn her, "Don't go into this, 'Oh we're just so happy. We've never been any happier.'" People will suspect her, her friend advises, of "just putting on." When her husband makes public jokes about marrying her for money or her mother's cooking, she is upset that people will believe that "he really truly doesn't love me" but "just married me for some off-the-wall reason." Her sensitivity to what people think about her marriage is manifested in her constant worry that a variety of specific individuals and groups approve of it and judge it a success. Her concern focuses now on her family, now on her parents-in-law, and now again on her friends:

1W–4: I'll tell you what I don't want. I don't want anybody saying, "Well Kay and Bobby are doing something stupid. They shouldn't have done such-and-such," or "They shouldn't have done this." I don't want to give anybody any reason to talk about me bad. Because I don't feel like we deserve it. I think that what Bobby and I do is our own business. It's our private life but people have a bad habit of talking about you, family included. They're going to say, "I think that's a stupid mistake they're making." Something like, "They shouldn't be getting married. They're too young." Mainly I heard that from guys that were friends of mine but didn't think I should get married. Not to Bobby, just in general they didn't think I should get married. Most of them didn't know Bobby. But things like – you know, my brother just getting married. Everybody was saying, "I just think Ernie's too young to get married."
I: Is this your younger brother?
W: My younger brother. And so they don't think he's responsible enough. I don't want people to say that to me and they didn't. It's like my father, when I called and said, "Daddy, I'm getting married." He said, "Fantastic. When?" When we called to tell him Ernie was getting married he said, "Kay, can't you talk him out of it?"
I: Is that because he feels you're mature and he . . .
W: Evidently. And my older brother did the same thing. Frank says, "Kay, when you got married that was one of the best things you ever did." He says, "You were ready for it." He says, "But Ernie's not."

1W–5: I want – my parents and my friends, you know, I don't want – I'm bad, Bobby gets on me for it, I'm bad about not wanting somebody to talk about me or to say, "I told you so." And I don't want anybody to be able to say, "Well they blew it. They couldn't make it. They couldn't work things out." And people – I mean somebody else's opinion of me matters.

1W–5: But their [her parents-in-law's] approval means a lot to me when you get back to approval. Only on my part, I couldn't care less what they think about – I know they know that our marriage is okay because they see us enough to. But I just want them to be sure. I want them to know that I'm trying my best to, you know, have a good marriage.

1W–5: I want them to like Bobby the ones that don't know him, I want them to like him, you know, I want them to say, "Oh, Kay he's – she's got a really nice guy," or something. You know you always want somebody to – I'm sure it's the same way with your children, you want people to like him and enjoy being around him. And as far as approval of my marriage I mean, at first I wanted that but now I don't give a damn. I mean I couldn't care less. I've proved to myself that I can make my marriage work or that I have made it work for a year and a half. And that everything's fine. I think when I first got married people were just so – were standing by waiting to see what's going to happen. You know I – one of my friends got married and the whole time during the whole wedding Bobby and I kept looking at each other and shaking our heads. This was like three or four years ago. Saying, "It'll never work. It'll never work." And sure enough they stayed married like a year and a half and they were divorced. Got a divorce. And I said, everybody knew – people were saying, "It's a farce. It'll never last." And I guess because of that I've always wondered if people were saying that about me. I was wondering if somebody was going to say – I wonder if people say they really think Bobby and I are going to make it together. Because I was in that kind of group where – of friends where everybody was close and everybody knew each other and knew what everybody else did so I guess, you know, friends' approval or what they said or talked about meant a lot to me. Because there was such a big group of us always together doing things. I mean we would go on beach trips together and there would be twenty-five or thirty of us. And we were all real good friends.

She says, in sum, that if her marriage were to fail she "would feel like I had let down a whole lot of people who thought that I had something good in my life and I lost it."

Kay is quite aware of the source of her concern for so many people's approval. Her own sense of self-worth is closely tied to the poor marital track record of her parents and her brother and other family members:

1W–1: I guess like I said, my parents were divorced, my brother was divorced, you know, everybody I was around was divorced and I felt like, "I'm not going to let that happen to me." Somehow I was going to pull a marriage together that was going to be good.

1W–1: I've always wanted a home. My parents are divorced so I always wanted to have a happy home because I really wasn't in one. And I guess I just kept thinking I was going to make my marriage so perfect because I'd seen everybody else's fall apart and I knew what not to do but that's not true. But I still think that's what I wanted.

1W–5: I guess what I'm saying about my marriage, I don't want my father to think that because he and my mother had problems, or because he ran around on my mother or he did this or that I'm going to end up letting something like that happen to me.

Most especially, she sees herself as avoiding what happened to her mother:

1W–3: We were better off with one parent but what I'm saying is that as long as my parents were together and there was so much trouble I know what it did to me. And I know what it did to my mother. I just don't want that. So it has influenced me a lot in my decisions on getting married and my ideas of marriage.

The lesson of her mother's unhappy third marriage to Kay's stepfather, and ultimate inability to keep this husband either, is contradictory however. On the one hand, her mother's experience suggests accommodation, as when Kay trains herself, early in her marriage, not to lose her temper or make issues over minor matters that, she says, are "not something to break up a marriage over." This is the lesson Kay's mother herself counsels. At one point when Kay and Bobby are still dating, her mother warns Kay that if she persists in the way she is treating him, "You're going to lose Bobby. You're going to lose the only good thing you've ever had in your life." After their marriage, Kay confesses, she prefers to talk over marital problems with her girlfriends than with her mother, who "takes Bobby's side on just about everything," urging Kay to give in for the sake of the marriage. But some indication that Kay shares her mother's fear of losing her husband is given by occasional dreams she has in which Bobby is terminally ill or dead, and her imaginings, when he fails to phone and let her know his whereabouts, that he has been killed in an auto crash. It is a willingness to do whatever necessary to keep Bobby and make the marriage succeed that prompts Kay to perform her "wifely duties" in the end.

A different conclusion can be drawn from her mother's experience, and it is the one that Kay arrives at when she remembers the older woman's suffering: her mother calling a small Kay to come downstairs and interrupt the vehement quarrels that started after she and her little brother had gone to bed at night; or her mother waiting up long hours for the return of her philandering husband.

1W–4: And she was always sitting downstairs waiting for my father to come home. She would be knitting or she would be reading and I always remember her sitting downstairs waiting for my father to come home.

The lesson Kay derives from these painful childhood memories is one that suggests a much less conciliatory approach to marital relations:

1W–2: He didn't tell her where he was. It's things like that, my mom would get so furious over what was going on and she would lose her temper with him and it would make it worse. He would get madder and I feel like, if she had just kind of took it very calmly and said, "Look. I'd prefer if you're going to run around to pick up and leave." Instead, she would let him do it. I wouldn't let someone walk all over me like that. But maybe it's because I've seen it. My mother had – you know, she came from the country with a family that always stayed together and stuff and she had already been through divorce and so – I don't know if she just felt like she had to try to make it work or what. Which everybody wants to make it work. But still, I mean, husbands treating you that bad, you don't just sit there and let them do it.

Kay's musings over her mother's marriage suggest that the conflict in her mind between being the kind of wife who could make a marriage work, and being treated fairly by her husband, was one that was established, and repeatedly reinforced, early in her life.

"That's what you owe to your husband"

The inner conflicts of other wives revolve around other complaints than Kay's about housework, complaints likely to be equally familiar to married American readers. Nan, for example, has a deep sense that a wife owes her husband an unconditional emotional commitment she herself cannot seem to summon:

4W–12: In a sense I always feel like I'm cheating Tom, you know. That he has a right to have a wife who has the sort of emotional commitment to him that many couples seem to have, and one part of me says, "Well you probably do have at least as much emotional commitment to him as almost anybody would have but you don't have the mindless 'I'm in love' kind of losing yourself, pu—surrendering your judgment and perspective and stuff like that." And some part of me must keep saying to me, "That's the way you're supposed to be, in love, that's why you're supposed to be married, that's the ideal," you know, "That's what you *owe* to your husband." I know some part of me is saying that and another part of me is saying, "Well," you know, "that's not what I've got, and I just – I am what I am and I . . ."

4W–12: That, you know, one part of me is saying, you know, "You creep. Poor guy, you know, here he is married to a wife who's not going to walk through fire for him" and the other part is saying, "Be realistic. You love him as much and are as committed as much as almost anyone but a total romantic could ever be able to achieve, why are you chastising yourself or feeling a lack?"

Nan views the obligation to be emotionally committed to one's spouse not as a singularly wifely one but as a reciprocal one; her guilt arises in part from the fact that unlike herself Tom seems to experience no lack of involvement, but is totally committed to her and the family.

Her emotional withdrawal, which she describes as thinking, "We're just going to put some brakes on right here," and taking "one giant step backwards out of my involvement in the marriage," first occurred at some point in the course of her husband's recurrent bouts of depression and his long-term inability to pull his life together, a time when she decided, "I wasn't going to put my eggs in that unsteady a basket in a sense – emotionally."

Emotional disengagement also "inevitably for me meant a giant step backward out of my sexual involvement," and the beginning of sexual tensions in the marriage. In his time of stress, Tom's attitude toward sex became "totally utilitarian – 'I'm uptight so I've got to get Nan in bed and . . .' – totally perfunctory, nothing to do with me or anything else. Just a release of tension was all that it involved." By unfortunate contrast, Nan describes herself as having never been able to disconnect sex and emotion in her mind or in her body. At the very worst moment in her marriage, it was her realization that "I don't want this man anywhere near my body" that alerted her to the extent of her own negative feelings and made her examine the rest of her relationship with Tom and her wish to be out of it. As she remembers that time,

4W–12: I felt prickly. I felt like every hair on my body was a porcupine spear saying "Keep away," you know. "Don't, don't, don't ask anything, don't come near me, don't . . ."

While she has sympathy for what her husband Tom is going through, Nan also still has doubts about her ability to "stay married to a manic-depressive." She worries that during one of his low times, her resilience will reach a breaking-point and something will snap:

4W–12: . . . I think if it snapped again that I would just – I would snap into a resolve, "Okay, I'm going to end this relationship before the children and I are drowned in it." I would never want to cut him out of my life because I love him too much. I mean I really do like Tom so much and in – and just really love his company and everything, there's – and I would feel very bereft if I didn't have him, but, I might – I could see – my imagination could see a point where if he – if his depression was too prolonged and too severe, something inside of me would say, "This is not for me day to day. I'm going to have to make my day to day life count on someone who's more dependable, and that's me." You know, in the sense more emotionally dependable.

Nan feels that her own strength to endure these episodes of depression "gets less and less as time goes by." Her "romantic" idea of the emotional commitment a wife owes her husband conflicts with a "realistic" sense of self-preservation:

4W–12: It's not as much emotional commitment as I want to have because I would feel happy with – as I think Tom deserves. I'm certainly committed emotionally but there is a part that I'm holding in reserve. There is that part that says, "Well, there may come a time when I have to dissolve this relationship because I can't deal with it anymore." It's a realistic kind of thing.

Her dilemma, the impossibility of involving herself emotionally in her marriage while protecting herself from the negative consequences to her own mental health of this involvement, is never more acute than when she attempts to deal with her husband's recurrent anxiety attacks. She thinks

4W–13: . . . that I'm basically le—a more stable person than he is, and that – so we tend to use me as the rock and try to pin him to it or, you know – and I get tired of that sometimes. And that is the issue of support. But I forget where I read it not long ago, someone making a comment about marriage and staying married and so on and so forth that you may find yourself married to someone who has characteristics or some problems or whatever, that you really don't like but you never will be able to change and that you'll just have to learn to accept. That's a thorn in your side, and that you can live with it. And I thought about that a lot because I think it might help me and it might help us for me to say to myself, "Tom has a lot of anxiety. And that's just the way it is." And I have to separate myself emotionally from that to some extent. Not let myself get swept into anxiety with him but just to say, "Well that's old Tom's anxiety working again." And not get thrown off balance every single time. But I have a fear that it will mean a disconnecting of emotional ties. That it's very hard to balance out – to be able to say, "Oh, that's just Tom's anxiety working," and not really be concerned about him. Because somehow you're disconnecting yourself when you do that. And then if you disconnect yourself, then why are you married to someone, you know, and this . . .

4W–13: That by kind of putting a little shield between his anxiety and me because the anxiety's catching and it's not good for me or for the kids, that I'll also be putting a shield between other things. I mean how can you just filter out that one thing?
I: Like you mean in general his sensitivities, or . . .?
W: Yeah, and feelings. I mean, what if I learned to say, you know, "That's just your anxiety, don't worry about it," or, you know, just learn to say and feel those things, I might also be at the same time, cutting myself off from other parts. So I – you know, it's just an idea I'm working on now, because I don't think that To—, I'm coming to believe that Tom's anxiety proneness will never change and it'll be a lot more under control, but it'll never change. And that, instead of me reacting like, "Oh, here's another crisis, my life is in crisis all the time," it would be much better just to say, "Oh, that's just another one of those things," and not get in a crisis feeling about it, even though he feels it's a crisis. But then won't he feel . . .?
I: That you essentially lack sympathy with him, or . . .?
W: Yeah. And that he's not getting support that he needs because I'm not involving myself in his crisis.

Countering this guilt over her inability to support Tom through his crises as a wife should is an assessment of inequality and a resentment over what she perceives as the unequal exchange of emotional support over the longer course of her marriage. Nan suspects Tom could develop the same tools and resources she has, and resents

4W–12: . . . his counting on it, wanting to lean on it, because I think it costs me a lot and I don't think he's measuring that cost. And I'm scared it's going to cost too much and leave me without being able to stay in the relationship.

4W–12: I think it feels good to be competent and I think it's realistic to say some people do have more skills than others do and it's not something that I can attribute to my own self. It's something in a sense that's a happy accident or birthing experience and everything else. But I feel like I can expend it happily a lot of the time but there's times when it's too much to ask. Everyone's asking me and nobody's giving and that – and I've just had it, I don't want it anymore. Somebody come support me for a while. And I think that's what I told Tom and so I feel like you got to – I have to have the belief that there'll come a time when he's going to turn around and say, "Lean on me honey. I feel up to it." And he's not sure that that's going to happen and I'm not sure that that's going to happen and I maybe even don't need as much of it as I think I do but I need some of it anyhow. I need to have the hope that it's going to be there as the occasion might demand.

So that her warning that she is reaching a breaking-point is simultaneously a complaint about the long-term imbalance in their relationship. If she is cheating her husband out of the total commitment he deserves from a wife, he is denying her the support she has a right to expect from him in exchange for her support of him. Just as Kay's concern to make what she regards as a perfect marriage conflicts with her indignation about the unfairness of the resulting division of household labor, Nan's desire to fulfil her ideal of the committed, supportive spouse conflicts with a felt inequality in the division of emotion work in her marriage. It is an inner contest, once again, between an obligation of role and a standard of equity.

Many American husbands and wives share Nan's attitude about the total emotional commitment one ought to feel for one's spouse. Nan says that her expectations regarding this commitment "certainly go back to my mother's Christian ideals or whatever – you know, what I was taught in Sunday school." This code of conduct she was taught includes a strong sense of responsibility to marriage and family and a determination "about fulfilling your part of the bargain" that marriage incurs. It includes marital fidelity and "a very narrow Puritan attitude emotionally that you're supposed to love the person you go to bed with," a notion that she associates with her own "image of what kind of young southern woman I was supposed to be" and her "feeling that my mother was the paragon of southern womanhood and everyone in the world said so, and my grandmother was, and I could never possibly live up to that but I had to anyhow." The expectations of her family and her high-school crowd, and "the whole standard of the whole town and where I fit into it" would have made a more experimental, casual attitude toward sex a "terrible disgrace." Regarding sexual possibilities, "The only concept I had," she says, "was good girl or bad girl."

Nan left the small southern town where she grew up to go to college, and, after that, partly to prove that she could take care of herself, she traveled around the world for the better part of a year. Yet, she reports, "deep down inside I still wanted to get married and have children and be taken care of." Her father had died when she was quite young, and her mother had not remarried for a number of years, a circumstance that perhaps heightened not only her desire for a husband who would take care of her, but also her idealistic standards for marriage and her felt lack of realism about marital relations. She "had no sense at all of what happened between men and women emotionally or sexually, really," she says.

Something that happened to her subsequently, when she was a young woman, is a key to Nan's story. What is most problematic in this story is her felt inability to live up to the emotional commitment she is so intent on making. She traces this shortcoming to her prior experience of another lengthy and significant relationship, with a man who left her not long before she met her husband-to-be – a relationship that she characterizes as "unfinished."

4W–12: Newton was the first person that I ever really went out with seriously for a number of years and – basically we lived together. And whenever the relationships between us were okay emotionally then certainly the sexual relationship was fine and pretty open and relaxed. I never really thought about it very much, I mean just very spontaneous and good humored kind of thing. But I think that towards the end of our relationship when there was a lot of kind of not so good stuff going on, that I started having this feeling of having committed myself way too much. And kind of equating this sexual openness and not ever thinking about holding myself in reserve with having been betrayed by him. That there – those two are kind of linked in my mind. That that total emotional giving in to him, total emotional involvement with him, is very linked with the sexual.

4W–12: I think that I fairly much, not very wisely, committed myself emotionally to him in a way that was not sensible. You know, I knew – I – some part of me must have known realistically that he wasn't a good person to trust those emotions with. He was not trustworthy about those sorts of things, but I went ahead and did it anyhow, thinking that, you know, true love will prevail, that – you know. And that – so that there is a tie that even I don't understand between that mindless, in a sense, really stupid sort of commitment, and the kind of spontaneous attitude that I had to sex at that time. You know, not ever – just was – it wasn't – just fairly open and good humored. That's all I can say about it.

Her sexual and emotional relationship with Tom was initially open and spontaneous too. This changed, we saw, in response to Tom's exhorbitant demands for support and his utilitarian approach to sex. Her attenuated commitment to Tom, with the sexual reservation this entails, are tied in Nan's mind to her earlier and unwise overcommitment, sexually and emotionally, to Newton.

4W–1: And I think some of the difficulties of – that I've had in committing myself to Tom in different kinds of situations ... There'd be either sexual situations or situations in which he wants me to be very, very supportive through a difficult time in certain ways and that I don't want to do that, I feel very strongly about not doing that, is tied up in the rela—, the previous relationship with Newton in which my role was always supposed to be supportive. And I realize that there's a limit to that. And that it – that I might even be more supportive to Tom if that didn't still linger.

Nan's withdrawal and withholding from her marital relationship are intended to prevent a repetition of the mistake she made in committing herself too unreservedly to this other man. Tom's demand for support, in particular, is too reminiscent of Newton's unreciprocated requirements of her in this regard. Tom's pursuit of instrumental sex seems to trigger another painful aspect of the experience with Newton, her unguarded emotional and hence sexual commitment to him and the subsequent hurt she must have suffered when he "betrayed" this commitment by disregarding her needs and then leaving her. It is as if the first serious relationship of her adult life taught Nan that the emotional support she had found it so natural to give is not automatically returned, priming her to be wary of such unequal exchanges in future relationships, including her present marriage. Similarly, Kay's lasting anger over her stepfather's treatment of her mother sensitized her to unfair treatment in her own marriage.

"I'm a lot more traditional than I wish that I were"

The third wife, Patsy, is on the academic job market with her husband. She worries endlessly about the compromise they may be called upon to make in seeking two positions in the same geographic locale. On the one hand, believing that the two of them are equally capable at their professions, she is committed to finding them two equally satisfying jobs:

9W–2: We're seeing a number of places where I fit what they want pretty easily, Rich doesn't and then at the other place he fits pretty easily, I don't and it's causing a lot of anxiety. My greatest fear – again I'm using the word "fear" – my greatest concern is that he'll find the job he most wants in this whole world and it'll be in Boston. And I'll find a job I want more than anything else in the world and it'll be in Los Angeles, that sort of thing.
I: Uh huh. Have you talked to him about that? I mean, specifically?
W: Yeah we talked about it and his response was something to the effect that, "I just hope that doesn't happen." Or otherwise he responds with, "Well, we just don't take them. We find something where both of us have something." Which is what we'll do, I'm sure of that. I'm sure that we will not take something at which the other person would be in a professional position that is totally unsatisfactory. One may be more satisfied than the other, but the one party has to be reasonably satisfied.

On the other hand, she is anxious that her husband secure a position commensurate with his professional capabilities and aspirations. She wants very much for him to have what he wants (even though, she confesses, she doesn't yet know him well enough to be sure that is what he wants). She holds her own determination also to have a career responsible for handicapping him in the job search, and worries that because of her, he will not maximize his potential:

9W–6: Part of it is that as a schoolteacher and from the way I can remember being pushed in education is that one has this obligation to oneself. To maximize one's potential. And then as a teacher that was sort of the ideal that I operated from. That I wanted all these students to do the best they – develop themselves to their fullest potential. And now here was the person that I loved the most, and I'm limiting his – he's not developing himself to the fullest, I guess. But you really, in going to graduate school, develop a sense of pecking order of jobs – you know, the prestige jobs. And of, you know, being in a top department. And Rich has that potential and because he has a wife who also has a career, he can't do that.

Aware of the contradiction between her desire for her husband's career to flourish and her unwillingness to sacrifice her own, Patsy rationalizes her situation in a way that manages to preserve the rightness of a "traditional" world in which the woman puts her husband's career first, while making herself an exception to this rule. She reasons that "It's too late for me to become the other kind of woman anyway," because of the years she spent in a Catholic convent and the education she received during that time:

9W–6: What I refer to as traditional. I guess that I don't – I think that if I had lived a normal life, you know, I probably would have been what my sisters were – are. Mothers and housewives. And I think I'm now at a point where I just couldn't change it anyway. I can't turn the clock back. I can't deny my brains. I can't deny my education and that I'm now just too well trained to forget it all. Too old to be a mother and so I really have no choice but to be a career woman. And I like it. I mean if I had a choice it was twenty years ago. There's no choice anymore. I'm already committed too far. I mean I can't decide to be a mother anymore. And so . . .

She goes on to argue that she has been made unfit for a traditional marriage by higher education, which has overtrained her for home-making, raised her aspirations, and pushed her to maximize her potential. The problem, Patsy reasons, lies not with traditional expectations about women's roles in marriage, but rather with schooling for girls, which unfairly teaches them a conflicting set of expectations. The startling conclusion to this line of reasoning is that girls should be excluded from higher education:

9W–3: But I started to think about the equality bit. I'm not sure what it would be like to be a woman with, say, an average IQ, who didn't go to college. What I would, you know, expect in a marriage. I mean, I don't know that equality would mean much to me. I'm not sure that in lots of ways, I couldn't – I don't think I could now be happy in a real traditional marriage. But I don't know that at one time I couldn't have been. In one sense I think the educational system isn't really fair to young women. I mean, you go through school and in grade school you make A's and, you know, the boys are always in trouble or whatever. And girls are going through making good grades. You go through high school and you keep making those good grades and then you go to college and you're still making those good grades. And somewhere along the line somebody forgets to tell you that, you know, you're being trained to use your mind and – through this process of getting these grades – and at the end of that you could well want a career and then that affects how you see marriage. Sometimes I think it's unfair to women and that really the world isn't all that open for career women. And men aren't all that ready for career wives. And somehow or another somewhere along the line they should kick the girls out of school.

In spite of her unusual aspirations, and in line with her accepting attitude toward "traditional" marriage, Patsy does anticipate some accommodation of her own career to that of her husband. Finally she justifies her willingness to make this kind of adjustment with the observation that Rich is more "career-oriented." Evidence is his ability to sit at his desk and work single-mindedly, ignoring the parade of distractions in their graduate-student office:

9W–2: And I'm quite the opposite. I'll go looking for conversations. That's – so he really concentrates more on, I guess, the career. For me it's different. I would say – I don't know, I'd generalize to most women. But you get so involved in things like, "Oh so-and-so is really worried today about something, I'll go and talk to her and see how she's feeling," or "I wonder what happened to so-and-so, I'd better go check." "Anne's been upset because her daughter's been crying at college, I'll go talk to Anne, see if they've worked it out." So that it's really been a learning process for me to learn to sit and do my research, write this paper, and be very concentrated on the career, as if your time – you've got so many hours in the day and somebody needs your help and you've got a computer program that has to be run, that you say, "No, I can't do it." For me that's been a real change in behavior and with Rich if it ever was a change it occurred when he was nineteen, not when he was thirty-nine. So in that sense I want him to have the kind of career that he dreams about. For me, being that career-oriented is sort of a new thing anyway. I haven't been unhappy all of my life, so I doubt if I would be unhappy, you know, adjusting.

Patsy repeatedly refers to herself as "traditional" for taking this view, that it is more important for her husband to have the prestigious job. She attributes her adherence to traditional values to the fact that, an older returned student, she was raised in an earlier era:

9W–6: I think my values are still the same as what I think are the predominant values of anybody raised in the fifties or becoming eighteen in 1950. Now maybe I just assume they were the dominant – predominant values but – I think my value system, or what I think is right I mean maybe I shouldn't call it values – my moral sense of what's right, or the way things should be, are still pretty much the same. That a woman has children, I think she should be proud to be home with them when they're young. When they go to school then it's all right for her to work, sort of thing. If she wants children, I think I believe she should be with her children. I: You mean until like the first grade, or . . .?
W: Until about the first grade, yeah. I think I have a tendency to really believe that if she's in that position of being a mother and she isn't able to maximize her own career because of her responsibilities towards her children, she should support

maximizing her husband's. And I guess I really do see that women make a choice when they decide to be mothers.

Patsy hints broadly at the primary source of these traditional ideas when she tells about going home to her parents' house for Christmas:

9W–5: When we go home at Christmas, which we will be doing soon, my mother will say, "Take care of your husband." She'll ask me, "Does Rich have a fork?" If he's eating in the living-room. "Does he have a fork," or something. "I don't know." And "I didn't notice, but if he needs one he'll get it." But that's not what she means. She means for me to go out and see that Rich has everything he needs. Go get him anything he needs and to keep him supplied. You know, "Does his glass need refilling?" or whatever. And that is what she does. That is what my sisters do. They're models, and negative models. I mean it hasn't – that isn't the way Rich and I pattern our marriage.

How firmly she rejects these particular models of the wifely role, in favor of a more equitable division of household labor, is told in an anecdote about her own early relationship with Rich:

9W–5: When we were living together, and weren't married, Rich was always willing to help me through things. But he never – he wouldn't initiate it. And one of the times that I remember was – the laundry needed to be done and I had taken it downstairs. And I went down after it, and I carried the laundry up and I was really hurt and Rich started to help and – but I was hurt. And he couldn't figure out what I was hurt about. And I said, you know, that – telling him that he was really great about helping but like he was *helping* me. It wasn't me he was helping it was our work, our laundry. It wasn't my laundry for him to help me with and that I really wish that he would initiate some of the housework that needed to be done. And he said, well, that he was sorry he really tried but he didn't know when to try. That it was his mother, she'd be mad at him for interfering in her work. And he never saw his father do anything like it. So he had no model to work on.

Yet Patsy is not entirely free of her "negative models" of what her wifely role should be, as reflected in the concern she expressed again and again to Rich before their marriage, that she would not be a suitable wife for him:

9W–4: I did everything to make Rich think about all the problems of marrying me. I mean I invariably made him mad with some of the things I would tell him. He really should think about the fact that he could marry a very attractive young co-ed. And that there were definite advantages to that. Like getting your laun—, meals cooked. You know there were real advantages of marrying someone who was not as career-minded as he was. And there were real advantages to marrying someone who could be a real hostess for him. And could have his children. He's very close to a woman named Alicia Gruening, who was a friend at Penn, and I asked him a million times why he didn't marry Alicia, that it would just seem natural that they would become very close friends – and I – I think I might have put it – he really told me it was unnecessary when – what I was doing.

9W–5: The best thing about Rich, for me, is that he fits me so well. I mean the best thing to me is that he's a liberated man, or whatever. That he – it's a – I'd die if I was some of those women that had to come home to cook supper every night. I mean I'd die if I had to come home and clean house. And I had – I mean that would just be – I couldn't, physically couldn't do it. I could not have the energy to be a housewife and to be a wage-earner. And I don't think I could be happy not being a wage-earner or to have my career or whatever. And that seems to be so necessary for me or otherwise I should have been kicked out of school after high school. I should never have been allowed to develop intellectually and then be told, "No career." So since I was allowed to develop intellectually and have a career, the greatest thing in the world to me is to have a man that makes it possible. That I don't have to fit into the traditional role of the homemaker. Because I just, physically, could not be a homemaker and wage-earner. I would just die, I mean I just physically could't do it. I don't have that kind of energy, endurance, or whatever. When I think about what women do who are – who work, and come home and cook the supper, and do the dishes, and do the laundry, get the kids to bed, help them with homework – that whole bit. And I have – you know my younger sister does that. Her husband helps a little bit with taking care of the kids and occasionally washes dishes. But basically she runs the house, she has her four children. Right now she's just – she just finished her bachelor's degree, is finishing this semester, and – to be a schoolteacher. But – and she's hoping that next semester she'll find a job. And that it will be a stable job and not just substitute teaching. But she's a homemaker, mother, and she'll be a wage-earner. I don't see how she does it. I also don't see how she carried a full courseload and did it – that sort of thing. But I couldn't do it, and that's the best thing about Rich, is that I can be married and have my career. And I would think that in many, many situations I couldn't have both. And he lets me. And back before we were married I kept asking him, "Are you sure you don't want to marry a nice co-ed? She'll look pretty on your arm and you won't have to do any of the housekeeping."

Rich, a wholly career-oriented person who does not want children and a "liberated man" who not only "lets" her have a career, but is willing to share the housework so that she can pursue it, resolves a large part of Patsy's dilemma.

However, Patsy's aspirations go beyond being allowed to have a career of some sort. Her traditional values require that she put her husband's career first, and that he find a suitably prestigious academic position, certainly one not inferior to her own. At the same time, she is not entirely willing to settle for a job that is secondary to his. This conflict between her traditional views regarding husbands' and wives' careers, and her concern for the equality of Rich's and her outcomes and the fulfillment of her own aspirations, becomes clear in the course of their job search. She admits,

9W–2: I'm finding out that I'm a lot more traditional than – I guess, than I wish that I were in some ways. I mean I just know at the present – I had a – at Ohio State I'm in a small group being considered for a job. They had two openings, but they decided Rich didn't fit their areas of interest. So I'm in and he's out. Well,

Ohio State's out, because I'm not going to go without him. But I also know now where I used to think I could go and have Rich take, oh, a position that was with a research center, or something that might work into a part-time position, I couldn't. I couldn't do – couldn't take a job in which I came out to have more prestige than he would – or a more secure job. But not the reverse. But I don't know the other yet either, because every time something comes up where it's really great for him, and really not so great for me, I can only say for one day it'd be okay. By the next day I'm saying, "I don't want it, Rich. I couldn't – I don't want that job." So I don't – we're in a sense trying to thrash this out. I mean, this is going to be difficult. I don't know that much about myself yet to know what I'm going to do, nor do I really know that much about Rich. And I'm very afraid that we'll each make a sacrifice that we can't live with after we've made it.

Patsy imagines various scenarios, establishing the limits of inequality acceptable to her:

9W–2: So I guess I think I can do that [accept a less prestigious position], especially if he's in the same kind of work. And maybe that makes a difference. If he's going to do it I can do it too. If he's going to go the traditional route [of a research and teaching job], well, then I want it too.
I: That probably is a whole lot of it.
W: I can do whatever he can do. That doesn't make me feel as insecure, or jealous even. If he would have a good traditional job, and I – a good job where it would be research and teaching, and I would have the real lower job, I don't think I could take that. I could take the compromise where we both go on less good jobs – I could take that pretty well.

Regrettable as might be the latter solution for her husband's career in particular, she cannot help finding a certain comfort in the prospect of equally poor outcomes for them both:

9W–3: Well like I said last week there – I am somewhat traditional. In that I don't think if a really great job opened up for me in an area and something not – something hardly adequate for him opened up, that I could ask – could do that. I think I really do need for him to have – oh, I don't want – really want to say a better job, but a good job, you know. The other would be a problem, I think – the reverse would be a problem. He's conscious of that too. In that he said he thinks I have a ten—, that I might have a tendency to sacrifice for him. But I do know what I couldn't sacrifice. You know, I do have an idea of the kind of job I couldn't take in order to give him a great job. You know, I know I couldn't take a really poor job to give him a great job. He'd have to have a poor job too. I mean really, if I have to have one he has to, you know. It's literally – there are times when it's really tit-for-tat thinking.

Fretting about the near inevitability of unequal outcomes, Patsy summarizes her quandary:

9W–2: Like if he gets something then I start, "What happened to me?" I wonder what's going on and sort of needing the assurance that I'm getting the same thing or that he's getting the same thing. Or else we are both going to get bad or possibly both get good, but sure that in most of these something's going to happen where one gets better than the other. I don't want him to ever get hurt. And I don't want him ever to not have something he wants so I hope that everybody wants him. On the other hand I don't want me to get hurt either.

The substance of what is at issue varies across the three marriages, as does the particular concern each wife brings to fulfillment of her marital role. Kay wants to be recognized as the kind of wife who is able to make a good marriage, Nan wishes she were the ideal wife who gives her husband the total commitment he deserves from her, while Patsy tries to be the "traditional" wife who puts her husband's career first. But once again, this third wife's conflict, like those of the other two, is a conflict between this latter powerful understanding of what her marital role entails and an equally compelling understanding of what in her view would be fair to her. Each woman, then, is divided between some commitment to marriage or spouse that leads to a felt inequality in the relationship, and an insistence on equality. The three experience these internal conflicts differently. Kay tells of finding herself doing what she does not believe in. Nan holds conversations between different parts of herself. Patsy oscillates from one day to the next.

Things about themselves, personal attributes, contribute to the inner conflicts experienced by Kay and Nan. Although she denies it, a tendency to seek approval from others may play a role in Kay's incessant quest for approval of her marriage, feeding her attempt to make it work, while Nan's involuntary emotional withdrawal from hers inhibits the commitment she would like to have – "I am what I am," the latter says. But it is Patsy's case that illustrates how understanding and enactment of one's marital role may be not merely enhanced or impeded by one's personal inclinations, but a part of a larger, and impelling, conception of oneself as a person of a certain kind: one, Patsy finds out, who is "a lot more traditional than I wish that I were." While Kay's explanation for how she came to have the attitudes she does toward marriage is a psychodynamic one, Patsy's explanation for how she got to be a traditional person is historical: she grew up in the fifties. Her wistfully expressed wish to be different and Nan's resignation over "what I am" both expose the same assumption that attributes of the person are unalterable or, at least, exceedingly difficult to change.

Still another conception of herself as a certain kind of person – a woman – comes into play at a critical point in Patsy's thinking. Like most women, and in contrast to her husband, she is less than single-minded about her career, liable to subordinate work to the friendship and emotional support of other women, happy adjusting to a less prestigious job. As a woman, her needs are simply different. Patsy in this 1979 interview parallels the arguments of Nancy Chodorow (1974, 1978) and other academic feminists – for she and they are drawing on a culturally shared model of men as more invested in achievement, women in relatedness. The assumption of gender difference, unlike Patsy's understanding of herself as a traditional person, needs no historical explanation, for it is an assumption of natural difference between men and women – although whether it is natural because biologically innate or deeply culturally ingrained, Patsy leaves unclear.

Interpretation

How do these three cases help us to think about the motivational force of cultural models? We are now in a position to see that many of their stated goals are explicable as lower-level ones that are recruited by the higher-level goals these wives pursue. The three, for example, share an American belief in the rights of all human beings to equality, and a modern, "feminist" insistence on the application of this principle to women. From this shared upper-level goal flows Kay's demand for an equal division of housework, Nan's expectation of reciprocal emotional support from her husband, and Patsy's insistence on an equivalent job and equal career opportunity – each a marital arena in which the general principle of equal treatment applies.

The wives' understandings of their marital roles are related to upper-level goals in further, more complex ways. Because Kay believes that being a certain kind of good wife is the way to make her marriage work, the overarching goal of having a successful marriage recruits that of being a good wife. That is, the latter goal is a strategy for obtaining the former. Nan's goal of supporting her husband wholeheartedly through his attacks of anxiety, to the point of getting swept up herself in this anxiety, is recruited by her higher-level goal, of being emotionally committed or "connected" to him the way you are supposed to be when you are married. The lower-level goal in this instance is related to the higher one, as she explains, through a psychological process of emotional spread or contagion. There is no way to limit the effect of "disconnecting" oneself from the other person to its original context; rather, this lack of connection becomes a general emotional alienation. Patsy's lower-level goal of putting her husband's career first is recruited by the higher-level goal of being a traditional wife, which is recruited in turn by the upper-level goal of living by traditional values. Each lower-level goal in this hierarchy is entailed by the one higher as part of her self-conscious program for enacting a cherished set of values. Thus means–end relations between hierarchically related goals can be various.

Now we re-encounter the question left hanging at the very beginning of this paper: How is it that goals embedded in upper-level schemas, such as human equality, marital success, wifely commitment, and a traditional value system in these examples, have the motivational force they do? It is because these schemas and these goals have become, in each case, the woman's understanding of herself – and because these self-understandings cast her as a natural being and a moral actor. To see how they partake of moral necessity and inherent naturalness, we can examine more closely some of these upper-level schemas.

Equality of outcome is expressed in a language of economic transaction and exact calculation, investing marital equality with the added moral force of fair economic exchange in the free-market system that is so central to American ideas of what is right. Nan says, "I think it costs me a lot and I don't think he's measuring that cost." Patsy talks about the "tit-for-tat thinking" that leads her to insist that "if he's going to go the traditional route, well then I want it too." Similarly, Kay says about housework, "I wouldn't ask him to do anything I wouldn't do," and thinks that when children arrive her husband should do "fifty percent" of childcare. For all three women, these attitudes about marital equality are powerful ones. Patsy vascillates daily, reporting that when considering a job opportunity that's much better for her husband than for her, she "can only say for one day it'd be okay. By the next day I'm saying, I don't want it, Rich. I couldn't." Nan is "scared it's going to cost too much," imagining the "time when I have to dissolve this relationship because I can't deal with it anymore," and anguishes," there's times when it's too much to ask. Everyone's asking me and nobody's giving and . . . I've just had it, I don't want it anymore." Kay argues incessantly with her husband that he is not being fair. She is the one who makes the moral basis for this claim to equality explicit, when she tells her husband she, too, is a human being with feelings – she gets just as tired as he does and doesn't like doing chores any more than he does. All three wives appear to share the unquestioned conviction that, as human beings, they have a right to equal exchange. This is a natural right that none finds it necessary to defend; that they are incontestably human is enough.

If their language of equivalence and fairness reflects a moral assumption about the equal outcomes due to every human being, these women's talk about their family roles reflects another kind of moral imperative: that people are bound to honor their socially assigned role obligations. Kay and Nan each appear to be torn between the treatment they believe they deserve as human beings, and the responsibilities they believe they incur as wives. Nan's language of contractual obligation – "owing" and "cheating" – makes this latter moral assumption explicit. Although her view of marital role obligations is a reciprocal one, it is she who is guilty of cheating her husband of the unconditional emotional commitment she owes him. Kay views her social obligation as one to her community rather than to her husband; she feels as if she will "let down a whole lot of people" if she does not make a good marriage. Interestingly, Kay rejects the cultural understanding of her marital obligations reflected in her husband's phrase, "wifely duty." In its place, she has her own version of "the good wife" – one that adds a layer of moral compulsion to her definition of the situation. By analogy to the morally laden idea of what a good mother does for her children, the good wife makes her husband happy and presentable to the world, and in so doing makes her marriage work and gains public approval for its success. Kay exempts her husband from any responsibility for the success of the marriage, whether out of recognition of her own unequal investment in it, or by extension of her view of wives as mothers, and husbands as their children.

Patsy too believes strongly that husbands and wives have certain role obligations; she holds, for example, the "traditional" beliefs that wives should be supportive of their husbands' careers and that mothers should stay home with their young children. These ideas derive from what Patsy calls her "moral sense of what's right or the way things should be," values she grew up with. They gain their moral force from being associated not with timeless sacred ideas about common humanity, fair economic exchange, the fulfillment of contractual relations or the duties of motherhood, but with an entire way of life in an earlier, and morally superior, time. Patsy must go to ingenious lengths to reason why she herself is at least partially excepted from the role prescriptions of this "traditional" world. She has been highly educated, leaving her with career aspirations it would be "unfair" to thwart. She has foregone having children, making a career possible. And she has married an unusual man who, thankfully if inexplicably, supports that career. Still she feels uncomfortable demanding that her professional advancement be taken as seriously as his. As she tells it, this persistent ambivalence is founded not only on her understanding of her role as a traditional wife but also on her understanding of herself as a woman – though it is hard to tell whether the latter explanation is more of a cause or an excuse for accommodation to her husband's career. With this claim about gender difference, Patsy reinforces an appeal to what is right with an appeal to what is natural.

Far from sharing the kind of global cultural understanding of themselves as women and wives that the academic literature on gender identity often assumes (see Davidson 1984 and Holland and Davidson 1983 for a critique of the literature on this point), three different women give three quite different renditions of what it means to be a wife. Rather than reflecting some larger whole in which each wife's conception represents a piece, these are alternative definitions of the wifely role, having no necessary connection to one another. Kay's view of the good wife appears to include nothing about unstinting emotional commitment or wifely devotion to her husband's career, for example. Patsy is quite clear that seeing to her husband's laundry and other personal care of the sort Kay gives Bobby are simply not, for her, the crucial elements of "traditional" wifehood. A better way to think about these women's differing views of wifehood is to imagine that they have each drawn, selectively, from a cultural repository of complexly interrelated but separable schemas available to them for conceptualizing this role. From this pool of possibilities, each has taken that cultural understanding of her wifely role that holds force for her. In the way these and other married people adopt alternative schemas for their marital roles, and then elaborate these schemas, weaving them together with other schemas they have selected, for, say, motherhood, contractual obligation, or traditional values, a great variety of individual ideas about how to be a wife or a husband is produced from a relatively limited stock of cultural components. To hold that motivational force resides in each wife's particular construction of the wifely role, not in some shared overarching conception of this role, is not to beg the question of how cultural understandings gain such force. It is simply to reframe the question as one about particularities.

Again, and importantly, it is not simply the abstract moral rectitude or inherent naturalness invested in these cultural ideas about human fairness, wifely obligations, and women's proclivities, that make these ideas compelling for these women. In each case, the ideas in conflict have become the woman's understandings of herself as a moral actor and a natural being, human and female. Unfortunately, the interview material at hand lends itself more readily to retrieval of the adult conceptions of themselves these interviewees hold, and speculation about the probable early sources of these concepts, than to reconstruction of the processes by which these notions of personhood became incorporated into self-understanding. There is a hint of such process in Patsy's description of her mother's relentless socialization of her, even into adulthood: "Take care of your husband"; "Does Rich have a fork?" It is easy to imagine an adolescent Patsy being told, "Take care of your father," or watching her father seated in the living-room while her mother brought him a fork. Yet, even here, it is not clear why these insistent messages, far from having their desired effect, came to constitute a negative model for wifehood in Patsy's mind, though other messages about how wives and mothers ought to behave, that may have been impressed upon her equally insistently, took hold.

Kay's story, more than the others, suggests the long process by which her ideas about marriage and wifehood became incorporated into her understanding of herself. Identification with her mother must have figured large in this process. We can speculate that Kay's unusual concern with others' approval of her marriage derives from the shame her mother, who "came from the country with a family that always stayed together," must have felt at being the first in that family to divorce. That Kay experiences a good marriage as a matter of community approval certainly accords with a picture of close-knit rural origins. Kay's willingness to conciliate and to do more than her share in order to make her marriage work, we can further surmise, echoes her mother's injunction about giving in so as not to risk losing "the only good thing you've ever had in your life," amplified through her mother's pain at having been herself deserted. This mother, too, is attempting to socialize an adult daughter. At the same time, Kay's fierce defense of herself as a human being with equal rights in her marriage can be related to the inner determination that grew in her as, a helpless child, she watched her mother suffering: "I wouldn't let anybody walk all over me like that," she said to herself, "Husbands treating you that bad, you don't just sit there and let them do it," as her mother had sat, waiting.

Nan's story like Kay's suggests the power of community approval and threatened disapproval. And this story makes a new point about the continuation, on into adulthood, of the process by which understandings of self are learned. In this ongoing process, early messages, in Nan's case messages about the importance of emotional commitment and its connection to sex, can be transmuted into powerful new imperatives by subsequent experience of a traumatic variety.

Cultural ideas like these about how humans are to be treated, how marital roles should be enacted, and what men and women are like, have the potential for motivational force because they are simultaneously structures for adult understanding and vehicles of child socialization. When particular ideas about human relations, about role obligations, or about types of people have force for us, rather than just being possible interpretations of the social world, it is because as children and young adults we have been socialized by means of appeals to these very ideas. We have been taught that this is our role, our nature, the way we should be treated and treat other people. I want to argue that these more or less explicit messages from socializing agents, and these lessons extracted from the behavior modeled by these socializers, are effective precisely because they depend upon cultural assumptions about what is moral and what is natural.

In a different context, theorists attempting to explain the power of ideology to rationalize domination and exploitation have pointed out that, to be persuasive, ideological appeals must draw upon shared assumptions either about the rightness and legitimacy, or about the naturalness and inevitability, of the social order. In a recent discussion of the ideological legitimization of inequality, Lewontin, Rose and Kamin (1984: 64) say succinctly why this should be so: "If what exists is right, then one ought not oppose it; if it exists inevitably, one can never oppose it successfully."

Thus, for example, these and other students of ideology point out that in the course of western history, class exploitation and imperialist domination have been rationalized by those who have done the exploiting and the dominating, in ideological terms that picture the status quo as the inevitable outcome of natural processes such as "the survival of the fittest" or the just outcome of a morally superior social order such as "the free enterprise system," and in terms of the inevitable biological superiority of some classes and "races" of people, and the rightful obligation of those superior people to rule and civilize the rest. Similarly, it is said, gender inequalities have been rationalized by the men who benefit from these inequalities in terms of ideas, not unlike some of those revealed in the material that has been presented in this paper, about the biological, hence inevitable, nature of women and about the rightful, hence unopposable, roles women occupy.

Similar appeals to legitimacy and inevitability are embedded in the schemas about human rights, about role obligations, and about the inherent nature of different kinds of people, through which children are taught how to behave. In fact, the analogy between ideological persuasion and child socialization fits precisely because the socializing agent, to be effective, must utilize the very techniques of the ideologue. Self-understandings taught in the course of one's socialization are doubly persuasive: at the same time that they provide ready, coherent interpretations of one's own behavior, they make ideological appeal, offering themselves as the way one must behave. It is, of course, this powerful prior process of socialization to what is right and natural that provides the hook for ideology. As adults, individuals are willing to accept and even embrace ideological appeals to what they have already learned to be true about their own nature, even though in this way of thinking theirs is an inferior nature, and about their own place in life, even when this designated place is one of subordination. Of course, when people have learned different, conflicting, assumptions about what is right and what is natural, as have the women described in this paper, a basis is laid for resistance to given ideological appeals. In these cases we see evidence of such resistance.

The story is not entirely finished even here. Ideas about the self may be taught in a variety of ways – through direct preachment in the style Patsy's mother adopts, or with more indirect demonstrations of approval and disapproval, such as may have suffused the world of Nan's upbringing, for instance, or more or less inadvertently by modeling and identification, as Kay has learned to identify with her mother. The effectiveness of a given technique may be enhanced by the association and cultivation of any of an array of matching feeling states that come to overlay and reinforce what one learns is the moral or proper or the only way to behave and "overdetermine" this behavior (D'Andrade 1984:98). There is pleasure in social approval, nostalgia for an earlier, better way of life, guilt over cheating others, or high indignation over others' perceived mistreatment, to name some feelings that might easily have figured in the lives of the women considered here. D'Andrade has put this a little differently:

There appear to be two major intrinsic motivational systems involved with cultural meaning systems: The first is relatively direct personal reward; the second is reward because of attachment to a particular set of values. Typically the two are mixed: For example, in the cultural meaning system involving success, accomplishment may be rewarding both because it satisfies personal needs for recognition, achievement and security, and because it represents the "good" self. (1984:98).

The present discussion broadens D'Andrade's schema, adding to the intrinsic motivation of attachment to ideas about the "good" self, that of attachment to ideas about the "natural" self. At the same time, this discussion illuminates something about the workings of the latter of the two intrinsic motivational systems he distinguishes. In particular, the cases argue that potentially motivating ideas about selves "good" and "natural" are incorporated in schemas for social relations and role enactment as well as those for personal attributes.

An unavoidable limitation of the material that has been discussed, I have admitted, is that we are able to retrieve, from these women's interview descriptions of their marital conflicts, only glimpses of the actual socialization experiences that led them to associate rewarding and un-rewarding feelings with given understandings of the good self and the natural self. By the time one is adult, one is long practiced at thinking the thoughts and feeling the associated feelings that emerge from an inter-action of particular lessons about what is right and what is natural with particular inducements for learning these lessons: "I'm not going to take what my mother did," or "I'm not going to disappoint people," or "I fulfil my obligations to other people," or "I can only be expected to put up with so much," or "I won't violate my traditional values," or "it's only fair for me to be allowed to fulfil my potential." In internal messages such as these, culturally given conceptions of "the good wife," or the "ideal wife," or the "traditional wife," or "the typical woman," or "the human being" fill in the details of what it is one is supposed to do, be, or accept. These goals are linked to other, low-level goals by means–end relations. Even though she doesn't think it fair, Kay makes the sandwich.

That particular outcome, or any other, is less important to the argument of this paper than the demonstration of how Kay felt compelled to make Bobby's sandwich by her understanding of herself, and the equally valid observation that competing views she held of herself made her doing so neither wholly predictable nor necessarily final.

NOTES

1 Indeed, marriage served for Searle (1969:51) as a prime example of such constitutive rules.

2 This "inner sense" of self is close to the "especially strong conviction" with which actors hold cultural beliefs that they have been internalized at Spiro's fourth level of acquisition (Spiro n.d.:38, quoted in D'Andrade, this volume: 37). At this level, says Spiro, "believing that Jesus died for man's sins, the actors are preoccupied with their own sins; and believing that one ought to care for the poor, their assistance to the poor represents a personal sacrifice." The task of this paper could be rephrased, in Spiro's terms, to say that it is an attempt to sketch the process by which cultural beliefs achieve this deepest level of internalization.

3 I take the self, and the process by which cultural schemas are converted into self-definitions, to be universal, while of course the particular cultural schemas so incorporated into self-understanding will vary cross-culturally. Relatedly, Wierzbicka (1989:46) has observed that ideas of "person" and "self" appear to be conceptual universals.

4 D'Andrade (1984:97) coined the term "directive force" to talk about this goal-providing property of schemas. If we stick to the meaning assigned to this term in the typology of illocutionary force from which it is drawn, reserving the term for the specific kind of motivation that is experienced as a sense of obligation, as D'Andrade (this volume: 36, and pers. comm.) originally intended, we need a more general term to include all kinds of motivation that schemas can incorporate. "Motivational force" would seem to be a straightforward and unambiguous choice.

5 The initial research on which this chapter draws was funded in 1979–80 by National Institute of Mental Health research grant No. 1 R01 MH330370–01. Research analysis and write-up have been pursued under National Science Foundation research grant No. BNS–8205739, a stipend from the Institute for Advanced Study in Princeton, New Jersey, where I spent a year as a visiting member, several grants from the Duke University Research Council at my home institution, and, most recently, a National Science Foundation Visiting Professorship for Women, grant No. RII–8620166, hosted by the University of California, San Diego. I presented the original version of this chapter at a session

on "The Directive Force of Cultural Models," organized by Roy D'Andrade and myself and held at the 85th Annual Meeting of the American Anthropological Association in Philadelphia, December 1986. Successive revisions have benefited from substantive comments by Roy D'Andrade and Dorothy Holland, and from extensive suggestions by Claudia Strauss about how to say what I really mean. I am also grateful to Laurie Moore for conducting the interviews with the third of the wives quoted in this paper, 9W, and to all three women for sharing with Laurie and myself their understandings of their marriages.

6 This is a fictive name, of course, as are the names of the other two women introduced in this paper.

7 The code at the beginning of this and later interview segments contains, in order, an interviewer identification number, a W for wife (and elsewhere in published accounts of this research, an H for husband), and the number of the interview from which that segment was drawn in the sequence of interviews with that individual. As in the segment to follow this one, comments or questions interjected by the interviewer are prefaced by an I, and resumption of the interviewee's part of the conversation is indicated by a W. All the interview passages reproduced in this paper have been regularized for stammers, stutters, elisions, slips of the tongue, and hesitations.

REFERENCES

Chodorow, Nancy
1974 Family Structure and Feminine Personality. In *Woman, Culture, and Society*, M. Z. Rosaldo and L. Lamphere, eds. Stanford: Stanford University Press. Pp. 43–66.
1978 *The Reproduction of Mothering: Psychoanalysis and the Sociology of Gender*. Berkeley: University of California Press.
D'Andrade, Roy
1984 Cultural Meaning Systems. In *Culture Theory: Essays on Mind, Self, and Emotion*, R. A. Shweder and R. A. LeVine, eds. Cambridge: Cambridge University Press. Pp. 88–119.
1990 Culture and Personality: A False Dichotomy. In *Personality and the Cultural Construction of Society: Papers in Honor of Melford E. Spiro*, D. Jordan and M. Swartz, eds. Tuscaloosa: University of Alabama Press. Pp. 145–60.
Davidson, Debra
1984 Transmission of Gender Knowledge in College Women's Peer Groups. Unpublished M.A. thesis, University of North Carolina, Chapel Hill.
Holland, Dorothy and Debra Davidson
1983 Labeling the Opposite Sex: Metaphors and Themes in American Folk Models of Gender. Unpublished manuscript, Department of Anthropology, University of North Carolina, Chapel Hill.
Hutchins, Edwin
1980 *Culture and Inference: A Trobriand Case Study*. Cambridge, MA: Harvard University Press.

Lewontin, R. C., Steven Rose, and Leon J. Kamin
1984 *Not In Our Genes: Biology, Ideology, and Human Nature.* New York: Pantheon Books.
Lutz, Catherine
1986 Goals, Events, and Understanding in Ifaluk Emotion Theory. In *Cultural Models in Language and Thought*, D. Holland and N. Quinn, eds. Cambridge: Cambridge University Press. Pp. 290–312.
Mainardi, Pat
1970 The Politics of Housework. In *Sisterhood is Powerful: An Anthology of Writings from the Women's Liberation Movement*, R. Morgan, ed. New York: Random House Vintage Books. Pp. 447–54.
Shweder, Richard and Edmund J. Bourne
1982 Does the Concept of the Person Vary Cross-Culturally? In *Cultural Conceptions of Mental Health and Therapy*, A. J. Marsella and G. M. White, eds. Dordrecht, Holland: D. Reidel Publishing Company. Pp. 97–137.
Spiro, Melford
n.d. Cultural Ideology and Social Reality: An Essay on Cultural Internalization. Unpublished manuscript, Department of Anthropology, University of California, San Diego.
White, Geoffrey
1985 Premises and Purposes in a Solomon Island Ethnopsychology. In *Person, Self and Experience: Exploring Pacific Ethnopsychologies*, G. M. White and J. Kirkpatrick, eds. Berkeley: University of California Press. Pp. 328–66.
Wierzbicka, Anna
1989 Soul and Mind: Linguistic Evidence for Ethnopsychology and Cultural History. *American Anthropologist* 91:41–58.

6 The directive force of morality tales in a Mexican community

Holly F. Mathews

This chapter addresses the issue of how meanings come to direct behavior by analyzing the ways in which the cultural representations contained in folklore operate both to teach schemas and to motivate listeners to act in accordance with the goals they generate. Research on this topic was conducted in a rural, agricultural community of 2,000 people located in the state of Oaxaca in Mexico. The inhabitants, of mixed Zapotec and Mixtec descent, now label themselves ethnically as Mestizos. The community economy is based primarily on subsistence farming. Residents live in patrilocal, extended households and continue to regulate their own internal affairs through participation in a hierarchy of civil and religious offices known as the cargo system (see Mathews 1985). Traditionally, folklore has been an integral component of everyday activity as well as of ritual practice. Many types of lore abound in the community, but one genre in particular, that of the morality tale, stands apart as a form that has compelling directive or motivational force.

Morality tales are concerned with evaluating and shaping courses of action. The texts of such tales contain a great deal of information about cultural expectations for behavior as well as about the bases of individual motivation for such behavior. I chose to explore these bases for motivation by analyzing sixty informant accounts of the morality tale of *La Llorona* or the "Weeping Woman."[1] This tale is particularly appropriate for a study of motivation for two reasons. First, it is extremely prevalent in the daily conversations of community members who use its message to interpret local events as well as to socialize the young. Second, there is an interesting divergence between the genders with respect to the way in which the tale is told. This divergence provides important clues about how the cultural schemas that motivate behavior vary for the members of each sex.

The *La Llorona* tale is about a mythical woman's marriage and the problems she encounters. Each version of the tale concludes with some dire consequence that people are enjoined by the moral of the story to

127

avoid. The following account is a typical example of those told by male informants:

La Llorona was a bad woman who married a good man. They had children and all was well. Then one day she went crazy (*se puso loca*) and began to walk the streets. Everyone knew but her husband. When he found out he beat her. She had much shame (*pena*). The next day she walked into the river and drowned herself. And now she knows no rest and must forever wander the streets wailing in the night. And that is why women must never leave their families to walk the streets looking for men. If they are not careful they will end up like *La Llorona*.

This tale is an overtly cautionary one. It was collected during a conversation in which an older man used it to scold his newly married daughter for wandering unchaperoned in the streets. The tale illustrates the worst possible result of her illicit behavior – she may end up dead and doomed to wander as a restless spirit. In order for the tale to succeed in its purpose, however, the daughter must be convinced that the outcome is a plausible result of the conditions set in motion in the story.

The *La Llorona* tale incorporates directive force on two levels. On one level, the tale is employed consciously as a dramatic device to direct behavior. It does so by demonstrating how an individual who fails to adhere to marital obligations may come to suffer the same fate as the characters in the story. To that end, the tale is used in natural settings as a device to teach unmarried youngsters about marital role requirements, as an illustration of potential problems for newly married individuals, as a warning to spouses to be vigilant about their own marriages and those of others, as a precept to guide the interpretation of ongoing marital disputes in the community, and as a justification for actions taken to settle such disputes.

For the tale to succeed in directing behavior, however, it must also have motivational force for the individual listener. It depicts characters attempting to achieve cultural values, often perceived by them as needs or as obligations to do something. The achievement of these values is defined as moral, and the frustration of such attempts, either by circumstance or by the deliberate actions of self and others, is defined as immoral. The tale attempts to inhibit immoral behavior by illustrating the terrible consequences that may result from a failure to act in accordance with culturally prescribed values. On this level, convincingness is dependent upon believability. The actions of the characters in the story must make sense in terms of generally-held beliefs about real-life possibilities. I suggest that the *La Llorona* story succeeds as a morality tale because the motives of the main characters draw upon culturally shared schemas about gendered human nature and the life goals valued by the members of each sex, spousal duties and obligations in marriage, and the emotional responses and resultant actions likely to occur when the expectations generated by these schemas are violated. These schemas give meaning to the actions of the characters and serve, therefore, to supply links between the seemingly disparate events contained in the tales.   .

These linkages, moreover, are expressed in a structure or grammar peculiar to the genre of morality tales. This grammer chains together whole episodes, each of which consists of a precipitating action on the part of one character and a complex reaction linking the experience of emotion to the formation of a goal and a consequent plan for action on the part of the other. One character's actions motivate the emotional and behavioral reactions of the other in a step-wise fashion until the dire consequence is reached. The grammar is thus a kind of general schema, or template, for the construction and understanding of the *La Llorona* stories. Any particular version of the *La Llorona* tale would be an instantiation of that general schema.

The subsequent discussion of the types of directive force contained in the *La Llorona* tales begins by analyzing the story grammar itself as a schema which functions to link events in a causal chain. Next, the different levels of cultural schemas operating to generate and give meaning to the actions pursued by the characters are described. The focus of this analysis is on the form and meaning of the tales themselves. A consideration of how the tales are actually employed by individuals to make sense of everyday experience is the subject of another study (see Mathews n.d.).

A story grammar for the *La Llorona* morality tales

Literary forms like fairy-tales and myths are an important domain for the study of the organization of cultural knowledge because they represent, as Abelson (1975:276) notes, a stylized world with "moderate size, moderate realism, and substantial interest." Psychologists have documented the various structures internal to story forms across domains of knowledge. These structures are often invariant regardless of the content being portrayed in the narratives. Such structures can be captured in a grammar that consists of a set of rewrite rules that do for the stories what rules of syntax do in describing the structure of all English sentences without regard to their content.

Story grammars were developed from transformational generative grammars. In the latter, rules are formed to generate certain elements of sentences. For example, the entity SENTENCE can be rewritten as a

NOUN PHRASE plus a VERB PHRASE. This would be diagrammed as:

SENTENCE ⎯⎯⎯⎯⎯▶ NOUN PHRASE + VERB PHRASE.

Similarly, we might find that the entity STORY can be rewritten as a SETTING plus an EPISODE or:

STORY ⎯⎯⎯⎯⎯▶ SETTING + EPISODE.

Setting and episode are technical terms just like noun and verb phrase. They describe elements of the story's structure regardless of the particular instance of setting or episode being represented and have rules that tell how they are to be treated in the story. Thus, as J. Mandler writes:

A story grammar is a rule system devised for the purpose of describing the regularities found in one kind of text. The rules describe the units of which stories are composed, that is, their constituent structure, and the ordering of the units, that is, the sequence in which the constituents appear. (1984:18)

There are various story grammars in existence developed to represent the structure of folk-tales the world over (see, for example, J. Mandler 1984, Johnson and Mandler 1980) and of stories in general (see Rumelhart 1975).

In my attempts to pinpoint the regularities underlying the different versions of the *La Llorona* tale, I referred to each of these approaches. However, I found none of them was able completely to capture the elements which I now believe may be unique to the genre of morality tales. Consequently, I devised my own grammar, represented as a set of rewrite rules in Fig. 6.1 to depict the structure underlying these tales.[2] In the interpretation of any particular tale, those who hear it will use this schema to parse it into these constituent elements and their interrelations. However, to understand the meaning of the tale, listeners must draw on a number of upper-level, culturally shared schemas of different types which, although not directly stated, give meaning to the events of the story.

In devising this grammar, I have followed the conventions employed by J. Mandler (1984:24). Nonterminal units that can be rewritten into other units are shown in upper-case letters. Terminal nodes are not rewritten into other units but are expressed by the states and events that make up the actual events of the stories. These are written in lower case. Brackets indicate mutually exclusive choices in the rewriting of a nonterminal node; i.e., any option may be used, but only one can be used at a time. Simple parentheses indicate optional elements. Superscripted parentheses indicate sets of elements that are used at least once when the rule is applied but many be used recursively (cf., J. Mandler 1984:23–5).

These rules are capable of generating any of the folk-tales I collected because episodes may be embedded in other episodes at certain key points. The rewrite rules are diagrammed schematically in Fig. 6.2. Connections between the units are either represented in the tales as causal (diagrammed with a "C") or as temporal (diagrammed with a "T" for then) or as having proximity within the store structure (diagrammed with an "A" for and). As J. Mandler notes, in most stories the connection between the setting and what follows is atemporal or an "and" connection. Within episodes, the connections are usually causal or occasionally temporal ones. Episodes themselves, she writes, "can be either causally or temporally connected. Causal connections occur through the embedding property of several of the constituent units. Typically, embedding occurs at the outcome or the ending of an episode..." (1984:23).

The *La Llorona* folk-tale consists of a setting and an episode. The setting's introduction presents the main characters, the locale, and sometimes the time at which the story takes place. In addition to the introduction, the setting of the *La Llorona* tale also contains a scenario which depicts how an ideal marriage is proceeding and, occasionally, makes a comment on the emotional status of the partners to that ideal marriage.

The body of the folk-tale consists of one or more episodes which are the plot of the story. Each of these episodes, regardless of content, follows a particular form. Each episode possesses three constituents: a beginning, a development, and an ending. The beginning constituent consists of both a precipitating event or series of events (episode) and an actual initiating event. In the content of the tales, the precipitating event(s) sets in motion the condition for the disruption of a cultural schema while the initiating event is the actual disruption of the plan to achieve the goals embedded in the schema. It is this disruption that elicits a response reaction from the protagonist character (i.e., the one who is wronged in the story).

The second episode constituent, the development, has several parts. The first thing that happens is that the offended spouse, or the protagonist, reacts in some way to the disruption of expectations. This complex reaction includes an emotion that causes a desire which, in turn, leads the character to formulate a plan to achieve that desire. The plan itself may consist of certain preactions necessary to bring about the desired action or it may involve only the action to meet the desire and the consequence of that action. The consequence may be either a success or failure, and it may cause the ending to the story or it may instead lead to the enactment of another episode embedded in the consequence. The embedded episode usually involves a reaction by the offending spouse or the antagonist to the action just perpetrated by the protagonist. This second, embedded episode, like the first, will involve a beginning, a development, and an ending

STORY ⟶ SETTING and EPISODE

SETTING ⟶ introduction and scenario

EPISODE ⟶ {BEGINNING cause DEVELOPMENT cause ENDING
EPISODE ({and / then} EPISODE)^n

BEGINNING ⟶ (precipitating {event / episode}^{n} then) initiating event

DEVELOPMENT ⟶ {COMPLEX REACTION cause PLAN
emotion cause desire
DEVELOPMENT (cause DEVELOPMENT)^n}

COMPLEX REACTION ⟶ emotion cause desire

PLAN ⟶ (preaction)^n then action cause CONSEQUENCE

CONSEQUENCE ⟶ {event^n / EPISODE}

ENDING ⟶ OUTCOME (and moral)

OUTCOME ⟶ {Ending event / EPISODE}

Fig. 6.1 Rewrite rules for a story grammar of morality tales.

constituent consisting of the same elements. The episode concludes with an ending constituent that involves both an outcome (either an event or an embedded episode) and some kind of commentary on the preceding events – the moral.

To show how this grammar depicts story structure, I have diagrammed one folk-tale in Fig. 6.3. In the diagram, the numbers represent the separate propositions in the folk-tale as outlined below:

M-30   (1) *La Llorona* was married to a hard-working man.

(2) They had many children and worked hard to get ahead. All was well.

(3) But one day she began to walk the streets and everyone knew, but her husband did not know.

(4) When he found out,

(5) he had much *pena*.

(6) And he wanted to chastise her.

(7) So he beat her and cursed her

(8) and told her that her actions had caused him much *pena*.

(9) But the beating gave her *pena*.

(10) And late that night she walked into the river
(11) and killed herself.
(12) And now she knows no rest and must forever wander as a wailing spirit,
(13) and all because she was a bad wife.

This tale is moderately complex. It contains two complete episodes; the second is embedded in the consequence of the first. I will describe briefly the structure of this tale as diagrammed in Fig. 6.3. The tale begins with the setting where the characters are introduced. The scenario paints a rosy picture of the marriage. The episodes or plot of the tale deal with what went wrong and disrupted this rosy picture. The first episode begins with an immoral event that precipitates the trouble, *La Llorona* begins to walk the streets. The real trouble is initiated, however, when her husband finds out about it. His discovery generates the development constituent of the episode. He reacts to the discovery by experiencing the emotion of *pena* which causes him to formulate the desire to chastise her which he then attempts to do by formulating a plan for action. His plan begins with the preactions of beating and cursing which set the stage for his main, goal-satisfying action of telling her what her behavior had done to him.

The consequence of his action is a second episode in which his wife's reactions to the chastisement are played out. The initiating event becomes his verbal chastisement. This causes her to experience the emotion of *pena* and to walk into the river preparatory to taking the action of killing herself. In this episode, the suicide is both the action and the consequence. What is left out of this second episode is an explicit statement of the desire that motivated her actions. The listener is left to infer one or to assume that the action was motivated directly by the emotional experience. Finally, both episodes end with her fate to wander forever as a restless spirit. The moral of the story is the comment that implies that the same fate awaits all women who are bad wives and act immorally towards their husbands in the way of *La Llorona*.

This story is unusual in that it includes explicitly all of the constituent units outlined in the proposed story grammar. However, in the majority of the tales, certain of the constituent units are omitted. Consider the following example diagrammed in Fig. 6.4:

F-28   (1) *La Llorona* was married to a man
(2) and they had many children.
(3) But one day he started drinking,
(4) and he lost all their money.
(5) She had much *pena*
(6) and so she became cold to him.
(7) But he kept drinking,

134

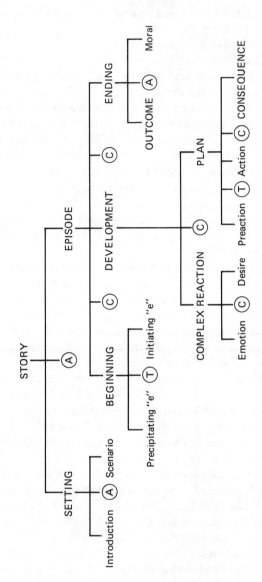

Fig. 6.2 Diagram for the rewrite rules for a morality story grammar.

(8) and one day he lost all their money when he passed out in the streets.

(9) And so she killed herself

(10) so that he would have no one to care for him and no one to help him.

(11) And so he ended his life with no money and no friends.

This folk-tale is fairly complete except that it omits the expression of a desire in the first episode and of an emotion in the second. As J. Mandler notes, there are relatively few deletions or movements of units in the surface structure of traditional stories probably because it makes them easier, as oral forms of expression, to comprehend (1984:25). The setting in general, or the scenario in particular, may be omitted from a story without destroying its sense. However, the episodes which form the plot are never omitted. A story would not be a story without them, although certain of the internal elements of episodes (the units that comprise the beginning, the development, and the ending) may be dropped. The most common omission by far includes elements of the complex reaction and the plan. This is because, in terms of the cultural schemas for self, marriage, and emotion to be described in the next section, the reactions likely to result from a disruption of expectations are easily inferred from the context of the situation.

Nonetheless, in some accounts, the links are made very explicit while in others they are left extremely vague. In this latter case, a story may jump from a precipitating event by one character to an action and consequence on the part of the other without reference to the emotion felt and the desires it generates. Consider this example:

F-29   *La Llorona* married an older, more experienced man. They had children and she was content. But then he stopped coming home and he never had any money. A neighbor told her he was with another woman, but she did not believe it. But one day she saw him in the street giving her money, and late that night she walked into the river and killed herself.

What is interesting about this account is that the listener is given no clue as to what the woman's intention was in killing herself. It is not explicitly shown to be the product of an emotion nor of a desire to end suffering or to exact revenge on her husband. It is up to the listener in this case to decide. In these more cryptic versions, then, there is room for some variability in the interpretation of motives although the number of plausible ones is limited by the schemas operating in the cultural model.

Based on an examination of a small number of tales collected in natural settings, I hypothesize that these extremely cryptic versions of the folk-tale are most often recounted in the context of group negotiations about the

136

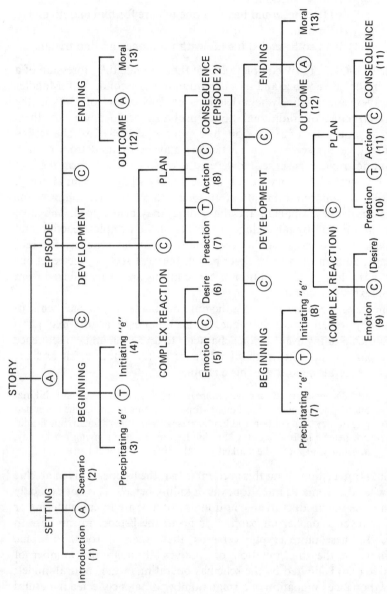

*Parentheses enclosing a constituent indicate that it was not explicitly mentioned in the folk-tale.

Fig. 6.3 Diagram of rewrite rules for folk-tale M-30.

attribution of blame in ongoing marital disputes. The more fully instantiated accounts, on the other hand, are used to convey strong moral opinions in the contexts of socializing the young and/or in justifying the actions taken by one spouse or the other in the source of marital disputes. In other words, the more fully instantiated accounts are didactic. They make connections explicit in order to teach others just which emotional responses are appropriate in certain situations and how such emotions can be expected to lead to goals and actions. The cryptic versions, on the other hand, are deliberately vague because the teller, for some reason, is either unwilling to commit to a particular interpretation or seeks to generate group discussions about the character's motivations.

In all cases, the story grammar underlying these morality tales structures events in sequences of episodes that are causally and temporally linked. Thus one event is shown to trigger the next until the final outcome is reached. Because these connections are fixed, and because the story grammar itself is a shared form of expression, the chains of events they create in the stories have a sense of naturalness and inevitability that is convincing to the listener. The grammar itself, moreover, gives force to the meanings conveyed because the ordering of the events depicted captures a general cultural model of human behavior that links thought to action. In this model, an offensive or immoral action by one person leads to an emotional experience and consequent reaction by the other. The experience of the emotion itself, in terms of this model, is the motivation causing the person to formulate a desire to react and a plan for doing it. To the extent that the structures of grammars for morality tales are shared across cultures, the underlying model of human behavior may be also.

But while the grammar serves as a template for the construction and understanding of the *La Llorona* stories, the listener must bring more to the interpretation of a single tale than a knowledge of its constituent units. In order to understand why certain episodes belong in certain settings, or why certain events precipitate or initiate certain complex reactions, or why certain complex reactions give rise to certain plans, the listener must draw upon a number of upper-level, culturally shared schemas of different types which, although not directly stated in the story itself, give meaning to the events that unfold.

The directive force of cultural schemas

D'Andrade suggests that the directive force of meaning is experienced by people as "needs or obligations to do something" (1984:97). In other words, the same meanings that represent and explain the world to people also define goals for them. The assumption is that once a goal is perceived

138

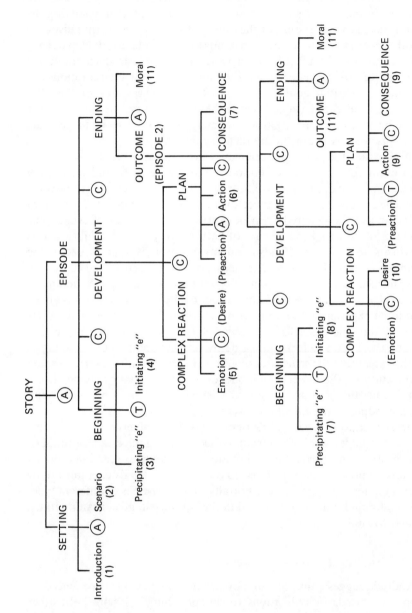

Fig. 6.4 Diagram of rewrite rules for folk-tale F-28.

as a need or obligation, the individual will respond by formulating and carrying out a plan of action to meet that need or fulfil that obligation.

Yet how do certain meanings come to be perceived by individuals as needs or obligations? D'Andrade notes that while many researchers have emphasized the importance of external sanctions and conformity pressures in motivating individual behavior, empirical evidence indicates that such extrinsic motivators are probably not the primary type of control in society. Instead, he draws on the work of Melford Spiro to propose that:

> More commonly or typically, the goals stipulated in the cultural meaning system are intrinsically rewarding; that is, through the process of socialization, individuals come to find achieving culturally prescribed goals and following cultural directives to be motivationally satisfying and to find not achieving such goals or following such directives to be anxiety producing. (1984:98)

From this perspective, it is useful to think of a cultural schema and the goals embedded in it as a motive (see D'Andrade this volume: 28). Morality tales are all about attempts to realize culturally valued goals. The tales usually attempt to inhibit immoral behavior by depicting the terrible consequences that stem from the failure to achieve culturally prescribed goals.

The main problem or plot of the morality tale begins when a character's plan to meet a culturally prescribed goal is disrupted. The disruptions in the plot are those which violate expectations implicit in the schemas motivating the characters' actions. For example, plans may be disrupted by the occurrence of unexpected events that do not fit with the ongoing interpretation of the world being made by the character. They may also occur when events "expected" in terms of the schema of the character do not happen (see G. Mandler 1984:188).

The disruption of a plan, moreover, may cause the character emotional distress. The degree of distress will depend on how much of a discrepancy there is between what is encountered (i.e., the disruption) and what is expected in terms of the schema (ibid.: 202). Usually, this emotional distress motivates the character to seek some way either to complete the original plan or to find a new way to meet the goal.

G. Mandler suggests that this tendency for completion usually leads to one of four strategies for action by people in general. The person may try and complete the original plan to meet the goals of the schema despite the disruption (i.e., try again), or the individual may attempt to substitute a new plan of action that will remove the source of interruption and allow completion of the original goals. However, if the elimination of the disruptive event is not possible such that the original goals can be met, then the individual is faced with the need to assimilate expectations to some new or alternative schema with a different set of goals. If such an acceptable alternative schema cannot be found, then the individual will be forced to make alterations in the existing schematic structure. This latter effort at accommodation may or may not be successful, but in either case, the realization of lack of fit between expectations and reality is likely to produce an intense emotional response (ibid.: 202–24).

In applying Mandler's idea to the analysis of the *La Llorona* tales, I suggest that the emotional consequences of the disruption of goals, as well as the strategies then pursued, vary in accordance with the level of the schema in operation for the characters. D'Andrade, in chapter 2 of this volume, proposes that hierarchies of schemas have three levels. At the top are those which he labels master motives because they give us our most general interpretations of what is going on, and they typically contain the most powerful set of goals (p. 30). Middle-level schemas are those that require other, higher-level ones to generate some of their goals although they also generate goals of their own. Schemas at the lowest level are those that only generate goals when other, higher-level schemas interact with them (ibid.: 31).

In the *La Llorona* tales, the higher-level life goals are embedded in schemas about the ideal self-schemas that are gender specific. These are examples of D'Andrade's master motives because they are complex representations of highly general conditions which people want to bring about or avoid. Thus women in the community define a major life goal as being a mother. The cultural schema of marriage itself is located at the middle level of the hierarchy. Marriage, in the research community, is a means for achieving a number of life goals defined by a sense of the ideal self. Yet marriage is also a culturally created entity that generates some goals of its own (see Quinn 1981 and this volume). Finally, emotion categories in the community represent lower-level schemas because they only generate goals when other, higher-level schemas interact with them. For example, the emotion of *coraje* (anger/rage) often generates the action goal of redressing the offense which caused the emotional experience. This judgment as to whether an event or action merits an emotional response and subsequent reaction, however, depends on the conditions established as normal and expected by the higher-level schema in operation at the time. For example, if the schema of marriage states that husbands have a moral obligation to provide financial support to wives, then the husband's failure to do so may cause the wife to experience the emotion of *coraje* and to activate the goal for redress of a wrong this emotion sometimes entails.

In order to understand how cultural meanings come to define goals for people and hence to be perceived as needs or obligations to do something, it is necessary to describe the cultural schemas that organize the moral values and goals pursued by the characters in the *La Llorona* tales in more detail. From this base it is possible to see how the disruption of plans to achieve cuturally prescribed goals leads the characters to experience certain emotions and, in response, form certain desires and plans of action.

Life goals and a cultural schema of marriage[3]

The most important life goal for women in the Oaxacan community I studied is to have children. Children mark the achievement of adult status and are valued for the companionship they provide and the assistance they render with farm and household labor. Moreover, women believe that their children will provide financially for them in later years thereby helping them attain some measure of independence from their husbands and their husbands' families. In keeping with this emphasis on self-definition through children, it is crucial to women to be recognized both within their families and in the larger community as the mothers of their husbands' legitimate offspring. This status implies a legal and legitimate marriage. Several different types of marriage are recognized in the community depending on the type of ceremony performed. Women who run off with men and live with them in common-law arrangements have no legal or religious basis upon which to claim legitimate status. They are usually looked down upon because of this. Officially recognized marriages require only a civil service, but a truly legitimate marriage in the eyes of the community requires a church service. A woman who has a legitimate marriage to a man expects that she and her children will be accorded a place of status among his family members and in the community whether or not he has other women and children from illegitimate unions.

Men value the achievement of success and public status above all. This success can be measured in personal, family, and community terms. On the personal level men want to attain a reputation as sexually accomplished as evinced by having many affairs and fathering many children. At the same time, however, a man wants to be respected for maintaining control at home as evinced by the sexual fidelity of his wife. Success on the family level is measured by a man's ability to provide for his wife and his legitimate children. Does he meet the material needs of his family and has he increased the productivity of his household? Such household success is also valued because ultimately it enables participation in the community-wide status system known as the civil-religious hierarchy or cargo. In this system households compete for prestige and influence by hosting elaborate festivals involving expenditures of household wealth (see Mathews 1985). The men from households that have completed the entire service hierarchy become political leaders with considerable influence.

For both men and women there is a fixed prerequisite to the attainment of these life goals. The individual must marry. Marriage is necessary in order to achieve adult status, establish a household production unit, have socially legitimate children, and enter cargo service. Until very recently, marriages in the community were arranged by families and although a principle of free choice is often employed now, it is still the norm for bride and groom to be virtual strangers at marriage because of limited opportunities for young men and women to interact in social settings. Residence after marriage is patrilocal, and the extended family consisting of a father, his sons, and their families is the valued ideal. In reality, however, conflicts among sons makes the achievement of this ideal family form difficult. In-marrying wives are expected to work under the direction of their mother-in-law with the wife of the eldest son being accorded the highest status as the eventual successor to the mother-in-law in administering the household.

It is not surprising, then, that my informants conceptualize marriage in a very different way than do Quinn's American subjects (1981, n.d.). Marriage is not the institutional realization of love. Indeed, couples seldom talk of love and marriage in the same breath, and if relations with a spouse are cordial then the marriage is considered to be going well.

Marriage for my informants is both a necessity for the achievement of adult status and a means to achieve other ends. Women want children and the status and security they provide; men want success and community-recognized status. Marriage makes the attainment of these life goals a possibility, and marital expectations are framed accordingly. Couples want marriages to function smoothly so that life goals can be met. Thus women, who are concerned with raising their children successfully, expect a husband to father children and support them financially. They do not expect a husband to be sexually faithful or to take much of an interest in raising children. But he should accord his wife and legitimate children a primary place of respect. Consequently, he should be discrete in his extramarital affairs and continue always to give his financial and moral support to his family.

Men who want to achieve public status expect that their wives will bear children and support this status quest. A wife must willingly meet her husband's sexual needs, although she is not usually expected to enjoy the experience. She should be faithful sexually to her husband so that the legitimacy of his children is never questioned. To that end a wife should uphold the household's reputation as well as her husband's by comporting herself in public with dignity and decency. A wife is also expected to work hard and place her service to the family and the household ahead of her own personal gratification. She must meet the needs of the family as well as fulfil her role in furthering the household's cargo service.

These general marital expectations which consist of both higher-level life goals, like a man's desire to marry in order to achieve adult status, and middle-level marital goals, like a man's expectation that marriage will provide him with regular sexual activity, are expressed in the opening sections of the *La Llorona* tales. Most begin with conventionalized scenarios about how a successful marriage should progress and the emotional satisfaction that results. Female versions portray this progression from the vantage point of a woman's life goals while male versions do the opposite. These scenarios are illustrated in the following excerpts from informant accounts (F is female informant, M is male informant; the numbers were assigned in the order that the interviews were completed):

F-2   *La Llorona* was a beautiful young woman who married an older, more experienced man. She had three children, and she was a devoted wife and mother...

F-4   *La Llorona* got married when she was very young. They had children and were very content...

F-6   *La Llorona* married an older man. She went to his house and worked hard for her mother-in-law. They had a baby and she saw that the baby was well fed and wore clean clothes...

F-7   ...she was very innocent when she married. And she had a child and worked hard for her mother-in-law...

F-8   ...she had children and cared for the home. And everthing was good. They built a little house and a fence and grew their own corn, and her mother-in-law said, "See what a good wife my son has"...

These scenarios from women's tales depict the main character achieving valued life and marital goals. The woman is shown to be a devoted wife and mother who has children and works hard to care for them. She is also shown working hard for her husband's family in order to build a successful household.

Male narratives begin with these types of scenarios:

M-17   *La Llorona* was an evil woman married to a good man. He worked hard and everyone liked him...

M-24   Well, it begins like this. There was a woman who married a man. The man married her because she was a decent girl from a good family. She was not beautiful, but he thought she would stay home and raise his children and work hard. They built a separate house and were content...

M-25   She was a good woman who married a hard-working man. At first all was well. She worked hard and they had children. They began to have cargo festivals...

M-26   She was a woman married to a good man. He worked very hard and
everyone liked him. He built a house and saw that his children had the
best clothes. They were content...

In the male version of the ideal scenario, the husband is shown achieving
important goals. He has children and provides for them; he is well liked in
the community; his household begins to have cargo festivals; and his wife
is faithful and dutiful.

Although each of these stories begins with the conventionalized scenario of how marriage should proceed, the body of the plot of the folk-tale
is devoted to explaining how and why the marriage goes wrong. What
goes wrong initially is an action on the part of one spouse that violates
what the other spouse expects from marriage. This violation of marital
obligations is viewed as a serious problem because it may threaten the
attainment of life goals. The offended spouse usually takes some counter
action to try and stop the violation and, in the course of the narrative, one
thing leads to another until the terrible outcome is reached.

Before I trace the logic structuring sequences of events in the folk-tales,
I will discuss briefly how expectations come to be violated in the first
place. In these tales, female informants pin the blame for marital problems
on men while men do the opposite. Problems begin when the spouse of
one sex reverts to type and fails to fulfil a marital obligation. I say reverts
to type because the initial violations, as portrayed in the narratives, result
from what community members define as "typical" male or female
characteristics. These attributes are rooted ultimately in more basic
notions about gendered human nature.

Male and female informants agree that marital disruption may occur
when selfish human desires cause people to neglect social obligations such
as those required by marriage. The difference between the two sexes is one
of perspective. Each sex views the other as weak and undisciplined and
hence apt to fail in meeting marital obligations. The likely types of failure,
however, differ for each sex in accordance with differential life goals and
expectations.

The male perspective on the violation of marital expectations

Men, for example, view women as being sexually uncontrolled. A woman
may be able to fool a man by acting decent and respectable, but in the end
her true nature usually comes out causing her to pursue her own desires at
the expense of her marital obligations. The way in which a woman reverts
to type is by "going crazy" and seeking sexual gratification outside the
marriage. This behavior is captured in a powerful exemplar known as

"walking in the streets" which is used by men to encapsulate bad or undesirable behavior in women.[4] Women who are decent and respectable do not walk alone in the streets where other men can take advantage of them. To do so means that a woman is interested in and receptive to male advances. A wife who begins to "walk the streets" is problematic because her behavior threatens her husband's public status and reputation since he may be seen as no longer able to control her or guarantee that his children are really his.

Women are expected not only to be faithful to their husbands but also to meet their husbands' sexual needs. A woman who is "cold" to her husband by refusing him sex is violating a marital obligation and will probably be suspected by her husband of seeing other men. However because wives, paradoxically, are not expected to enjoy or need sex, a wife's "coldness" may be tolerated by the husband as long as she does not have affairs with other men.

Women may also attempt to pursue their own pleasures by engaging in visiting and gossip at the expense of performing household duties. Ultimately a failure to work hard in the household may jeopardize that household's productivity and ability to compete in the cargo system. Moreover, such activities along with time spent "walking the streets," are often perceived by community members as taking away from the care given to children.

In summary, wives can disrupt the marital expectations of their husbands by going "crazy" and beginning to "walk the streets," by visiting and gossiping instead of performing household duties, by neglecting children, or by turning "cold" to their husbands and refusing them sex. Each of these disruptions is depicted in the following excerpts from the folk-tales:

M-24   ...They built a separate house and were content. But then one day she began to walk the streets. And everyone knew, but he did not...

M-25   ...They began to have cargo festivals. But then she began to gossip all the time. She was always gone visiting other women...

M-3   ...La Llorona was an evil woman. She did not care for her children or her husband. All the time she walked in the street...

M-4   ...They had four children and then she did not want any more. And so she became cold to him [stopped having sex with him]...

A man whose wife evinces these behaviors is likely to take steps to try and keep the disruption from interfering with the achievement of his marital goals. I suggest that the type of step he takes in the folk-tales falls into one of four categories of strategies to deal with disruptions. The first three categories include efforts to deal with or put a stop to the disruptions. Interestingly enough, these never succeed in the tales. Instead, as the early efforts to handle the disruption fail, attention is focused on the main moral problem which must eventually be handled by the fourth category of strategy: a drastic attempt to alter the existing reality or schema.

In attempting to deal with the disruption, the husband may, for example, renew his efforts to complete his original plan to meet marital goals despite the intial disruption. Usually this response involves the husband in either going on as usual with daily activities and denying that the disruption happened, or it may involve him in attempting to escape the situation temporarily in the hopes that the same plan can be tried again successfully at a later time:

M-14   ...She did not care for the child. When her husband found out, he had much *pena* (shame). He did not know what to do. But he did not tell anyone else. He went on as usual...

M-12   ...Then one day she began to walk the streets and look for men. When he found out, he had much *pena* (shame) and did not want to show his face. So he thought he would go to work for another farmer for a few days. But when he came home...

A second possible strategy is for the husband to attempt to substitute a new plan of action that will remove the disruption. This strategy usually involves the husband in attempts to correct the disruptive behavior of the wife in order to put the marriage back on the same footing. Thus men may try and shame their wives into a change of behavior by beating, cursing, or otherwise humiliating them in public. Similarly, a man may turn his wife out of the house in the hopes that her own parents to whom she returns will reprimand her. Alternatively, he may turn her out in an effort to deny her the privileges of marriage and family until she corrects the disruptive behavior. Finally, men may attempt to punish their wives physically through private beatings designed to force a change of behavior through intimidation. The goal in each situation is to correct offensive behavior so that the marriage can return to normal. At the same time, each particular plan, whether it be to turn the wife out or to punish her physically, satisfies, when completed, a more limited subgoal such as "deny her the privileges of marriage" or "physically punish her." Moreover, certain actions like turning one's wife out of the house can subsume multiple subgoals at the same time. The excerpts from the folk-tales illustrating these actions often include statements about the goals and subgoals being pursued:

M-10   ...He never knew until one day someone told him . . . He put her on the street and yelled for the neighbors to come. Then he told them all that she was a whore and a cheat and a liar – that she was a bad woman. She tried to hide her face with the *rebozo*, but he yanked it away and made them see her...

M-8   ...His mother told him of her laziness and he had much *pena* (shame). He did not know what to do. And so he locked the door to her and told her not to return. He knew that she would go to her parents and that they would scold her and tell her to return and be a good wife...

M-9   ...But one day he heard some men in the cantina talking about her and he had much *pena* (shame). And so he locked the door to her and told her never to return. He knew her parents would not want her and that she would have no where to go...

M-27   ...his mother told him about the visiting. He had much *coraje* (anger) and took her inside and beat her and told her she should obey him or he would beat her again...

If it does not appear possible to eliminate the source of the disruption, then the husband may have to assimilate his expectations to some new or alternative schema of marriage. This third course of action is only pursued in the folk-tales when the disruption does not necessarily threaten the completion of life goals. The one disruptive action that wives take that falls into this category is that of "turning cold" to the husband and refusing to have sex with him. If this behavior should be motivated by the wife's infidelity, then it would threaten a life goal – that of ensuring the legitimacy of one's children. However, if it is not, representing for example the wife's supposed innate dislike of sex or her unwillingness to get pregnant again, then men usually adjust their expectations of marriage slightly by finding another woman to provide sex. Such a tactic is illustrated below:

M-4   ...They had four children, and then she did not want more. She became cold to him. The man had to look elsewhere for his needs. So he found another woman...

M-5   ...But then one day she became cold to him and slept away from him. At first he was filled with *tristeza* (sadness) and he did not understand. But then he found another woman and began to visit her...

The final set of strategies occurs at the point in the story when the disruptive behavior is so severe that it cannot be corrected or threatens the satisfaction of life goals to such an extent that no acceptable alternative schema of marriage can be substituted. This realization is experienced as intense negative affect by the protagonist who is then driven to remove the negative affect by either ending the marriage or by killing the offending spouse. In either case, the marriage is terminated. In the folk-tales, the husband usually takes one or two actions in this situation. He either kills his wife and/or her lover, or he turns her out of the house forever thereby ending the marriage. The subgoals the husband hopes to accomplish with the plan may include either putting an end to his own public humilation or getting revenge against his wife. Each of these outcomes is illustrated below:

M-12   ...When he found out he had much *pena* (shame) and did not want to show his face. So he thought he would go to work for another farmer for a few days. But when he came home his wife was still gone, and he was filled with *coraje* (rage). So he found his wife and shot her so no one could tell gossip about them again...

M-28   ...he beat her and told her she had given him much *pena* (shame). She did not listen and started to walk the streets again. When he found out he was full of *coraje* (rage) and so he shot her and her lover. And now they will never know any peace and will be doomed to wander as restless spirits...

M-10   ...he made them see her. After he finished, he went in and locked the door and told her he would never see her again...

The female perspective on the violation of marital expectations

Women view men as being by nature lustful, possessing insatiable sexual appetites. They are compared with animals in that they are driven to seek their own satisfaction without regard to social and family obligations because they want sex but not the obligations that a sexual relationship entails. Consequently, although a man may try to be a good husband and provider, his true nature is like to come out at any time. Men violate obligations by establishing liaisons with other women such that family resources are given to these women. Similarly, men violate a wife's expectations if they use family resources for the pursuit of pleasures like drinking or gambling. A man's failure to provide jeopardizes a wife's goal of raising children successfully. A man may also violate the terms of marriage if he fails to give his wife and legitimate children the primary position of respect by publicly acknowledging the status of his mistress or illegitimate child. Each of these violations is illustrated in the following excerpts from the folk-tales:

F-4   ...They had children and were very content. But one day her husband took up with a widow and began to give her all his money...

F-16   *La Llorona* was a good woman. She worked hard to care for her children. But then her husband started drinking. He was always in the cantina or passed out in the street while the children had no food...

F-6   ...Then one day she found out he had another woman. And she heard him telling others that he loved her – that she was his woman now...

Wives in the folk-tales pursue the same four avenues of action as husbands do when their expectations of marriage are disrupted. They may choose to deny the situation and go on as usual or to escape for a few days in the hopes that things will continue as normal when they return. Alternatively, they may attempt to institute some new plan of action designed to correct the offensive behavior of the husband and allow for the completion of the original marital goals. Wives, however, use different tactics to correct behavior than do husbands although the subgoals they achieve with the correction are often the same. The wives' tactics include the shaming of men into compliance and the denial of the privileges of marriage and family pending a correction in behavior. The one difference is that women do not have the option of using physical punishment to intimidate men into compliance. This use of violence is a fundamental asymmetry between the sexes that is revealed in the folk-tales. Wives may attempt to shame their husbands into correct behavior by publicly humiliating them or by gossiping about them to others. For example:

F-21   ...So she went to confront them both, and she called to her husband and cursed him for his bad treatment in front of the neighbors...

F-13   ...And she went and told her mother why, and soon all the neighbors were talking about how her husband had wronged her...

Alternatively, the wife can deny her husband the privileges of marriage and family until he corrects the problematic behavior. This is accomplished in the folk-tales when the wife stops performing household work, denies her husband sex, or turns the children against him. For example:

F-11   ...One day he lost all their money when he passed out in the street. And *La Llorona* had much *pena* (shame) because the money was all gone from his drinking. And so she said to him, "Why should I work hard to give you money to waste? I will not work anymore until the drinking stops.".

F-27   ...But then when she saw him with the other woman she had *pena* (shame). And she turned cold to him and slept away from him. And he was sad and asked her what was wrong. And she told him she would not be his wife as long as he stayed with the other woman...

F-9   ...But she knew it was true and she told her children, "Your father is spending all his time and money on that woman. He is treating us badly." And so her children began to ask their father why he no longer cared for them...

If it does not appear possible to correct the source of disruption, women may also assimilate their expectations to a new schema of marriage and the goals it entails. This usually involves them in finding other sources of family income independent of or in addition to the money earned by their husbands:

F-18   ...But one time he stopped coming home some nights and he never seemed to have money when the children needed something. She thought that it was difficult for him to make money so she began to keep and sell animals to get money for her children...

However, when the disruptive behaviors are judged so severe that correction is impossible, or when they threaten the achievement of a woman's life goals, intense negative affect results. In such situations, the wife is driven to take a drastic action to alter the existing schema and end the marriage. This always involves taking her own life and sometimes the lives of her children as well. This action puts an end to the schema of marriage and may also enable the wife to take revenge against her husband by frustrating his ability to meet life goals as well, or it may be undertaken as a means to end the suffering and/or public humiliation she suffers at his hand.

There is one important difference in the options available to women and men in this response category. Men can lock their wives out of the house and thereby put an effective, if not legal, end to the marriage. Women in the research community do not have this option. Because the wife is the in-marrying spouse, the only way she could hypothetically terminate a marriage would be to leave her husband's house and return home. However, because most marriages are arranged by parents and involve reciprocal exchanges of resources, natal families are usually unwilling to take back a daughter permanently and thereby contribute to the break-up of a marriage. So the only option perceived to be open to a woman who wants to terminate her marriage is suicide:

F-28   ...But he kept drinking, and one night he lost all their money when he passed out in the street. And so she killed herself so that he would have no one to care for him and no one to help him...

F-8   ...and *La Llorona* heard it. She was wounded by his betrayal. And she said to her mother-in-law: "On this day I will leave my life" ...And so late that night she walked into the river and drowned herself...

F-11   ...and she was filled with *coraje* (rage) and so she killed herself and her children so that they would not suffer anymore...

Thus far, the analysis shows that the folk-tales begin with a conventionalized scenario of how marriage is expected to proceed. These scenarios often demonstrate the realization of both life and marital goals by the partners to the marriage. However, the body of the folk-tale is devoted to showing how a marriage can go wrong when one spouse acts in an immoral fashion. These immoral acts are behaviors that threaten the other spouse's expectations about marriage, causing him/her to experience extreme negative emotion. This emotional experience motivates him/her to attempt either to restore the original marital situation, to meet the original goals in some other way, or to end the marriage.

The link between the disruption and the plan of action formulated to deal with it is the feeling of arousal, expressed in the folk-tales as an emotion. Emotions thus mediate between the disruption of expectations and actions. The emotion itself, moreover, is depicted in the stories as the motivation that gives direction to the plan of action developed to deal with the disruption.

Emotion schemas

In the folk-tales under consideration, violations of marital obligations by one spouse lead to one of three emotional reactions on the part of the other spouse: *pena*, shame/embarrassment; *coraje*, anger/rage; and *tris-teza*, sadness/grief.[5] Each of these motion words is itself a schema with embedded goals. Furthermore, as Lutz (1987:300) demonstrates for Ifaluk emotion terms, each word does more than just signal the presence of a goal, it may also actively produce goal directionality by producing a motive or deepening and clarifying an existing one (ibid.:301). The goals generated by the emotion words in the *La Llorona* folk-tales are action goals which motivate characters to deal with their spouse's disruptive behaviors in accordance with the four types of strategies outlined previously.

The emotion of pena/shame

For example, the emotion of *pena*, translated as shame or embarrassment, implies some form of public humiliation. That is, the activities of one spouse have been publicly recognized as a violation of the expectations of the other thereby causing him/her to feel shame. In keeping with this usage, *pena* is expressed in these folk-tales as a mass noun conceptualized as an entity that one can possess. People who "have" *pena* have usually been "given it" by someone else. This is where the public aspect comes in. The emotion is not an internal state of existence nor is it the product of one's own actions. Rather it is a feeling directly caused by the actions of others. Thus one may appropriately say, *Tengo pena* ("I have shame"), or *Me dió pena* ("He/She/It gave me shame").

Entailed in this schema is a desire to rid oneself of that sense of shame and to restore one's public standing prior to the event. Consequently, spouses who experience shame in the folk-tales are motivated to formulate some plan of action to remove that sense of shame in a way that will restore their public standing as shame-free individuals. These actions, as outlined in the previous section, included attempts to deny the situation and go on as usual pretending that a source of shame does not exist as well as efforts to correct the behavior of the offending spouse and remove the source of shame.

These relations between events, emotions, and actions can be diagrammed as a series of proposition schemas in a format devised by Lutz (1987:292–3). These types of schemas are viewed as templates which specify the relationships that obtain between entities in terms of variable ranges of concepts (see also Hutchins 1980:51 and Quinn and Holland 1987:25). The instantiation of a schema occurs in my analysis when the ranges are replaced by specific examples of entities thereby forming a proposition which is itself a concept. In the notational system employed, schemas are labeled by key words representing the type of entity under consideration. These words are followed by square brackets which enclose the particular entities involved as described in simple English phrases. Broken arrows pointing from left to right indicate the direction of the causal relationship. I use broken arrows, following Lutz's system (1987:293), to emphasize the probabilistic nature of the causal link which is part of my informants' folk model of how these relations between entities are structured.

For example, the emotion of *pena* is represented in the following proposition-schemas:

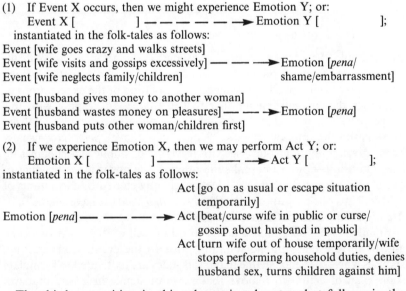

(1)   If Event X occurs, then we might experience Emotion Y; or:
    Event X [   ] — — — — — —➤ Emotion Y [   ];
    instantiated in the folk-tales as follows:
Event [wife goes crazy and walks streets]
Event [wife visits and gossips excessively] — — —➤ Emotion [*pena*/
Event [wife neglects family/children]   shame/embarrassment]

Event [husband gives money to another woman]
Event [husband wastes money on pleasures] — — –➤ Emotion [*pena*]
Event [husband puts other woman/children first]

(2)   If we experience Emotion X, then we may perform Act Y; or:
    Emotion X [   ] — — — — —➤ Act Y [   ];
    instantiated in the folk-tales as follows:
                              Act [go on as usual or escape situation
                                temporarily]
Emotion [*pena*] — — — –➤ Act [beat/curse wife in public or curse/
                                gossip about husband in public]
                              Act [turn wife out of house temporarily/wife
                                stops performing household duties, denies
                                husband sex, turns children against him]

The third proposition in this schema is a key to what follows in the remainder of the narrative of each folk-tale. The emotion experienced and the resultant action taken by one spouse may lead to a counter-action on the part of the other (i.e., the one who initially committed the violation). The link between the two actions is the emotional experience. Yet this linking emotion is often dropped out of the tales producing a proposition where action leads to action. Often whole sequences of events are chained together in the tales as one action generates another. This proposition is diagrammed as follows:

(3)   If a person performs Act X, then another person may perform Act Y; or, Act X [   ] —— —— —— —— —➤ Act Y [   ]; instantiated in the following version of the tale:

M-1   *La Llorona* was a very evil woman. She roamed the streets and visited other men in the fields. Her husband did not know, but everyone else did. When he found out, he beat her. She killed herself and her children. Now he has no wife, no home, and no pride.

The schemas in this tale can be diagrammed as follows:

Event [wife walks the streets] —— —— —— —— —➤ Act [husband beats wife]
Act   [husband beats wife] —— —— —— —— —➤ Act [wife kills herself and children]

or, Action leads to Action. Here the linking emotional experiences are not made explicit. The listener can infer that some emotion motivated the response, but such an inference is not essential to the plot.

Although the experience of emotion may motivate one spouse to take a counter-action, the other spouse reacts solely to the behavior, not to the emotional experience of his/her partner. Hence speculation about the motives of others is not a theme in the folk-tales, and the characters do not spend time trying to figure out what another person is feeling, nor do they take responsibility for the emotional reactions of others.

This ethnotheory of emotion expressed in proposition-schema 3 differs dramatically from that documented by Lutz (1987) for the Ifaluk. According to Lutz, the Ifaluk believe that each individual holds important responsibility for the emotions of others and for causing an emotion in another (ibid.:297). The Ifaluk ethnotheory treats emotions as social phenomena, not predominantly as internal states that correlate to social events (ibid.:296). Thus in Ifaluk discourse, the proposition: if we experience Emotion X, then another person should or might experience Emotion Y, (i.e., Em 1 [   ] —— —— —— —➤ Em 2 [   ]) is central. Lutz notes that propositions from this schema may be formed through a chain of inference linking the experience of an emotion to an action by one person that then leads to the experience of an emotion by the second person. However, the dyadic links between emotions are very common in discourse, and these omit all references to linking actions (ibid.:296). So for the Ifaluk emotions in one person are shown to lead more directly to emotions in another person than they are in the *La Llorona* tales.

The emotion of *coraje* – anger/rage

The second most common emotion recognized in the folk-tales is that of *coraje,* anger/rage. The emotion implies a rage that results from a perceived wrong caused by another person as opposed to a minor annoyance or a wrong caused by self or by chance. In the latter case the emotion word, *enoja,* from the verb, *enojar* (to anger/annoy), is employed. Thus a person might say, "I am *enojada* (mad)," when annoyed or mildly angry. *Coraje,* on the other hand, is a noun that implies an entity that someone has or possesses. Thus my informants might say, "I have *coraje*," or "He/she/it gave me *coraje*."[6]

The terms as they are used in the folk-tales imply a kind of anger or rage that is perceived to result from a deliberate affront or wrong. This emotion causes the victim to seek redress or revenge against the person causing it. There is also a sense of an overwhelming affect associated with *coraje* such that the person acts as much to get rid of the feeling as to carry out any particular plan of action. A survey of the occurrence of these emotion terms in the folk-tales revealed the following instantiations of the schemas for emotion borrowed from Lutz and outlined above for *pena*:

(1)   Event [wife walks streets] —— —— —— —— ➤ Emotion [*coraje*]
      Event [husband beats wife/for physical punishment]
      Event [husband wastes resources/causes neglect of child]

(2)   Emotion [*coraje*] —— —— —— ➤ Action [husband murders wife and/or
                                              wife's lover]
                          Action [husband turns wife out forever]
                          Action [wife kills herself or wife kills
                                  herself and children]

The actions motivated by this emotion are drastic in the sense that they put an end to the marriage schema. Consequently, for the emotion of *coraje,* there is no possibility that the retaliatory action will produce the same emotion in the spouse to whom it was directed. The following excerpt illustrates this terminating quality associated with *coraje*:

M-31   *La Llorona* was an evil woman married to a good man. They lived
       together and were content. She worked hard and had children. But then
       one day she went crazy and began to walk the streets. Everyone knew but
       her husband. And then his mother told him that his wife had been
       walking the streets and that other men were laughing about him. He had

such a great *coraje* that he went to look for her. He found her with her
lover and he killed them both so that she would never make a fool of him
again.

(1)   Event [wife walks streets] — — — — —► Emotion [*coraje*]
(2)   Emotion [*coraje*] — — — — —► Action [husband murders wife and
                                                    lover]

The emotion of **tristeza**/*sadness*

The third emotion term used in these folk-tales is that of *tristeza*, sadness/
grief. This term is also used as a mass noun in the stories to depict a
quality that a person can possess (i.e., "he had much *tristeza*/sadness") or
be given, (i.e., "He/she/it gave me *tristeza*/sadness"). The situations which
elicit sadness are depicted in the excerpts below:

F-6   ...Then one day she found out he had another woman and she heard him
       telling others that he loved her – that she was his true love. And she had
       much *tristeza* (sadness). So she took her children to her mother's and
       then she walked into the river and never returned. And now she still calls
       in the night for her lost children and all because her husband was no
       good.

F-2   ...One day, when her child was very sick, *La Llorona* went to find her
       husband to beg him to come and help her get the baby cured. He refused.
       The child died and it gave her much *tristeza* (sadness). In her grief, *La
       Llorona* killed herself and all her children so that they would never suffer
       again at the hand of their father...

M-5   ...But then one day she became cold to him and slept away from him.
       And he had much *tristeza* (sadness) and he did not understand. So he
       found another woman and began to visit her...

People who "have" sadness are likely to take some action and try and
get rid of it. The instantiations of the sadness schema are represented in
the following propositions:

Event [husband gives resources to another woman]
      [husband neglects child/death results] — — — —► Emotion [*tristeza*]
      [wife turns cold to husband]

Emotion [*tristeza*] — — — —► Action [husband finds another woman]
                               Action [wife kills herself; wife kills herself
                                       and children]

The only situation in which male characters report the feeling of *tristeza*
in the tales is when their wives turn cold to them. Since the action of
"turning cold" by wives can sometimes elicit *coraje* as well, it is useful to
examine the narratives to try and explain and differences in the labeling of
arousal. I suggest that the experience of sadness occurs when wives who

are known to be sexually faithful turn cold to their husbands. In such a situation, the coldness results not from the wife's actions in finding another man, but rather from her supposed innate dislike of sex. Hence it is not a deliberate action that she can control. Consequently, the man's response is to find another woman to meet his sexual needs, and the expectations the husband and wife have of the marriage are reframed accordingly. However, the husband's action of finding another woman often serves, in the folk-tales, to generate an intensely negative emotional response from the wife, sometimes expressed as *pena* and sometimes as *coraje*. In these cases, the emotion is produced not just because the husband finds another woman, since women expect men to do just that, but rather because he also gives to the woman resources or recognition that should be reserved for his wife and family.

In many versions of the tale, the experience of sadness leads the wife to take her own life or that of her children thereby ending the marriage and the pursuit of life goals. Men are most often motivated to end the marriage by the emotion of *coraje* which usually leads them to murder their wives and sometimes their wives' lovers. For women, then, the experience of *tristeza* is often the terminating emotional response that *coraje* is for men. This may reflect a cultural belief about the differential emotional responses appropriate for each sex to express in certain situations.

It is interesting that each of the three emotions experienced by the characters in these stories is used as a mass noun although each of them can also be expressed as an adjective that describes an interior state of being. It is appropriate in the folk-tale to use the form, "I have *tristeza*/sadness," but not to use the equally common expression of daily life, "I am *triste*/sad." This form of use is congruent with the purpose of the discourse. Morality tales are devised to portray the consequences of a person's immoral acts for others. Hence, the emotional reactions described in the tales are always presented as states caused by the behavior of someone else, not as internal qualities of the individuals.

The emotions expressed in the folk-tales are themselves schemas which define goals. These emotion schemas operate at the lowest or most basic level of the schema hierarchy. The goals they define may not be expressed unless recruited by the operation of a higher-level schema. In the body of the narrative, the particular emotion expressed in a certain situation is the product of the severity of the affect triggered and the type of goal disrupted by the "immoral" action of the offending spouse. Thus, a wife's act of turning cold to her husband may be interpreted in one situation as springing from her more serious act of "walking the streets" – an act that threatens the integrity of the marriage and the husband's life goal of creating and maintaining a public reputation. We might expect, in this instance, that the arousal resulting from the violation would be intense and would be labeled as either *pena* or *coraje* – emotions that are seen to arise for men from the deliberate, immoral acts of others. Once activated, these emotions carry with them the goal of doing something to alleviate the arousal by either removing the source of shame or redressing the wrong.

The actions these emotions are shown to generate, moreover, carry a double dose of directive force because they are depicted as both the natural and appropriate responses to the emotions experienced in the situation. The wedding of emotion to the planning of action makes completion of the plan an especially powerful goal for the characters. In this sense, cultural values are depicted as being highly salient for the characters in the tale since they engage their emotions, not just their minds (see also Spiro 1984:328).

Conclusion

The *La Llorona* stories incorporate directive force on two levels. As dramatic devices they are employed consciously in the research community to shape behavior. The stories succeed in this aim, however, to the extent that the actions of the characters are believable to the listeners. Believability in this case generates convincingness. Central to an understanding of how such convincingness is achieved is an understanding of how characters in the stories are motivated to act.

The actions of the characters make sense, and indeed seem inevitable and rational, in terms of generally held, cultural beliefs about the life goals men and women desire to achieve. These goals are defined by high-level schemas of self which are gender specific and are normally achieved through the institution of marriage. Marriage, however, defines certain goals of its own that spouses then want to bring about or cause to happen.

The folk-tales presented in this paper deal with moral issues. They are all about people doing "bad" or "immoral" things that cause problems for those who are trying to meet culturally valued goals. When a bad action disrupts the completion of a goal, the offended spouse pursues one of the four strategies outlined previously. Whatever the strategy employed, however, it is always the experience of an emotion caused by the disruption that is shown in the tales to motivate the actions that result. Thus emotions themselves are embedded in schemas that define goals. Moreover, these emotion schemas are recruited in the folk-tales by higher-level schemas of life and marriage and operate, therefore, to define motives for action when the goals defined by these higher order schemas are disrupted. It is this wedding of emotion to action that makes the behaviors of the characters seem especially believable in the context of the folk-tales.

The cement that holds pieces of these schemas together is the grammatical structure of the story form itself. Because the connections binding story elements are fixed, and because the model of human behavior which the grammar captures is shared, the chains of events created in the stories have a sense of naturalness and inevitably that is convincing to the listener.

This explanation for directive force may seem somewhat circular in that culturally shared schemas make the story believable and therefore compelling while the story itself, as an instantiation of those schemas, makes them more powerful and hence causes them to be more quickly and intensely activated by individual listeners. There is a certain real-world circularity found in the process of constructing and interpreting culturally salient stories. Many morality tales, including the Bible stories familiar to members of western society, take their believability from people's generally held beliefs such as belief in God. Hearing the story, moreover, activates and thus further strengthens such beliefs. Of course, stories alone do not cause people to internalize beliefs to that extent that they subsequently motivate behavior. Rather, real-world events and social practices must also be linked to the upper-level schemas about God and God's will for Bible stories, or to upper-level schemas about gendered human nature and marital goals for the *La Llorona* stories, if they are to succeed and be persuasive to listeners. This is no paradox – seeing a particular pattern which needs a certain schema to interpret it, strengthens that schema.[7]

The linking of realism to believability is not the only way in which different types of discourse incorporate some measure of directive force. Hutchins (1987), for example, analyzes a Trobriand woman's version of a myth which, as a disguised representation of Trobriand thoughts and fears, enables her to reason about relationships to deceased relatives. Because the myth works on an unconscious level, it does not need to be realistic in its depiction of real-life events to be meaningful for members of the culture.

On the other hand, the proverbs analyzed by White (1987) promote the enactment of the dictums they contain not by invoking motives that are inherently plausible or convincing but rather, he argues, by their formulaic and linguistic economy of construction which signals the presence of cultural wisdom. Because they are also cast in the present-tense verb form, they take on a timeless quality that further enhances their seeming validity.

Similarly, Abu-Lughod (1986) argues that the formulaic presentation of personal sentiments in the lyric poems of the Bedouins makes them persuasive to others even though the messages the poems convey contravene official cultural ideals. She notes that the poetic genre is bounded by a limited range of themes and metaphors, and that the style is public and conventionalized. Thus individuals are able to cloak their personal experiences in an impersonal, generalized content which, through association with the traditional Bedouin world, grants them a sense of social legitimacy and makes them seem less dangerous.

In contrast, morality tales motivate behavior both because they are consciously employed in natural settings to enjoin people to avoid certain dire consequences, and because they show how ordinary actions may plausibly lead to the very consequences they enjoin. These stories go to great lengths to outline the factors that motivate the actions of the characters and the events that cause them emotional distress because they are explicitly designed to teach the importance of adherence to culturally prescribed values. To a certain extent, then, the *La Llorona* tales are reflections of what happens in ordinary Oaxacan village life, and they are also guides to what *should* or *might* happen. Yet the act of listening to and learning a tale does not guarantee that an individual will necessarily follow the values it prescribes in any given situation. Rather, as Strauss's chapter in this volume demonstrates, individual understandings depend in large part on how the upper-level, culturally shared schemas interact with a great number of lower-level, more "context related" schemas, many of which are highly idiosyncratic. A complete account of how the cultural representations contained in folk-tales teach schemas and motivate adherence to the goals they contain requires that the next step in analysis focus on how individuals interpret the meanings taught by the tales and apply them in specific situations.

ACKNOWLEDGMENTS

Partial funding for the collection of these data was provided by an East Carolina University Faculty Research Grant. I would like to thank Roy D'Andrade, Naomi Quinn, and Dorothy Holland for helpful comments on earlier versions of this chapter.

NOTES

1 For a more detailed discussion of the history of the *La Llorona* legend and of variations in the tales told in different locales, see Janvier 1910, Horcasitas and Butterworth 1963, Kearney 1969, 1972, Kirtley 1960.
2 My grammar for the *La Llorona* morality tales incorporates elements developed in the grammars of J. Mandler (1984) and Rumelhart (1975). The main

difference is the depiction of the SETTING as a nonterminal node incorporating both an introduction of characters and a scenario depicting the ideal conditions existing prior to the beginning of the immoral acts. Similarly, I have rewritten the ENDING node as one that incorporates both an outcome to the episode(s) and a moral which involves commentary on the preceding events in the story. The remaining difference is some refinement of the elements in the beginning and development constituents to capture more accurately the actions occurring in these tales.

3 In addition to the sixty versions of the folk-tales, I collected in-depth interviews with a stratified sample of fifty male and female informants and a set of life histories from thirty male and female informants. This analysis draws on all of these sources.

4 Dubisch (1981) reports a similar exemplar used to describe women's behaviors in a Greek village.

5 This analysis is not meant to provide an exhaustive account of emotion schemas operative in the research community. Rather, it surveys only the schemas in use in the sixty folk-tales included in the study. Within these tales, only three emotion terms were recorded, and all of them were used as mass nouns depicting emotion as an entity that could be possessed. To understand fully the ethnotheory of emotion underlying this specialized use of the schemas, an investigator would need to do a field study to elicit the categories of emotion in the community and the range of use for them across situational contexts as Lutz (1987) did for the Ifaluk. Kearney (1969, 1972) has done some of this work for the Zapotec in Oaxaca.

6 Kearney (1969) discusses the emotion of *muina,* internalized anger resulting from envy, as a motivating factor in the actions of the *La Llorona* character in tales collected in a village in southern Oaxaca. Although *muina* is an emotion term used in daily life in my research community, it does not appear in the tales I collected where *coraje,* anger caused by the acts of others, predominates. This difference in usage may reflect the more traditional Zapotecan identity of Kearney's research site, or it may reflect differences in ethnotheories of emotion and the conception of the term *muina* between the two communities.

7 I thank Roy D'Andrade for suggesting this idea of paradox to me and for providing the parallel example of western Bible stories.

REFERENCES

Abelson, Robert P.
   1975 Concepts for Presenting Mundane Reality in Plans. In *Representation and Understanding*, D. G. Bobrow and A. Collins, eds. New York: Academic Press. Pp. 273–309.
Abu-Lughod, Lila
   1986 *Veiled Sentiments*. Berkeley: University of California Press.
D'Andrade, Roy G.
   1984 Cultural Meaning Systems. In *Culture Theory: Essays in Mind, Self, and Emotion*, R. Shweder and R. LeVine, eds. Cambridge: Cambridge University Press. Pp. 88–119.

Dubisch, Jill
1981 Culture Enters Through the Kitchen: Women, House, and Food. Paper presented to the meeting of the American Anthropological Association, Los Angeles, CA.
Horcasitas, Fernando and Douglas Butterworth
1963 La Llorona. *Tlalocan* 4:204–224.
Hutchins, Edwin
1980 *Culture and Inference: A Trobriand Case Study*. Cambridge, MA: Harvard University Press.
1987 Myth and Experience in the Trobriand Islands. In *Cultural Models in Language and Thought*, D. Holland and N. Quinn, eds. Cambridge: Cambridge University Press. Pp 269–89.
Janvier, Thomas A.
1910 *Legends of the City of Mexico*. New York: Harper and Brothers.
Johnson, N. S. and Jean M. Mandler
1980 A Tale of Two Structures: Underlying and Surface Forms in Stories. *Poetics* 9:51–86.
Kearney, Michael
1969 La Llorona as Social Symbol. *Western Folklore* 28:199–206.
1972 *The Winds of Ixtepeji*. New York: Holt, Rinehart, and Winston.
Kirtley, Basil F.
1960 La Llorona and Related Themes. *Western Folklore* 19:155–68.
Lutz, Catherine
1987 Goals, Events and Understanding in Ifaluk Emotion Theory. In *Cultural Models in Language and Thought*, D. Holland and N. Quinn, eds. Cambridge: Cambridge University Press. Pp. 290–312.
Mandler, George
1984 *Mind and Body*. New York: W. W. Norton and Co.
Mandler, Jean M.
1984 *Stories, Scripts, and Scenes: Aspects of Schema Theory*. Hillsdale, NJ: Lawrence Erlbaum Associates.
Mathews, Holly F.
1985 "We are Mayordomo": a Reinterpretation of Women's Roles in the Mexican Cargo System. *American Ethnologist* 12(2):285–301.
n.d. Why the Woman Weeps: Alternative Models of Gender in a Mexican Community. Unpublished manuscript, Department of Sociology and Anthropology, East Carolina University, Greenville, NC.
Quinn, Naomi
1981 Marriage is a Do-It-Yourself Project: The Organization of Marital Goals. In *Proceedings of the Third Annual Conference of the Cognitive Science Society*, Berkeley: University of California. Pp. 31–40.
n.d. Love and the Experiential Basis for American Marriage. Unpublished manuscript, Department of Anthropology, Duke University, Durham, NC.
Quinn, Naomi and Dorothy Holland
1987 Culture and Cognition. In *Cultural Models in Language and Thought*, D. Holland and N. Quinn, eds. Cambridge: Cambridge University Press. Pp. 3–42.

Rumelhart, Daniel
1975 Notes on a Schema for Stories. In *Representation and Understanding,* D. G. Bobrow and A. Collins, eds. New York: Academic Press. Pp. 211–36.
Spiro, Melford
1984 Reflections on Cultural Determinism and Relativism with Special Reference to Emotion and Reason. In *Culture Theory: Essays on Mind, Self, and Emotion,* R. Shweder and R. LeVine, eds. Cambridge: Cambridge University Press. Pp. 323–46.
White, Geoffrey M.
1987 Proverbs and Cultural Models: An American Psychology of Problem Solving. In *Cultural Models in Language and Thought,* D. Holland and N. Quinn, eds. Cambridge: Cambridge University Press. Pp. 151–72.

7   Learning to be an American parent: how cultural models gain directive force

Sara Harkness, Charles M. Super, and Constance H. Keefer

When John Whiting came to publish his dissertation research on child-rearing practices in a New Guinea tribe (Whiting 1941), he titled the work "Becoming a Kwoma." The title was deliberately chosen to express the idea that children are not born with an understanding of their cultural identity, but that they must learn to think and act like members of a particular social group. This theme has received renewed attention under the rubric of "the acquisition of culture" (Schwartz 1981, Harkness 1990), drawing meta-phorically from the field of child language to suggest the kinds of mental processes that may be involved in the child's learning of the culture. In both recent models of culture acquisition and earlier formulations of "childhood socialization," the role of parents is taken as central.

Strangely, however, anthropologists have rarely examined the processes by which parents learn to be parents in a manner consistent with the beliefs and practices of their own culture. In traditional societies where the ethnographer could at least imagine a time before contact with western culture, the task of learning to be a parent as part of learning the culture may have seemed fairly straightforward. Ethnographic accounts of tradi-tional societies in East Africa, for example, detail how children are trained to be child nurses at an early age, how they learn the lore of married life through the circumcision ceremonies, and how they begin married life and parenthood under the close supervision of their elders. This kind of "hands on" socialization lends itself readily to social learning theories of culture acquisition, whereby members of the culture learn to be parents through imitation, immediate rewards (or punishments) from authority figures, and the intrinsic rewards of culturally appropriate behavior (Whiting and Whiting 1975).

Theories of culture acquisition must deal with the reality of culture change, however. As LeVine (1980 :77) has put it, "All cultures, including our own, are in the process of disappearing." Although the rapid pace of contemporary culture change makes this more apparent, the history of peoples around the world reflects the changing nature of cultural settings for human development, from the migrations, conquests, and recombinations of tribal groups in Africa to the changing constitution of the family in western Europe. Whether the pace of culture change is overwhelming or imperceptible to its members, however, we believe that a fundamental shift in thinking is required as one progresses from one culturally framed developmental life-stage to the next, and the transition to parenthood is a prime example of this. To return to our initial example, the idea of "becoming a Kwoma" does not include "becoming a Kwoma parent" in the sense of having a well-developed set of cultural schemas available to deal with the normal range of situations that growing children present to their parents. Rather, the shift in thinking as one enters a new culturally defined role such as parenthood involves the integration of previous experience, general cultural models available in the parents' environment, and the day-to-day events of life with a particular child of a particular age. In this process, cultural models become elaborated and specialized, and they gain "directive force" as needed to shape parents' responses to the demands of their roles.

In this chapter, we present some preliminary findings from a study of American parents' theories of child behavior and development to illustrate the idea of cultural models as actively constructed for shaping behavior and thinking in everyday contexts. We will focus on two salient cultural themes in American parents' discourse, and discuss three processes that appear to be important in the construction of cultural knowledge that has directive force.

Sample and methods

Our observations come from a recent study of American families in the Boston area (see also Harkness 1990). The thirty-six couples in our study came from three cohorts, based on the age of their child at the beginning of the project: a newborn cohort, an eighteen-month cohort, and a three-year-old cohort, each divided evenly by sex and birth order (first-born versus later-born). The parents were interviewed by one of the authors (SH or CMS) each six months over the course of a year and a half, and the interviews were tape-recorded and transcribed. The parents also kept week-long "diaries" of their child's daily routines and behavior for each of the four interview cycles. Additional information was collected on the parents' background, the history and temperament of the child, and parents' general metaphors of child development.

The parents in this study were not representative, in the technical sense, of the American population or even of the population of the Boston area.

All were recruited through a large health-maintenance organization, and virtually all were American-born of European descent. All were members of intact nuclear families, and their children were healthy. These "Cambridge parents" (as we shall call them – most actually lived in the surrounding towns, and we also use fictitious names to refer to them here) were thoughtful, well-organized people who were interested in their children's development and willing to make a noticeable commitment of their time to our research project over the course of eighteen months. Many were highly educated and verbal, able to reflect on their own lives and their observations of their children. As such, this group of parents present a coherent and accessible view of cultural processes at work. At least some of these, we believe, are probably also relevant to a wider group of American parents.

The directive force of cultural models for parents: "stage" and "independence"

Two concepts have been particularly salient in the Cambridge parents' discourse about their children: "stage" as a marker for a perceived pattern of behavior associated with the child's growth and development, and "independence" as a central theme for the perceived pattern. Both these terms have a familiar ring to American ears, of course. They have their counterparts in formal psychological theory (Piaget 1970, Mahler, Pine and Bergman 1975), and they are also pervasive themes in the way that Americans think about themselves and the larger social entities of which they are a part (McClelland 1951, Whiting and Whiting 1975). The ideas of "stage" and "independence" are examples of what Quinn and Holland (1987:11) call "general-purpose cultural models which are repeatedly incorporated into other cultural models developed for special purposes." Here, we illustrate American parents' use of the ideas of "stage" and "independence" by reference to the discourse of two couples in the Cambridge study.

David (age three years, the younger of two brothers)

David's mother invokes a "stage" in talking about her son's recent behavior:

...he's very definitely been in a stage, for the last three or four months, of wanting to help, everything I do, he wants to help. I'm much more at ease with all that now than I was the first time around... Washing dishes, cooking. If I'm peeling a carrot, you hear chairs, you know, he sees me doing anything, you hear a chair coming towards me. He peels a carrot or, whenever I go into the bathroom working on laundry, he's there to put the clothes in the washer or in the dryer. He's at that helpful stage. It's a positive thing at the moment, I know that doesn't last forever... And now, I would say in the last month, the intensity of wanting to do everything himself is ... we're really into that stage.

The mother relates "wanting to help" and "wanting to do everything himself" to a larger theme of "independence," and illustrates the second part of this theme with another vignette:

I suppose they're all together... ya, I suppose they're two parts of the same thing. Independence, reaching out for independence. Anything he wants to do for himself, which is just about everything, that I might move in and do for him, will result in a real tantrum. Then we have to go back to the original state and set things up again, so that he can do it himself. I opened the car door today without thinking, he was having a hard time, I don't think he can open it. He was very upset, so we had to go back and... close the door, and he tried and he couldn't, and he said, "Can't open the door."

David's father also seems to link the two behaviors of "wanting to help" and "wanting to do everything himself," although he seems less sure of how to interpret these behaviors:

Well, this constant helping, he wants to get involved in what you're doing... but it's much more intense now, the last couple of nights, trying to get him undressed and ready for bed, he just doesn't want to do it, and flails around... I don't know why, he just... doesn't want to. He seems much more willful.

David's mother offers an explanation of why David doesn't like to be dressed, and particularly why he doesn't like to have his diapers changed, which further elaborates the idea of "independence":

It's probably... he's still in diapers, this is... we put cotton diapers, they're wonderful, but they really do require that you lay the child down, now if he were in paper diapers, it would be very different, you can really change those very quickly, in a standing-up position. He's getting... I was thinking about this today, he's getting to the point where it's insulting, and he doesn't want to be put on his back to have his diaper changed, unless you're telling him a real good story or... got him totally distracted, so that he's not thinking about what you're doing.

David's parents' idea of his current "stage" can be described in several different ways. First, the stage has a temporal dimension: the "wanting to help" started about six months ago, and the "wanting to do everything himself" started in the last month. Although each of these behaviors is described as "becoming more intense" over a period of time, there is also a sense of a developmental plateau that has been reached. Second, the behaviors which form the core of the perceived "stage" are in the context of frequently occurring routines, such as preparing food in the kitchen, doing laundry, opening the car door to go somewhere, having his diaper changed or getting undressed for bed. The vignettes presented by the parents to illustrate this "stage" seem to function as "prototypical event sequences" (Quinn and Holland 1987:23) that constitute the core meaning of schemas for "wanting to help" or "wanting to do everything himself." That is, simplified representations of these event sequences constitute "best examples" of the more general ideas of "wanting to help" or "wanting to do everything himself," in part because of their frequency of occurrence and in part, perhaps, because the evidence of exactly what the child wants appears very straightforward in these instances. The schemas for "wanting to help" and "wanting to do everything himself" are, in turn, related at a more abstract level as representations of the culturally constituted idea of "independence."

In our interview with her, David's mother also mentioned another behavior pattern: he has two-hour naps in the car, which usually start on a drive somewhere but take place mainly with the car parked in the driveway. The mother describes how this pattern developed:

It just evolved, I guess. He just fell asleep easily in the car. I guess because sometimes I'd have errands to do, and I'd put him in the car, and then I'd come back to the house to get something I'd forgotten, and in two minutes he'd be asleep, I hadn't even gone anywhere. Now I have to drive him somewhere [to get him to sleep]... But we never talk about it being a nap. We're going for a drive, to see such-and-such. He's beginning to say he wants to come home, I say we'll go home, we just have to go up here, and then we'll go home, and then he... He was eating some crackers today in the car. He was sound asleep practically, and still putting them in his mouth. But he goes to sleep so peacefully, without any struggle, usually.

This behavioral pattern is a routine which is repeated daily, with details such as a snack, extra covers, and a pillow to keep David comfortable and warm carefully worked out. Yet the mother does not label the behavior as part of a "stage." The behavior "just sort of evolved" in the context of interaction between her and her child, it is convenient, and she gives it no particular interpretation. This is remarkable in that David's acquiescence to being strapped into a car seat and taken for a ride that inevitably ends in a nap might be seen as inconsistent with his need for "independence," that is, like having his diaper changed and thus cause for being "insulted." We return to this apparent paradox after a look at how another couple in the Cambridge study talked about "independence" in their young daughter.

Cathy (age twenty months, the younger of two sisters)

Cathy's parents, like David's, see their child as being in a "stage" characterized by the central theme of "independence." Her father recalls the beginning of this stage:

Then she started having some difficulties, whether it was the terrible two's or whatever. Actually, it was about eighteen months that it started.

According to the father, the characteristic behavior in this stage is being "obstinate" (although not as difficult as her older sister used to be). Cathy's mother develops this idea by saying that what they've noticed in Cathy recently is "...the sort of independence thing she's into now, 'I'll do it,' and... wanting her own way, and the negativism."

Although both parents evidently agree on the idea that Cathy is in a stage characterized by obstinate behavior and a need for independence, it turns out to be rather complicated to specify a simple event sequence to illustrate this. The mother concludes her statement about Cathy's behavior, "I guess that's what we're thinking of now [the negativism], 'cause that's what she seems to be into."

Father: She's unpredictable about that too, because when you put her in a car seat, you don't know whether she's gonna straighten out and not allow you to strap her in, or whether...

Mother: Does she ever do anthing else for you?

Father: Well, she will, it seems to me, if you take her in the car, and you go to a store or, and then you come back and get her in then, it's like the second time you try to get her into the car seat in one trip, then...

Mother: She's worse?

Father: Ya. She seems to be all right sometimes when you put her in initially, so it's kind of like you catch her off guard and you sort of lull her into it. But she does do it on every trip, almost, wouldn't you say?

Mother: Brutal.

Father: She's pretty strong.

Mother (gesturing): Two handed, right before they slide down, because with the polyester snowsuit on, they slide right off. Then you give them a karate chop in the middle... What causes that behavior? Well, you're really sort of chaining them down, and it's exactly what they don't want to have happen, at this age. Because they have no control, they... you are forcing them to do something, and there's no way around it, they've gotta do it. And the more you force then into it...

Father: You can't trick them, because they know that the ultimate is that they get tied into the car seat, or that's my feeling.

Mother: And it seems like once she's in there, she is totally resigned to it, and she's fine. But just getting into it, is wicked. Why is control such an issue at this age? Well, I guess it's that whole stage of development, where they have to branch out, and do whatever it is they're going to do on their own, so they're testing everything. The first thing she says all the time is 'I'll do it, I'll do it, I'll do it.' Because they're not babies any more.

Father: The thing is, the thing that's interesting is that she allows you to clean her up, after changing her, a lot more easily than she used to. She used to hate to be cleaned up. She would twist and squirm, and...

Mother: And now she's wise there. I think she just doesn't like it in her pants. She'll always tell you after she's messed.

The directive force of parental theories

Critics of traditional personality theory, who hold that it predicts too little behavior in too few situations (e.g., Fiske 1974, Mischel 1968), would hear a familiar note in these parents' discourse about their children. David's parents offer the idea of a stage characterized by the theme of independence to explain his behavior in certain frequently occurring event sequences (e.g., having his diaper changed), but they do not seem to be troubled that his behavior in another frequent routine (the naps in the car seat) do not fit this pattern. Cathy's parents address the issue of how her response to being put in the car seat, which is initially offered as an illustration of "this whole stage of development," is modified in actuality: it depends not only on whether it's her mother or father putting her in the car seat, but also whether it's the first or second time on a given outing. Further, as they note, the "independence" that is manifested through not wanting to be manipulated doesn't seem to carry over to the similar event of having her diaper changed (oddly, the exact reverse of David's response pattern).

Why do parents turn to such general-level ideas as "stage" and "independence" to describe so little behavior? Like the idea of personality, the notions of stage and independence allow parents to cast particular experiences in a larger framework that gives them meaning. The idea of "stage" provides a developmental framework for conceptualizing the behavior of one's own child in relation to other children of the same age. "Independence," in American culture, is thought of as part of human nature, waiting to manifest itself in various different ways across the life-span. It is significant here that both ideas are positively valued. A new "stage" for a child implies growth, and thus, in some sense, achievement, another positive American value. The Cambridge parents showed in many ways that they valued and encouraged the development of independence in their children – for example, teaching their infants to go to sleep alone, or sending two-year-olds to nursery school or a baby-sitter.

As we have noted, the idea of "stage" is applied to behavior patterns which have changed at some identifiable point in the child's history, and they are associated with particular context-specific behavior patterns that seem to function as prototypical event sequences. What emerges from parental discourse is that these prototypical event sequences (like the idea of personality) may exist more in parents' heads than in the real world. This is not to suggest that they lack validity, but rather that they are idealized, simplified models that may infrequently be exactly replicated in experience. Parents construct these cultural models to facilitate organizing the flow of daily events and behavior into a larger meaningful framework.

In reviewing behavior to which parents do *not* assign the concept of "stage," it seems clear that "stage"-related behavior patterns are perceived as initiated spontaneously by the child – thus the association with growth or developmental achievement. Perhaps most important, behavior which is thought of as representing a "stage" is behavior which requires a new set of responses from the parent. These new responses require effort and may challenge the parent's ability to cope successfully. Thus, David's naps in the car, although they are a regularly occurring feature of a certain era in his life, do not represent a "stage" because they are the product of an interactive pattern with his mother, and because they resolve rather than raise a behavior issue. Cathy's recent acquiescence at having her diaper changed, although initiated by the child, is not actually labeled as part of a "stage" because it does not call for a new effort of response by her parents. In contrast, David's need to try to open the car door by himself, and Cathy's obstinacy about being put in the car seat, do require new responses, and the parents refer to the idea of "stage" in their descriptions of these behaviors. In summary, parents' recognition of a "stage" prompts a salient restructuring of their responses to frequently occurring situations that represent prototypical event sequences.

Parents' interpretations of new behavioral patterns which call for new responses and which, on the surface, may even seem difficult and irrational, are shaped by the directive force of cultural models, and it is here that "independence" as a positively valued cultural ideal is important. To see a child's behavior as a manifestation of a "stage" characterized by striving for "independence" is the first step in structuring a parental response designed to encourage the perceived underlying motivation while accomplishing the immediate caretaking tasks. When David became upset because he wanted to open the car door himself, his mother "went back to the beginning" and started the sequence again, allowing him to try although she knew he would not be able to do it. She did not spurn David's efforts to peel a carrot or load laundry, although they were probably not, in fact, very helpful. Both David's and Cathy's parents used distraction to get their children through situations which they interpreted as "insulting" to the child or assaulting the child's need for "control." Diapers do need changing and children do need to ride in car seats, but even the application of force – the "karate chop" in the middle to get the child into the car seat – was with a sense of humor, at least in retrospect.

The process of constructing parental theories

Thus far, we have argued that parental theories that have "directive force" are derived from larger "general-purpose cultural models" available through many channels in the wider environment. The application and elaboration of these models for the special purposes of parenting takes place in the context of responding to particular children at particular developmental points. Thus, the idea of a "stage" characterized by "independence" as an explanatory framework for understanding why a three-year-old boy wants to open the car door himself is constructed in the context of needing to respond to that behavior in a culturally appropriate manner. The notions of both "stage" and "independence," we have suggested, facilitate parents' responses by casting behavior which on the surface may seem negative or difficult in a culturally valued framework.

The process of constructing specific cultural models for parenting particular children of particular age is an active one, and the "directive-ness" is derived, as we have suggested, from the need to respond to the day-to-day needs of raising children. Many questions remain as to how this process is actually engaged. For example, how do parents choose from among the many general-purpose cultural models in the larger environment in constructing theories of child behavior? Which cultural models are perceived as relevant to child rearing and which are not? Further, if we imagine parents as developing a repertoire of relevant cultural models, how do they decide which situations any given model should apply to? In addressing these questions, we must turn to the culturally structured environments of parents themselves – thus returning to the question raised at the beginning of this chapter of how parents learn to be parents in any given culture.

From preliminary analysis of data from the Cambridge study, we have identified three processes that seem to be important in the construction of cultural models for parenting: (1) redefinition of the self as a parent through reflection on one's own past as a child and one's own parents; (2) the construction of informal networks for accessing experienced opinion and knowledge about children relevant to one's own; and (3) the utiliza-tion of formal "expert" sources of knowledge about children's behavior and development. We will describe each of these processes briefly, then discuss how they interact as a system to generate directive models for parental understanding and behavior.

Redefinition of the self as parent: reflection on the past and its reconstitution

The parents in the Cambridge study have come a long way, either literally or figuratively, from the worlds of their childhoods. Most now live in areas different from where they grew up, and spouses often do not come from the same area as each other. Even those who now live close to their original homes have returned there after an interlude of living elsewhere. Others live in what they consider transitional homes, places to stay until they can buy a home in a "real community." For all these families, the past has been central in setting schemas for how to construct family life; but in no case can the past simply be continued. In time, space, and social transitions, the present is separated from the past, and thus the task of becoming parents includes reconsidering and reconstructing past elements from the point of view of the present. The Cambridge parents show that they are doing this in at least three different ways. First is the process of sifting out the positive and negative elements in their own upbringing. In American middle-class culture this process can be formalized through psychotherapy, but more simply for these Cambridge parents the labeling of negative elements in their own background serves to organize thinking and action around a contrasting model. One mother, whom we shall call Elizabeth Clarendon, chose a woodsy suburb of Boston as a home for her family partly in response to her feelings about her California childhood:

I'm one of these strange California people who loves New England, and never wants to go back to live in California. I like the seasons... not today, perhaps [looking out of the window at a grey drizzle], but... I think people in New England are much more connected to the natural environment. You don't have to battle anything in California, it's all there, it's all manicured. I can see it when my mother comes here, she's so soft!"

For the Bakers, a couple who both came from rural southern backgrounds, the contrasting schema has been set up in the area of discipline. Meg Baker, the mother, describes the parenting style of her parents as "It was 'Spare the rod and spoil the child.' " Hardly a day went by that she did not receive physical punishment, and "everything was a sin." Her husband, Bob, recalls his father's unrelentingly critical teaching style as a formative influence on him to be different. Both parents, consequently, say that they never use the word "no" in talking to their nine-month-old daughter. This approach extends to their interpretation of negative behavior in the two-year-old son of some friends; as Bob puts it, "All that child says is 'No, no, no,' 'cause that's all he hears."

Along with the negatives, there are also conscious choices to replicate what are seen as positive elements from the parents' background. Brendan and Elizabeth Mills had their son baptized in the Catholic church despite their own sometimes agonizing conflicts with church doctrine, because of other experiences they found important. Brendan explains: "The values I grew up with had a lot to do with the church. I went to this Catholic school and I went to a Catholic college and I did a lot of work under the auspices of priests doing charity work, soup kitchens and volunteer work.

The group would get together and there would be a Mass but I would do the work... I think it's good for a child to grow up in association with a community that says 'Love they neighbor as thyself'; that's a pretty good basic thing."

It may be that positive elements of one's own past are less consciously directive than are negative ones. They are more likely to be expressed in apparent replication of behavior patterns which the parents describe without reference to why they have chosen to do these things. These behaviors are recognizable both through their partial parallels with salient aspects of the parents' own reported childhoods and because they are often distinctive in the present cultural context; yet they are presented as natural adaptation to particular circumstances that the family now experiences. George Clarendon, for example, recounts that, as an only child, he was taken on many trips by his father. As the study progresses, we find that George now takes his older son on a number of trips, while Elizabeth and their younger son stay home or go on trips of their own. In another family, the father reports in an interview soon after the birth of his baby daughter that he regularly reads to her – from his medical journals, the newspaper, or whatever is at hand. Later, when the baby is nine months old, it's *Good Night Moon* and other storybooks. In recalling his childhood, this father describes his mother as a voracious reader who took her children to the library every week. An interesting aspect of these replications of behavior from the past is that their function and meaning for other members of the family has probably been transformed from the original, without the awareness of the parent who brings them into the present. For example, trips with a son who is an only child are different from trips with one of two children, and taking school-age children to the library is quite different from reading to an infant.

The past is also represented metaphorically in the present through themes which can be applied across behavioral domains. Thomas McMahon, father of two-year-old Jonathan, speaks of the importance of letting his son know "Who's the captain." Thomas's family has sent its sons to military academies for the last three generations, and Thomas views himself as a successful inheritor of family values that he will strive to pass on to his own son. Another father feels that he should not force his three-year-old son to "go pee-pee" before a long trip in the car. In his account of his own development, the themes of freedom and personal autonomy are central, although there are no references to how his parents socialized his bathroom behavior.

The past, thus, is represented purposefully, implicitly, and metaphorically in the ways that parents think about themselves as parents and organize their child-rearing behavior. The cultural commonalities in how individual pasts are reconsidered and reconstructed, however, are derived in part from reference to present sources of cultural knowledge. We find it useful to differentiate these in terms of their informal versus formal characteristics, although the distinction is not always easy to draw. In relation to both informal and formal sources, parents engage in an active process of construction which then has directive force for the organization of responses to the everyday situations of bringing up children.

The construction of informal knowledge networks

The transition to parenthood requires the development of new child-centered networks which serve as primary sources of cultural knowledge about parenting as well as providing social and emotional support. The Cambridge parents belie the image of the "isolated nuclear family" in American life, but they create new networks for cultural learning through their own conscious efforts. As examples from among the parents show, informal knowledge networks can be constructed in a variety of different ways.

Jeff and Darlene Hopcraft's living arrangement provides an example of network-building on the basis of pre-existing household relationships. During the first two years of their marriage, Jeff and Darlene lived in an apartment by themselves. Then came an opportunity to "take care of" the first-floor apartment in Jeff's childhood home, and the couple moved in. Jeff's older brother Jim, his wife Mary, and their two children were already living in the upstairs apartment. During the next year, Mary had another baby, and Darlene quit her job as a sales clerk in order to become a family day-care provider in her own home. By the time her own son Eric was born, Darlene had settled into a routine of child care combined with informal social activities with her sister-in-law and young nieces and nephew, who were also home during the day. When asked about her plans for nursing Eric, Darlene cited the example provided by Mary: she would nurse the baby for eight months, then switch to a bottle.

The Hopcrafts' arrangements are striking in their resemblance to traditional and non-western aspects of family life, with the important distinction that this couple *chose* their extended-family arrangement rather than simply growing up into it. Families with other lifestyles can also find ways of constructing child-centered informal networks, however. For mothers who work, the day-care provider or the nursery school teacher as well as the other parents in this setting can become important resources. Three months after the birth of her second son, Joan Perlmutter put him in family day-care along with his older brother so she could return to work as a part-time teacher. Every afternoon at 3:00 when she or her husband picks up the two boys, the day-care mother gives them an account of her observations of the children during the day. When the older boy misbehaves at home, his parents send him to sit in a chair just as the day-care mother does.

The Cambridge parents have found a multitude of other ways to build child-centered networks, including attendance at town-sponsored parent-child activities, mothers' "support groups," employment situations where parents can talk about their children, and even the chance meeting with other parents at the local playground. For all the Cambridge parents, the common element is a sense of purposefulness about building these networks, and the recognition that they play an important role in the development of thinking and action related to children.

The utilization of "expert" knowledge

The role of formal "expert" knowledge in American middle-class parents' approaches to child rearing has been widely recognized (Clarke-Stewart 1978), yet it is problematic in some respects. Several generations of American children were purportedly "raised on Spock," and the same statement might be applied more generally to other widely read books of advice to parents. Conversely, social scientists have used such "expert" sources of cultural knowledge to study historical trends in the beliefs, values, and behavior of the consumers of this knowledge, reflecting a recognition that much "scientific" theory is itself a product of cultural paradigms (LeVine 1980).

The Cambridge parents have frequent recourse to books of "expert" knowledge about how to understand and cope with children's behavior. Most have a small library on the subject. These include books on how to provide adequate "stimulation" for infants, how to play with young children, how to deal with sibling rivalry, and the most compelling of current topics – how to get the child to sleep through the night. In describing the behavior of her four-year-old son, one mother said, "He's at the Oedipal stage right now, he really prefers to be with me, and he wants that closeness... I remember Jamie was just the same way at that age." Although she can no longer remember which book she read this in, she states it with the certainty of having read it somewhere and accepted it as an authoritative interpretation of her son's behavior.

These parents report what is probably a widespread pattern in consultation of expert opinion on child rearing through books: during the first pregnancy, and during the opening months of the first year of life, many books are acquired and read. As time goes on, there are fewer acquisitions and a great deal less reading. This trend seems to be the result of several factors. First, parents may feel that they have learned what the experts have to say on the subject, and there is no need to review it. Second, their own experience in dealing with children leads to a greater sense of being "experts" themselves who are not so much in need of advice. Third, informal child-centered networks take over part of this function as they become better established.

In addition, the non-interactive nature of formal knowledge sources can become increasingly frustrating to parents. One of the Cambridge mothers, interviewed when her first-born son was six months old, showed us an array of books she had consulted to understand her baby's difficult sleep patterns. Dr. Ferber's book *Solve Your Child's Sleep Problems* (Ferber 1985), she said, clearly stated that a baby of six months requires more sleep than her baby was getting, and this worried her. Other books seemed to suggest that her child's "sleep problem" was caused by a need to make up for time during the day that the baby was no longer spending with her mother, since she had recently started day-care. The mother herself was perplexed about how much sleep her child really did need, and how to figure out whether the baby was getting enough. In the process, she had come to question all of her own interpretations of the baby's behavior.

Finally, with the realization that experts disagree among themselves, some parents come to discount general advice books. Another mother of a six-month-old commented simply, "They all say something different. After a while I stopped reading." In this kind of situation, a living "expert" source of knowledge, such as the family pediatrician, can be especially helpful if he or she is able to respond to the particulars of a parent's concerns.

Summary and conclusions

The study of how cultural knowledge is acquired has focused new attention on the interface between individual and culture as a growing point for both systems. In contrast to more traditional ethnographic approaches, studies of culturally organized thinking in individual people have demonstrated that learning cultural knowledge is an active, constructive process that continues thoughout the life-span. Also more evident in recent work is a realization that, in most societies, the system from which cultural knowledge is drawn is itself dynamic and constantly changing. In the midst of this complex moving system, growing individuals nevertheless manage to construct seemingly coherent sets of cultural knowledge which are consistent with their own pasts as well as with the collective present.

The necessity of constructing new cultural knowledge is nowhere more apparent than in the transition to parenthood. Although future parents everywhere probably approach this new life stage with some general ideas about children's behavior and development, we believe that these ideas are elaborated and re-shaped in the context of living with particular children of particular ages. In this context, parents draw from their own remembered pasts as well as available knowledge from contemporary sources in the culture. The cultural models which result from this process have "directive force" in that they help parents to organize responses to children's day-to-day behavior in terms of culturally meaningful frameworks.

In this chapter, we have focused on two examples of general all purpose cultural models as applied to the specific concerns of parents of young children: "stage" as a concept for recognizing a new constellation of behaviors that require parents to modify previous response patterns, and "independence" as the unifying principle for understanding these. Although the definition of any particular "stage" is organized around frequently occurring behaviors that seem to function as prototypical event sequences, we have seen that exact replicas of these are not often found in everyday experience. Rather, these prototypical event sequences are idealized, simplified versions of experience in which the idea of "independence" is used thematically to link behaviors that on the surface are rather different, though they share the common feature of being problematic for the parent. The linking of cultural models of "stage" and "independence" directs the parent to respond to the child's behavior on the basis not of its surface characteristics, but rather in terms of the perceived underlying motivation. In this way, the two cultural models for "stage" and "independence" as culturally constructed in the context of parenting come to have a strong positive force for parents' own thinking and behavior.

In trying to understand how general cultural models such as "stage" and "independence" are applied for special purposes by American parents, we have explored three processes that seem to be important for the parents in the Cambridge study. The first of these, reflection on the past and its reconstitution in the present, is a central feature of redefinition of the self as a parent. Along with this is the construction of informal knowledge networks and the utilization of "expert" knowledge. Although consultation of expert sources is the most widely recognized feature of cultural learning among American middle-class parents, we suspect that the second process, the construction of child-centered networks for learning relevant cultural knowledge, may be most central. That is, parents' theories of child behavior and development are elaborated in their own micro-environments, which include not only having children of particular ages, but also interacting with other members of the culture who can help in giving meaning to parents' experience of everyday life at home. It is in this context that cultural models come to have directive force for organizing parental behavior.

ACKNOWLEDGMENTS

The research reported here was supported by grants from the National Science Foundation and the Spencer Foundation. All statements made and views expressed are the sole responsibility of the authors.

REFERENCES

Clarke-Stewart, Alison
    1978 Popular Primers for Parents. *American Psychologist* 33:359–69.
Ferber, Richard
    1985 *Solve Your Child's Sleep Problem*. New York: Simon and Schuster.
Fiske, Donald W.
    1974 The Limits for the Conventional Science of Personality. *Journal of Personality* 42:1–11.
Harkness, Sara
    1990 A Cultural Model for the Acquisition of Language: Implications for the Innateness Debate. *Developmental Psychobiology* 23(7):727–40. (Special issue, *The Idea of Innateness: Effects on Language and Communication Research,* C. Dent and P. Zukow, eds.)
LeVine, Robert A.
    1980 Anthropology and Child Development. In *Anthropological Perspectives on Child Development,* Charles M. Super and Sara Harkness, guest eds. *New Directions for Child Development* 8:71–86.
McClelland, David
    1951 *Personality*. New York: William Sloane.
Mahler, Margaret S., Frances Pine, and Anne Bergman
    1975 *The Psychological Birth of the Infant*. New York: Basic Books.
Mischel, Walter
    1968 *Personality and Assessment*. New York: Wiley.
Piaget, Jean
    1970 Piaget's Theory. In *Carmichael's Manual of Child Psychology,* 3rd edn. P. Mussen, ed. New York: Wiley. Vol. I, pp. 703–32.
Quinn, Naomi and Dorothy Holland
    1987 Culture and Cognition. In *Cultural Models in Language and Thought,* D. Holland and N. Quinn, eds. Cambridge: Cambridge University Press. Pp. 3–42.
Schwartz, Theodore
    1981 The Acquisition of Culture. *Ethos* 9:4–17.
Whiting, Beatrice B. and John W. M. Whiting
    1975 *Children of Six Cultures*. Cambridge, MA: Harvard University Press.
Whiting, John W. M.
    1941 *Becoming a Kwoma*. New Haven: Yale University Press.

Part III

Cultural models as motives reconsidered

8 Motivated models

Catherine Lutz

Talk of the motives, needs, or goals of individuals has been common in psychological anthropology, but it is only recently that cognitive anthropologists have become interested in the problem of how the cultural knowledge systems they describe are related to such things. Traditionally, there has been little attention paid to the question of how thoughts or cultural knowledge are related to desire, interest, affect, or motive. The problem has recently been raised and phrased in several different ways. D'Andrade (1984) has called attention to the "directive force of cultural models"; Quinn (1982) and Nardi (1983) have discussed goal-generated and goal-generating thinking; and Hutchins (1987) has explored the connections between repression and the shape of mythic schemas. These "cognitively" oriented anthropologists raise issues concerning what might also be termed the wanting in thinking (in psychological terms) or the group interests implicated in the forms of social knowledge (in more social terms) or the habitus (in Bourdieu's psychohistorical term).

The question of the relationship between goals and cultural models or knowledge has been discussed in broadly similar terms in many corners of the discipline of anthropology. One of the sources of this wide concern can be sought in the western cultural foundations of social science and particularly in the dichotomous terms our tradition provides or perhaps forces upon us. The dualisms of desire and rationality, of feeling and thinking, and of pleasure and reality provide much of the impetus for academic discussions in which these culturally provided tensions are worked with and against. Goals need to be connected with knowledge because they have first been culturally sundered.

Gergen's social pragmatics and motivated models

Rather then explore that latter question here,[1] I examine some of the pragmatic origins of the problem of the "motivation in models." I begin by explicating and drawing on some of the insights of Kenneth Gergen concerning the social pragmatics involved in psychological talk and, by extension, in the cultural models discernable in that talk. What Gergen offers is a paradigm for explaining how psychological talk originates and has its ongoing impetus in the requirements of social relationships. He also presents a way of rooting our accounts of the forms of cultural models outside the isolated thinking subject, going beyond the notion that models are learned or that they are constructed by the individual out of cultural resources. With some adjustments of Gergen's framework to take fuller account of cultural processes, I will use some of his insights in looking at the "motivated models" evident in talk about emotions among an interviewed group of middle-class American adults.

Gergen posits that psychological discourse in both its everyday and scientific versions takes the form that it does not so much from the veridical observation of mental functioning as from the problems of human relationship about which the language was designed to communicate. The entities with which the mind is populated, including such things as motivations, emotions, or goals, can be seen as "the objectification of linguistic practices born of pragmatic exigency" (1985:117). Cultural models of mind or of thought processes, in other words, can be seen as reflections of the social practices that surround their use. In other terms, cultural models of mind are "emergent" in ongoing social life rather than rigid or mechanical apparatus that exist independent of practice.

Three aspects of social pragmatics that shape psychological discourse are outlined by Gergen, including the principles of (1) intentionality, (2) seriation and singularity, and (3) pandemonium. The concept of intentionality is used to talk about the fact that human action is primarily described in everyday discourse in terms of the results, endpoints, or accomplishments of the action rather than in any literal rendering of body movements that constitute the behavior. The principle of intentionality results first from the fact that reference to other people's activities is obviously needed for coordinated or social life. In Gergen's view, however, observing human behavior is more like watching candle flames or ocean waves than it is like watching chairs. The vocabulary for describing the actions of humans *qua* bodies is, like the language for talking about waves and flames, a correspondingly thin and relatively unreliable vocabulary in comparison with that for furniture or even art styles. The pragmatic problem of referring to such inchoate phenomena as human action is solved by the more economic focus on its concrete results. Rather than describing the movements of bodies, generalized outcomes of the action stand for the behavior, and so people are described as helping clean up after dinner rather than moving an arm towards a plate, grasping the plate, dipping the plate into soapy water, etc. In many cases, however, the point of psychological discourse is to describe an actor rather than an act.

In that case, the action's result is taken as also the actor's aim. Helpful behavior is assumed to entail helpful intentions and aggressive behavior aggressive dispositions.

There are problems with Gergen's apparent assumption that it is more natural to want to explain bodies than meanings, as well as being more difficult. In addition, what Gergen describes, at least implicitly, as a universal desire to understand actors before the consequences of action is called into question by ethnopsychological research (e.g. Heelas and Lock 1981, Rosaldo 1980, White and Kirkpatrick 1985) in sociocultural systems where explanatory interest centers on more radically contextualized agents or the consequences of acts. Nonetheless, the centrality of the notion of goals and of the related notions of motivation or desire to our current discussion and to academic psychology more generally can be seen then as stemming from the difficulty of referring to human action in more concrete ways. Cognitive anthropologists, like others, find in the notion of goals one of the few parsimonious ways to refer to chunks of human activity. If goals are not necessarily things, they are at least handy ways of speaking.

The second set of Gergen's pragmatic principles includes seriation and singularity. This is to say that psychological phenomena usually are described in the lay and scientific worlds as series of temporally bounded, sequential, and singular events. This is in contrast to other possibilities, including descriptions of the psychological as a "continuous, multiplex flow." These tendencies toward singular and seriated psychological language arise from the dominance of the verbal mode for communicating about behavior, particularly in academic discourse. That is, it is in the nature of language to index the world in clearly separable or discrete ways: "a linguistic rendering of [mental life's] character, can do none other than characterize it in terms of independent events, structures, or occurrences" (1985:120).[2]

There are implications of this principle for academic discussions of "goals." The highly verbal mode of these discussions will lead us to tend to conceptualize people's aims as relatively isolable, discrete entities. Goals will be accessible and distinct rather than diffuse. When multiple goals are identified, there will be a tendency to hierarchize, sequentialize and otherwise interrelate those goals without violating each goal's integrity as a separate psychological or psychosocial fact. Goals will be seen as guiding action; the deployment of goals often will be seen as sequential (first someone would try to be well liked by co-workers and then they would try to succeed on the job); and multiple goals will not readily be said to be held simultaneously. At least one consequence of the latter will be a tendency to underestimate the importance of ambivalence or ambiguity, as each of these two concepts can be used to talk about fuzzy, multiple, or contradictory goals.[3] It is interesting to note in this regard that cognitive anthropologists, in their traditional emphasis on language, have devoted far less attention to this problem than have symbolic and psychodynamically oriented anthropologists, who have been less language centered.

The final principle of pandemonium is the most interesting and relevant for our purposes. Psychological statements seem logical or correct or appropriate in reference to other statements that can sensibly be made within the linguistic system. If someone claims to be anxious, we judge their claim on the basis of culturally current definitions of anxiety, in which the term is defined with reference to other terms within the psychological lexicon such as emotion or desire or worrying or tics. In fact, all terms of the lexicon are related, more or less closely, to all other terms. As a result, it is theoretically possible for a creative person to explain any psychological state in terms of any other state, to explain why, for example, one woman's goal of becoming President of the United States would explain why she liked apples. Gergen's notion here is that there are nearly infinite possibilities when we create statements. This openness of psychological explanation is not simply a linguistic fact; rather the flexibility or pandemonium has social causes and social implications. He notes that it gives people great latitude in explaining themselves and their compatriots to others. Those explanations often draw on psychological states such as motives or affect. According to Gergen, because the process of social accounting is one of mutual, cross-time negotiation, one is disadvantaged if a commitment must be made to one and only one mental state. In the same encounter, for example, one may need to redefine his or her friendship as affection, affection as love, love as desire, desire as need for spiritual merging, and so on. Or one may need to show why an intention to hurt was born of a desire to help, why an apparent intention to steal was the product of uncontrollable psychodynamics, or how a seeming criticism is based on deep regard (1985:123).

Gergen draws support for the utility of this view from the results of a study he conducted with American English-speakers in which items from the widely used introversion–extroversion scale were randomly paired with psychological trait terms. For example, one pairing included the trait term "shyness" and the statement "there is a direct connection between how hard I study and the grade I get." According to one of Gergen's informants, "such a rationale [as the latter statement about studying and grades] excuses the shy person from too much socializing and allows him to secrete himself in his room." Of the 120 trait-item pairs, there were only four of which respondents could not make sense.

The linguistic and cultural creativity and flexibility to which Gergen points needs to be balanced against the notion that certain types of statements within a cultural system have more force than others. To most middle-class Americans, the statement "He loves his mother" makes more sense than the statement "He loves his accountant." The latter statement does have cultural force and social impact, but it is by virtue of its apparent irony or seeming violation of some available and popular cultural models. In these popular models, love is an emotion felt for intimates; mother–child relations are among the most intimate; to call someone an accountant is to draw attention to his or her occupational niche and not to the closeness of one's affective ties to that person; and folk personality theory tends to portray those with an interest in numbers as relatively socially and hence emotionally withdrawn from others.[4] The notion of a pandemonious set of relations between elements of cultural idea systems also unnecessarily ignores the important point made by D'Andrade (this volume, p. 36–7, expanding on Spiro) that individuals differ in the degree to which they are (generally over time) committed to particular ideas – rejecting some, voicing some as clichés, others as held beliefs, and yet others are highly salient beliefs.[5]

These provisos aside, it appears useful, when talking about the directive force of cultural models, to take account of the phenomenon Gergen labels pandemonium. It alerts us to both the flexibility and the constraints that we operate with when using a borrowed cultural vocabulary – such as motives, goals, or thinking in academic discourse. We play with the terms of, but ultimately satisfy, western (cultural) common sense. It also suggests that we conceptualize models as serving social relations as much as or more than social relations following models. As Quinn and Holland (1987) point out, the question of the force of cultural models can be seen as continuous with a line of argument phrased in terms of ideological constructions and power differentials. To understand why some linguistic constructions have more rhetorical and/or directive force, it is necessary to look at who voices the model, who interprets the voice, and the power and influence of speaker, hearer, and audience. While all members of a cultural system are "moved" by their models, some are moved more than others or, perhaps more aptly, some are moved more often by others' models.

In sum, then, Gergen's work can be read to suggest, first, that the move to theorize about goals or directive force in cognitive anthropology follows a more general principle found useful in everyday descriptions of others' behavior; the strong tendency is to talk about action in terms of goals rather than the flow of acts. Second, the tendency to seriate, chunk, or singularize goals and other mental processes (itself a function of the use of language to describe them and therefore accentuated in academic work) leads to an underestimation of ambiguity, ambivalence, contradiction, simultaneity, and multiplicity in goals. And, finally, the pandemonious relationships between elements in available cultural models of the world means that individuals have a vast range of resources to deploy in thinking, conversation, and social persuasion. It suggests the relative subservience of the model as stable, unitary mental structure to the model as temporary, emergent construct motivated both internally by its own dominant cultural logic and externally by a particular social relationship or situation.

Emotions and motivated models: some American examples

The utility and the limits of Gergen's analysis can be seen in the following analysis of some Americans' talk about emotions. While diversity of voiced ideas characterizes this talk, patterns of thinking and value emerge. The value of talking about individuals' use of cultural models (however temporary or contextually shifting they are), can be seen in the transcripts of interviews conducted with a small group of American adults. Fifteen men and women of diverse class, age, and ethnic background were asked to join in a series of conversations about the topic of emotions. The cultural models concerning emotions used by Americans are diverse. Asking any two people to define "shame" or to explain why some people are more emotional that others can produce very variable responses. Class, gender, ethnicity, age, degree of prior exposure to academic or popular psychology, and other factors appear to make an important difference in the ways people think and talk about their emotional lives. Nonetheless, there are some common themes that occur across these groupings. Many people can make similar kinds of sense from the following statements: "emotions are irrational," "you can be lonely in a crowd," "jealousy is a useless emotion," "I may get an ulcer because I always hold my anger inside," or "emotions can be a hormonal thing."

These widely used cultural models about the nature and processes of emotions provide special examples of the concept of directive force. This is because the models do two things simultaneously: (1) they entail a large number of goals (for example, to express one's anger to avoid ulcers, or to be emotionally unexpressive to avoid being seen as an irrational person) and (2) they are about an aspect of personal experience in which something (the emotion) is seen as "moving" the person in a particular direction, or prompting action (for example, fear is defined in part as the impulse to protect oneself and anger as the desire to take revenge against another). After looking briefly at an example of each of these two aspects of emotion models, I would like to discuss how some of the goals people pursued in our interview conversations can be discerned in what was said. Emotion models, like those models used to understand any domain, involve goals. Seemingly simple declarative statements about emotion often entail their promoter in a set of goals. Marion,[6] a woman in her thirties, was asked to define boredom and said, among other things, that bored people

mope around, they sit around, tired of the things they're doing, that's being bored. You know, not being able to think of things to do. You know, use your life the way you want to use it maybe, being bored, I don't know. Boredom is self-inflicted, I think, by most people. It's just stale, people, you know they get stale after a while, get locked into a rut, I don't know, that's boredom. They're pitiful, they really, you know, boredom is awful.

The goals entailed in this model of boredom include thinking of new things to do and taking control of one's life more generally. Viewing boredom as "self-inflicted" implies that one is wounding oneself by failing to take the control needed. To fail to exercise that control makes one pitiful, and to be pitied is, in another part of the model of human emotions, to be seen as inadequate by one's pitier. On the other hand, the additional metaphors Marion used to describe boredom – as "staleness" and being "locked in a rut" – imply that the bored person lacks control over herself in contrast to the metaphor of self-wounding. While this model of boredom is articulated in a way that suggests directive force, the ambivalence is also clear.

In addition to entailing goals, the model of boredom is about a feeling that, in an oxymoronic way, motivates inertia. It directs the person to sit and do nothing or to feel incapable of changing the course of events. It is also both a noxious or "awful" experience and one with no redeeming social or personal value. Boredom thus carries its own more immediate and somewhat contradictory force or goal, which is to signal that change in one's current circumstances is difficult but necessary.

Although models can be and usually are spoken of as existing in individual minds, anthropological interpretations of cultural models both (1) emerge from some very special kinds of interactions, such as observations by a relative stranger, or interviews, and (2) are structured by the sometimes conflicting models of anthropologist and informant. The commonplace that cultural knowledge responds to context and practical exigencies bears repeating. In attempting to understand the relationship between models and goals, it is important to begin with the context in which our understanding as analysts was both discovered and created.

In much of the hundreds of pages of transcripts of people talking about emotions, a primary goal people seemed to be operating with is that of evaluating themselves and other people to me. They were not, in other words, simply describing or explaining emotional processes. People evaluated the situations that caused emotions, they evaluated the appropriateness of their behavioral response to the feelings they had, they evaluated each of the emotions such as anger or compassion, and they evaluated emotionality itself. This evaluative goal was evident even in those cases where I explicitly framed my questions in abstract, depersonalized, or relatively non-evaluative ways. While the details of the emotion models have directive force, as we have seen with the example of boredom, the models are employed in much of the discourse in the service of evaluating behavior and feeling, that is to say, in the service of making moral statements about what ought or ought not to happen. Much psychological talk has this character (Gergen 1984, White and Kirkpatrick 1985), although psychologists have tended to talk about schemas as if their function were primarily to identify objects and events.

Let us look at some examples of the moral inferences listeners can draw from this emotion talk and the moral directive force it articulates.

Anthropologist: All right, can you think of a time when you've experienced anger? Bob (man in his seventies): Yeah, last night. There was a matter of discussion amongst a couple of people, ah, one man, the man is very affluent and his thinking was that everybody should have everything that they desire. Now I'm talking about a man that's very affluent. He can afford anything he wants. So he told me that he had two large refrigerators in his house, he had a freezer and he had a small refrigerator. He has three television sets. He has this electrical, that electrical, microwave oven, etc., etc., electric can opener, and he said you ought to have those. And I had to hold myself back in order not to insult him so that what he has I have no desire to own, because I think it's absolutely a waste of money and the fact that he flaunts this in front of people that can't afford these so-called luxuries makes me so mad to think that another individual has so much and the other fellow on the other side of the fence has so little. And that provoked me to the point where I had to bite my tongue in order not to insult him. With all due respect to his money, he can afford it, fine. But why flaunt it? And that irritates me to the point where I really get mad inside... I'm not the materialistic sort of guy... And these people who feel as though they've got to keep up with the Joneses so to speak irritate me to the point where I boil inside and I walk away from it, cause I know if I should ever get involved in a discussion, ah, it would end nowhere.

Among the elements of the model with which this man worked are the following explicitly stated and/or inferable propositions (Hutchins 1980):

Wealthy people ought not to talk about their possessions.

People ought not to be materialistic.

There ought not to be great differences in individual wealth.

I get angry when people do what they ought not to do.

Anger can cause you to insult others.
People ought not to insult others.
Anger should be controlled.
I control my anger.

The directive force of this discourse sits on the surface. He evaluates himself, the situation of hearing someone speak about their wealth, and the appropriate responses to anger. While this man may in fact be observed to insult people regularly and angrily and to brag about his own possessions, the goal of his statements was both to order the world morally for himself and to convince me that he is a worthwhile person, someone to whom I should continue to listen, perhaps even someone from whom I should learn about how to feel and think.

While these are common goals, they are not the only ones entailed by talking about anger. When she was asked to describe an anger episode, Marion berated herself for the way she typically responded to anger-producing situations. What she describes below is her adherence to the goal of "doing" anger correctly despite a description of the inadequacy of her current anger.

Marion: I think the angriest I ever felt is when [Barry, her husband] finally did confront me and told me that he was carrying on with his girlfriend, you know, and told me the whole truth, and I was real angry. When I get that angry, you get so mad. I don't know, I feel like sometimes I'd just like to kill somebody. You know, when I get that real anger, anger. But what I wind up doing is usually crying. If I'm really, really angry I get very upset and usually I end up crying. I can't talk anymore, I start screaming to begin with, when I'm really angry. And then it turns to, then I can't even talk because I start crying and I can't scream anymore, cry anymore or do anything else anymore so it's um, that's what happens.

After describing this pattern in great detail, Marion goes on to discuss the problems it involves.

Anthropologist: In the time when you're angry and yelling, do you get everything that you want to say...
Marion: No, I won't even let you finish that. 'Cause you know why? I'm a terrible one, I don't know if you're the same way but a lot of people are. I feel that, later when I think about it, there were so many things I should have said or could have said when someone says something else to you, and you think about it later and I stew about it later. Oh, I stew terrible about, over things. 'Cause I think why didn't I say this, why didn't I do that, you know, why didn't I think of saying that. But it all comes to me later. I think the anger blocks out your thinking about what's going on...

Some of the embedded propositions involved in Marion's talk include the following:

I ought to be able to state why I am angry while I am angry.
Anger blocks thought.
Some people can state why they are angry when they are angry.
Many people cannot.

In describing the angry incident, Marion chooses to focus on the expression of anger and its inadequacy rather than on the infidelity itself or on her husband's response to the anger. Marion's discourse has the goal of evaluating the way the feeling of anger is organized and expressed by her as an individual. The evaluative focus is herself, rather than her husband, despite the fact that one central goal the concept of anger subserves is to evaluate and chastise others for their behavior. The negative tone to her self-evaluation comes from the implication that things could be otherwise, that she could "speak her mind" when angry. On the other hand, she notes that "a lot of people are" inarticulate during anger – that she is somewhat normal in this regard. She also states that "the anger blocks out your thinking" – that anger naturally takes control from her self. In switching from the first to the second person, Marion also shifts the focus from the uniqueness of her anger to its universality.

Quinn and Holland (1987) point out that the force of a model often derives from propositions about "what is right and what is inevitable." The force of Marion's statements in part relies on notions of the naturalness or inevitability and the social normality of anger's inarticulateness. The fact that some people seem to be able to speak their anger and the rightness of that approach to other's wrongdoing leaves Marion with some self-doubt and self-criticism, or at least with the puzzle that she finds important to talk about.

In an insightful article, Roy Shafer (1984) discusses the clinical picture for those who come to therapy complaining of depression (who are most often women) and those (often men) who seek help for having failed, in their own view, to succeed in life tasks including work. He attempts to explain the persistence of these emotional patterns or, in our terms here, he aims to understand the directive force of these painful cognitive/affective patterns. He describes many depressives as "idealizing unhappiness" and his second group of clients as "pursuing failure." In other words, sadness and task failure become goals and their pursuit is valorized.

These seeming "anti-goals" achieve their force by being "recruited," in D'Andrade's terms, into a higher-level goal. In the clinician's view and perhaps also in his clients', that more central or salient goal would be to see oneself as a good person. For the depressive individual, the model of sadness as something suffered by sensitive people and a model of oneself as sensitive might combine with conditions of loss and social denigration to make depression a kind of goal (see also Obeyesekere 1985 on culturally constituted goals involving suffering in Sri Lanka).

More broadly, however, powerful others or forces (e.g., the threat of unemployment, the denial of worth and resources to people on the basis of gender, race, or class) involved in the lives of these clients can be said to lead individuals to take on some of these models/goals. The psychological language of goals, in these cases, can unfortunately suggest (but ought not to) that individual choice explains their existence. Shafer recognizes that his models of his client's models bear his imprint and that of the therapeutic encounter and are not simply "discoveries" of his; and psychotherapy *is* generally predicated on the notion that the distressed get well when they *want* to. Here a path needs to be walked between the notion of goals and models as essentially emerging in the head and the agentless subject whose moves and voices are the predictable outcome of social forces.

In either case, the models Marion voices require her to do some additional mental, emotional, and communicative work if she is going to see herself and/or be seen by others as worthwhile or at least as sensible. The model of anger as something that blocks thinking in many people, a model of herself as someone unable to overcome that natural force of anger as some others might, and the view that it is good to speak anger all mean that Marion rhetorically must emphasize that part of the model that discusses the most stable and unchangeable part of the problem. That would seem to be the natural – because biologically based – emotion of anger rather than the more elusive and mutable personality characteristics that allow some people to verbalize their anger. Emotion talk would seem to play a crucial role in this regard, at least in American society, because emotions are seen as a fundamental natural fact of human functioning and as an explanation for much behavior. Doubt, ambivalence and multiple and drifting goals, however, would seem the natural accompaniment to the model that Marion voices here and the social situation in which she finds herself.

In sum, the American emotion models that have been examined can be seen to be goal-infused in many ways. Some of these are contradictory, as in the case of boredom or depression. The talk from which models were inferred was also seen to be highly evaluative, with the speaker morally ordering the world for him or herself through discussions of how s/he or another ought to have behaved. In addition, the importance of evaluation was also evident in the ways in which the interviewees (and as I note below, the interviewer) attempted to manage their self-image and present a positive, even if sometimes critical, view of themselves before the other.

Concluding remarks

The foregoing analysis has suggested that a large number of psychosocial factors are at work behind the voicing of particular ideas; we therefore focus on an individual psychological system of cognitive models at risk of missing the point that those models are deployed in social contexts which provide the primary structure and system in which the models operate and, more basically, are formed. It can also be taken to suggest that sociolinguistics might become a more appropriate or at least necessary adjunct model for cognitive anthropology, dislodging the tendency to rely primarily on either cognitive psychology or a linguistics focused on semantic meaning for insight into relevant processes. The focus of sociolinguistics on language use, its emphasis on speaker's communicative goals, on the influence of audience on codes and content has much to contribute to an anthropology that would place the thinking subject in a social world rather than either lost in thought or simply expressing thoughts when she or he speaks.

In this regard, a number of people have noted that the interview situation is undertheorized given its important role and frequent use across the social sciences, including anthropology in its cognitive and other variants (Briggs 1988, Mishler 1986). The practical demands of the interview provide the context in which people talk about the ideas from which we infer their models and influence the goals of both conversational partners. As a social situation, the interview entails differing role demands for anthropologist/interviewer and "native"/interviewee, expectations about what *should* be voiced (as either question, comment, or answer), assumptions about who the other partner to the exchange is or what his or her politics/personality/social background are. Briggs (1988) notes the value of identifying the interactional goals of the two participants in an interview or, by extension, in any conversation. Some respondent goals Briggs mentions include resocialization of the ethnographer, entertainment, obtaining cash or other quid pro quo, or protecting the self or others from scrutiny. The interviewer often simply assumes an identity between self and subject in those goals and may often rely on the implicit assumption that the interviewee's goal is to transmit information. For this and the other reasons identified above, the analyst's attention may be focused on the informant's talk about ideas and goals as stable psychological entities. Some of the goals spoken of may match those pursued in the interview, but others may not.

It then becomes crucial to examine our interview practices in close detail. As cognitive anthropologists have moved away from the highly structured interviews that were used in the past to elicit taxonomies, many have followed the lead of Quinn (1982) in attempting to hold interviews which approximate what she terms "natural conversation" and what is perhaps more standardly called the unstructured interview. Many anthropologists interested in indigenous understandings and the building of a "dialogical" anthropology have made similar methodological moves; to reject a structured interview is to avoid control by the ethnographer and, similarly, a "monologic" anthropology which effectively erases the other's voice under the agenda of the ethnographer (e.g., Dwyer 1982).

Nonetheless, the prescriptions both for dialogue and for interview as natural conversation entail some hidden assumptions about what conversation can and ought to be like; these assumptions guide our behavior and as a result that of our informants as well. They include the assumption that it is possible to avoid disagreement with informants or effectively to hide disapproval when it occurs. When one of my informants tells me, as she did, that some women get so emotional when they menstruate that they pose a threat to others, the pleasant-faced nodding that I tried to do despite my feminist values might not immediately signal a dissembling and untrustworthy communicative partner to her, but it cannot give the kind of enthusiastic support, friendly challenge, or angry dismissal that would occur in other kinds of conversations (including interviews with another person, perhaps non-feminist or more interventionist in style). The models the interviewer is working with – models involving what the informant is likely to say, what human conversation can accomplish, appropriate methodology, etc. – all influence the voicing (and of course interpretation by the observer) of models by an informant.[7] The goal of critical analytic distance might often be replaced by the interactionally constructed goal of sympathetic listening and shared ideas.

The way Marion and Bob implicitly and explicitly articulated their goals and ideas to me was conditioned by their assessment of who I was, whether I was powerful or weak, like them or different, how I thought about the issues we discussed, and from these latter notions, their assessment of what they ought to say to me. One could say that the directive force of cultural models is always relative to some particular audience in front of whom they are implicitly or explicitly voiced. As an audience, I found myself motivated, too, to be seen by these people as a pleasant person, and by a series of assessments I also made about their social positions and likely values. In a sense, then, the goals attributed here to Marion and Bob are in fact goals we created together, and the models constructed with a multitude of motives.

ACKNOWLEDGMENTS

An earlier version of this paper was presented in the symposium on "The Directive Force of Cultural Models" organized by Roy D'Andrade and Naomi Quinn at the meetings of the American Anthropological Association, Philadelphia, December 4, 1986. I thank Clifton Amsbury, Roy D'Andrade, and Claudia Strauss for their helpful suggestions for improving an earlier draft of this paper.

NOTES

1. See Lutz (1988), Lutz and Abu-Lughod (1990), and Rosaldo (1984) on this issue.

2. This critique is in keeping with the Derridian identification of logocentrism that Stoller and Olkes (1986) have extended to ethnographic description.

3. This is, of course, a problem frequently identified in social science but far less often rectified (but see White 1978).

4. These statements have no real meaning outside an actual context of use. "I love my accountant" voiced by an adulterous husband at a party to his physician wife in a defiant tone of voice is but one, still fictitiously thin, example.

5. While these two academic models may seem contradictory, the point is to balance the rigidity of the structure of motivation and cognition suggested by D'Andrade and Spiro with the total fluidity of Gergen's system (which fluidity, at least implicitly in his view, must attend both thinking and social relations). The social pragmatics of academic discourse in this case incline toward an attempt to maintain conversation amongst otherwise non-conversing viewpoints.

6. All names of those spoken with in interviews are presented as pseudonyms.

7. Handler (1985) describes how the sharing of models and goals between anthropologists and the nationalists whom they sometimes study and interview leads much research on ethnicity to fail to distance critically or even distinguish the analyst's models from the models of those with whom s/he speaks.

REFERENCES

Briggs, Charles L.
    1988 *Learning How to Ask*. Cambridge: Cambridge University Press.
D'Andrade, Roy
    1984 Cultural Meaning Systems. In *Culture Theory: Essays on Mind, Self and Emotion*, R. Shweder and R. LeVine, eds. New York: Cambridge University Press.
Dwyer, Kevin
    1982 *Moroccan Dialogues: Anthropology in Question*. Baltimore: Johns Hopkins University Press.
Gergen, Kenneth J.
    1984 Aggression as Discourse. In *Social Psychology of Aggression*, A. Mummendey, ed. New York: Springer-Verlag.

1985 Social pragmatics and the origins of psychological discourse. In *The Social Construction of the Person*, K. Gergen and K. David, eds. New York: Springer-Verlag.

Handler, Richard
1985 On Dialogue and Destructive Analysis: Problems in Narrating Nationalism and Ethnicity. *Journal of Anthropological Research* 41:171–82.

Heelas, Paul and Andrew Lock, eds.
1981 *Indigenous Psychologies*. New York: Academic Press.

Hutchins, Edwin
1980 *Culture and Inference*. Cambridge: Harvard University Press.
1987 Myth and Experience in the Trobriand Islands. In *Cultural Models in Language and Thought*, D. Holland and N. Quinn, eds. New York: Cambridge University Press.

Lutz, Catherine
1988 *Unnatural Emotions: Everyday Sentiments on a Micronesian Atoll and their Challenge to Western Theory*. Chicago: University of Chicago Press.

Lutz, Catherine and Lila Abu-Lughod, eds.
1990 *Language and the Politics of Emotion*. New York: Cambridge University Press.

Mishler, Elliot
1986 *Research Interviewing: Context and Narrative*. Cambridge, MA: Harvard University Press.

Nardi, Bonnie
1983 Goals in Reproductive Decision Making. *American Ethnologist* 10:697–715.

Obeyesekere, Gananath
1985 Depression, Buddhism, and the Work of Culture in Sri Lanka. In *Culture and Depression: Studies in the Anthropology and Cross-Cultural Psychiatry of Affect and Disorder*, A. Kleinman and B. Good, eds. Berkeley: University of California Press.

Quinn, Naomi
1982 "Commitment" in American Marriage: A Cultural Analysis. *American Ethnologist* 9:775–98.

Quinn, Naomi and Dorothy Holland
1987 Culture and Cognition. In *Cultural Models in Language and Thought*, D. Holland and N. Quinn, eds. New York: Cambridge University Press.

Rosaldo, Michelle
1980 *Knowledge and Passion*. New York: Cambridge University Press.
1984 Toward an Anthropology of Self and Feeling. In *Culture Theory: Essays on Mind, Self and Emotion*, R. Shweder and R. LeVine eds. New York: Cambridge University Press.

Shafer, Roy
1984 The Pursuit of Failure and the Idealization of Unhappiness. *American Psychologist* 39:398–405.

Stoller, Paul and Cheryl Olkes
1986 Bad Sauce, Good Ethnography. *Cultural Anthropology* 1:336–52.

White, Geoffrey
    1978 Ambiguity and Ambivalence in A'ara Personality Descriptors. *American Ethnologist* 5:334–60.
White, Geoffrey and John Kirkpatrick, eds.
    1985 *Person, Self and Experience: Exploring Pacific Ethnopsychologies.* Berkeley: University of California Press.

9   What makes Tony run?
Schemas as motives reconsidered

Claudia Strauss

It is obvious that people's wants are shaped, to a large extent, by their culture. There are probably few goals shared by !Kung hunter-gatherers, United States businesspeople, and Hindu renouncers. But how, exactly, does culture shape motivation?

Following some recent work by Roy D'Andrade (1984, 1990, this volume), I assume that insight into this problem can be provided by looking at the cognitive representation of cultural knowledge. Unlike D'Andrade, however, I argue that cognitive representations can differ in the kind of motivational force they provide. This paper focuses on five Rhode Island male blue-collar workers' talk about "getting ahead." I also know about some significant choices they have made in their work lives. What I found is that their choices have been directed by three types of knowledge. These three types of knowledge differ not just in content, but also in form of cognitive representation, manner of verbal expression, and type of motivational effect.

Schemas and directive force

D'Andrade's central thesis[1] is that culturally formed cognitive schemas not only determine our interpretation of the world but also direct our actions in it, often serving as goals. To appreciate this claim it is necessary to understand what a cognitive schema is.

Casson (1983) provides a helpful review of the cognitive science literature on schemas. Although this notion has received different treatments by different theorists, and has even been presented under different names (e.g., "scripts," "frames," and "scenarios"), the core concept is that

Schemata are conceptual abstractions that mediate between stimuli received by the sense organs and behavioral responses ... not all stimuli are stored in memory; rather, schemata are employed to provide "a general impression of the whole" and to construct (or reconstruct) "probable details." (1983:430)

Rumelhart provides a similar explanation:

According to schema theories, all knowledge is *packaged into units*. These units are
the schemata. Embedded in these *packets of knowledge* is, in addition to the
knowledge itself, information about how this knowledge is to be used.
   A schema, then, is a data structure for representing the generic concepts stored
in memory. (1980:34; emphasis mine)

One famous example of a schema is our knowledge of the typical
sequence of events when we eat at a restaurant. This schema organizes our
perceptions of ongoing restaurant experiences and our memories of earlier
ones. It is also the basis for interpreting others' discourse, because
speakers in this society can leave most of this background knowledge
unsaid when talking about particular dining-out experiences (Schank and
Abelson 1977). Finally, this schema clearly has directive force for us: if we
are eating in a restaurant, we generally feel motivated to follow the
restaurant "script" (i.e., pick choices from a menu, tell them to a waiter or
waitress, eat, wait for a check, pay it, leave a tip, and go out). To put it as
D'Andrade does, the restaurant schema has goals "embedded" in it.

Gerber (1985) provides another good example of a schema with
directive force. The Samoan term *alofa*, loosely equivalent to our "love,"
is linked to the following scenario:

an old person, often portrayed as a stranger, is seen walking along the road,
carrying a heavy burden. It is hot, and perhaps the elder seems ill or tired. The
appropriate response in this instance is a feeling of alofa, which implies helpful or
giving actions such as taking over the burden or providing a cool drink and a place
to rest. (Gerber 1985:145).

In other words Samoans have an *alofa* schema, which links this term to
the above scenario. The Samoan *alofa* schema, like our restaurant schema,
has embedded in it certain goals for action: if one sees an old person who
is hot, tired, and overburdened, one should offer refreshment or help.
Thus, the Samoan *alofa* schema is a good example of a cultural model
with directive force.

The goal-embedded schema model of motivation has many advantages
over previous approaches. D'Andrade notes that earlier motivational
research searched for a small, cross-culturally applicable set of measurable
motives that worked like the drives of hunger and sex. If goals are seen as
embedded in schemas, on the other hand, there is room for cross-cultural
variation and no need to specify a single, fixed list of human motives. The
fact that the goals embedded in any schema are not always activated – as
D'Andrade points out, we know chairs are for sitting in, but we do not feel
motivated to sit just because we see a chair – can be explained by seeing at
what level a schema contributes to the interpretation of a situation. Thus,

One recognizes some chair as part of the "finding a seat" schema, which is part of the "attending a lecture" schema, which is part of the "finding out what's going on" schema, which may be for some people part of the "doing anthropology" schema . . . (this volume: 30).

D'Andrade proposes that the schemas at higher levels of interpretation (e.g., doing anthropology or getting ahead) will trigger their embedded goals more than those at lower levels of interpretation: "*a person's most general interpretations of what is going on will function as important goals for that person*" (this volume: 30).

I agree with D'Andrade that a goal-embedded schema theory of motivation has the advantages he cites over earlier motivational research. My own study of five working men's success discourse has led me, however, to the conclusion that high-level cultural schemas do not necessarily serve as important goals. The motivational effect of cultural knowledge depends on other features of its cognitive representation. My interviewees' discourse about getting ahead, and the career choices they have made, reflect three different types of cognitive representation, each of which has qualitatively different motivational effects.

Consider first the widely shared, easily verbalized values that underpin the "American Dream": with hard work anyone in America can get ahead, and everyone should strive to do so. Although my interviewees voiced this success model, they appear to hold it in a bounded way. By "bounded" I mean these ideas are only weakly linked to the rest of the belief-holder's knowledge structure. Furthermore, my interviewees were able to see these values *as* values. Their discourse shows not only an acceptance of success values, but also an awareness that these values are dominant ones in our society. Success values are a good example of what D'Andrade calls "a person's most general interpretations," which are supposed to act as motivators. Yet success values did not greatly influence the career choices most of my interviewees made. This surprising finding is discussed in the next section.

In the following section I turn to a more class- and gender-specific schema held by my interviewees. Much of their discourse about being breadwinner suggests that they are not aware of these values as values, seeing them instead as inescapable reality. Breadwinner values, unlike success values, *did* direct my interviewees' routine behavior.

Although my interviewees share many beliefs about work and success, each also has a unique outlook stored not in the bounded way of the success model, but as an unbounded network linking key symbols, emotionally salient experiences, and ideas about himself. These personal semantic networks, the third form of belief discussed below, have had a still different sort of directive force, guiding each man toward idiosyncratic self-defining goals and general styles of behavior. This is illustrated, in the penultimate section, with the discourse of one interviewee, Tony D'Abrosca.[2] Tony's accomplishments as a runner fit into a personal semantic network linking athletic achievement to childhood memories, feelings of distance from others, and current political values.

The final section speculates that these different forms of cognition are the products of different sorts of cultural messages and briefly considers the implications of these findings for a theory of culture.

American success values

D'Andrade (1984) has used American beliefs about success as an example of a cultural model with strong directive force. He notes that from some interview data he has collected:

It seems to be the case that Americans think that if one has ability, and if, because of competition or one's own strong drive, one works hard at achieving high goals, one will reach an outstanding level of accomplishment. And when one reaches this level one will be recognized as a success, which brings prestige and self-satisfaction. (1984:95)

He adds about the American emphasis on success:

There are external sanctions involving money and employment, there are conformity pressures of many kinds, and there are the direct personal rewards and value satisfactions already mentioned. Perhaps what is surprising is that anyone can resist the directive force of such a system – that there are incorrigibles. (1984:98)

I found that in certain contexts, several of my interviewees voiced the same ideas about success as D'Andrade's interviewees. The main difference is that D'Andrade's interviewees seem to have had a model that transcended purely economic criteria, whereas most of my informants, like the white-collar managers and professionals interviewed by Robert Bellah and his colleagues (1985) associate high goals and hard work with upward mobility.

In 1985 I conducted a series of semistructured interviews with four neighbors (two male, two female) and six union and management employees (all male) of a batch-processing chemical plant in Cranston, Rhode Island. This plant, owned by Ciba-Geigy Ltd., a multinational pharmaceutical and chemical company, had been a source of local controversy, first for its noxious discharges, later for its decision to close and leave the state. Over the course of six to seven lengthy interview sessions we talked about the Ciba-Geigy controversy, the role of business in American society, current events, general political and economic questions, and their own work experiences and life histories. The first five interview sessions with each person were very loosely structured around a common set of topics that got covered sooner or later with each interviewee. In the sixth interview session I asked a series of open-ended but standardized questions about our social system.[3] The interviews were tape-recorded and transcribed.

This analysis focuses on the responses of the five working-class men in the interview group. Four were employees and one was a neighbor of the Cranston Ciba-Geigy plant. The men are all native Rhode Islanders in their forties or fifties, are married and have children, had between nine and twelve years of schooling, and have (or had – some are now retired) skilled or semiskilled blue-collar occupations. All are white and their ethnic backgrounds cover the four most common Rhode Island ethnic groups: Italian-American, French-Canadian, Irish, and Yankee.[4]

The questions that most reliably elicited shared American success values came from the standardized series used in the last interview. At one point I asked (one at a time): "What things keep people from getting ahead in the world?" "Who or what is to blame for this?" "What things help people to get ahead?" and "Is the system fair? Does everyone pretty much have the same chance to get ahead?" Later in the same interview I asked each man if he agreed strongly, agreed somewhat, disagreed somewhat, or disagreed strongly with the statement, "Anybody can get ahead if they just work hard enough." Here are the answers four of the men gave to one of those questions. (Underscore indicates my emphasis; italics the speaker's.)[5]

1. CS: If people can't get ahead in the world, who is to blame for that?
   Jim Lovett: I don't know that you could *blame* any one. You, you are the one to blame. It's you. Because . . . you can achieve anything your mind can conceive. If you can thin—, if you have an idea. [del] And if you think about it hard enough. And you want it bad enough. Then you can achieve it. There's nothing on this, in this country or on earth that if you were willing enough to work at it, that you cannot achieve it. So we all have the potential of being a millionaire, if that is your goal. You've got to have a goal. And if you're willing to work at it, *hard* enough, then you can achieve it. So, it goes right back down to you. [del] If it's your own personal *drive* if you will or your goals. Goals. Everyone should have a goal. (6:17–18)

2. George Gauvin [responding to "Anybody can get ahead if they just work hard enough"]: I would say that's true. You've got to work, you've got to really try to better yourself. Even if you're not – you don't have to be on top, but improve your job, improve your class. You start off as a helper, you become good, you become a journeyman – have to work hard at it. (6:24)

3. Daniel Collins [responding to "Anybody can get ahead if they just work hard

enough"]: I *strongly* agree with that ... I believe if you put an effort into *anything*, you can get ahead. Just [like] myself, where I have to put the effort into learning, again. You know. If I want to succeed, I'll succeed. It has to be, come from within here. Nobody else is going to make you succeed but yourself... And, if anybody disagrees with that, there's something wrong with them. (6:27–8).

4. CS: "What things keep people from getting ahead in the world?"
Anthony Gallucci: Brains and ... not having any initiative or ... money. Some people don't want to get ahead. Too much responsibility, I guess, you know, in some [cases?]. [del] It could be laziness. [In answer to later questions, he adds] I would think if you were trying to bring your kids up properly and ... show them, I mean, try to show them what the advantages of having a good job – or disadvantages of digging a ditch. [del] It all depends how bad you want something. Your kids going to school now, pump gas and work at hamburger places and everything else, trying to save a few bucks, help pay their way to college, anyway. I think if you want it bad enough, there's ways. (6:12–13).

Each of these men claims that anyone can get ahead and either states or implies that one should want to.

Only one man, Tony D'Abrosca, seriously disputed in response to these questions[6] the premise that anyone can get ahead and the value of doing so:

5. CS: "Does everyone pretty much have the same chance to get ahead?"
D'Abrosca: [del] That's the old saw, you know. "Anybody can get ahead." "Lot of opportunities." Nah. There is for some ... There is for some. They get the opportunity to skin the small guys. That's how I look at it. (6:32)

One thing that is distinctive about the way these ideas were held by my interviewees, compared to many of their other beliefs, is that they could see them *as* values. This is obvious from D'Abrosca's statement ("That's the old saw, you know" [5.]), but the values embedded in this model were not accessible only to someone who disputed it. Every man but one spoke at some point as if he were aware that he might be judged by the criteria of the success model and found wanting.

Some particularly clear examples of this awareness come from Jim Lovett's speech:

6. I'm happily married. And I've got three terrific kids and wonderful grand-children. I feel so, that with my education, which was only to the ninth grade, I've been fairly successful, um,[7] raising my family. (1:2)

7. So I was always able to provide a decent living for my family. We never had a lot of – my own, my *own* family – a lot of *elaborate* things perhaps. We always were the last one in the, in my group that I grew up with or went to school with, to have a new car. *But.* We – our children never went without

clothing. They never went hungry. And Irene and I would probably not get to go to the movies or go out to dinner as often as the others did, but our *children* never went without. So we were in a sense good parents or providers or whatever. And we look back on it now with the others that did afford, could afford themselves night clubs and, and restaurants and new cars. That their children, because of it, have to've been left with a babysitter a lot more than my children because we did stay with them. We were *involved* with them and they weren't. So . . . their children have grown up and gotten married and divorced where – and fallen away a little bit because maybe they weren't attended to by their family, or, or afforded their parents as they grew up as much as my children were. (5:18)

What is the meaning of the pause in 6. after Lovett says he was "fairly successful?" The construction of "I feel so, that with my education, which was only to the ninth grade, I've been fairly successful," which implicitly contrasts his "success" with his education, suggests that Lovett was starting to say something about his success in monetary terms. Probably he was starting to say that even though he dropped out after the ninth grade, he still made a fairly good living. But then he stopped, perhaps realizing that most people would *not* say that he has made a good living, would not judge him to have been successful in those terms. (When I interviewed Lovett, he had been out of work for seven years with a crippling occupational disability. His workers' compensation payments, frozen at a rate determined by his wages when he left work, put him just over the poverty line.) So in 6. Lovett pauses, then completes the thought by saying that he was successful at raising his family. Passage 7. shows the same realization that others (perhaps the friends who can afford the new cars and movies and night clubs) might judge him to have been a failure by the goals of the success model.

A similar awareness is apparent in the following remarks by Anthony Gallucci:

8. CS: Is there anything about your life that you would do over, if you could?
   Gallucci: [del] I had a good time at Ciba-Geigy. I mean, I wouldn't, if I could find something better, naturally, I would do something better, but if I – for a poor working man, I had a good time there, over the years, for the most part. (5:20)

9. [Gallucci mentioned that some workers at Ciba-Geigy can get enough overtime and holiday pay to make a salary of $40,000. He added] Which isn't bad for, you know, nobodies. (5:32)

Gallucci, more than anyone else I interviewed, used terms like the ones highlighted above to put himself and fellow workers down. It may be that he actually is embarrassed to be a working man or it might be something more complicated – that he anticipates that I will look down on him and so talks about himself and his fellow workers from what he imagines is my point of view, which is not one he shares necessarily.[8] In any case, Gallucci shows an awareness that the dominant social judgment is that one should strive to be more than a "poor working man."

Even D'Abrosca anticipated and reacted to the social judgment that he had not made enough money:

10. CS: "What things keep people from getting ahead in the world?"
     D'Abrosca: [del] like me, I'm not cut out for business. I couldn't charge a guy ten bucks for something I paid five for. You know. And . . . There's a certain makeup there you [?] have to be, to be a businessman. I did the best I could with my education and knowledge and skills. I'm not rich, I'm not poor. I'm happy with what I have. I've got a home and the kids have grown up pretty good. (6:15)

Daniel Collins spoke with greater pride and less defensiveness than some of the others about a key decision that kept him from getting ahead. Twice he was offered promotions into management at Ciba-Geigy, and both times he turned the offers down. The second refusal came when Collins held an elected position in his union's local. He felt he could not betray the men who had elected him by becoming a foreman. At one point Collins recollected a conversation with the plant manager who had offered him that promotion:

11. He said, "You stupe," he said, "You could have been a boss there." I said, "Well, I chose to do what I'm doing." I said, "Maybe in later life," I said, "It might haunt me." [laughs] [del] I look back and I'm not mad at myself. I'm happy that I, you know, didn't take that type of job instead of what I had to contribute to my fellow workers and the union and international. [del] I don't kick myself in the fanny as some people would say for not taking it. (2:12)

Collins had spoken earlier of how much more money he could have made as a foreman than as a worker, especially in severance benefits from the plant closing. So this statement, too, is a reply to the judgment that he did not make the smartest moves he could have to get ahead.

Collins's decision to remain in the union may seem surprising, given his explicit assertion of success values. (Later he said that he agreed with the statement, "I usually admire successful businessmen," adding, "I do, anybody who succeeds, I admire him" [6:32].) In fact, of the four men who endorsed success values in response to my questions about getting ahead, only one made career choices consistent with those values.

The one man whose behavior was strongly directed by the goals of the success model was George Gauvin. Gauvin presented his life history as a success story, stressing how he overcame a physical handicap, learned a trade, and was able to support his family fairly well through a strategic series of job moves when he was young. He said that when he was young, his friends never knew where he was working, because if he learned he could make a few more dollars somewhere else, he would be there. Even after he had settled in at Ciba-Geigy, he persistently applied for the position of lead man in his department in an effort to get ahead.

Jim Lovett, like George Gauvin, learned a trade so that he could make more money than an unskilled worker would. Unlike Gauvin, however, Lovett stayed at a job that did not pay especially well and did not pursue promotions. He considered but decided against moving to another state where his skills would have brought a higher income, because he and his wife felt they should remain near their ageing parents.

Gallucci, like Collins, turned down an opportunity to take a foreman's position at Ciba-Geigy. Collins had been interested, however, in advancing in the ranks of his union's international. Gallucci, on the other hand, consistently placed working conditions and personal relationships above economic advancement. He left a better-paying job with the railroads to begin working at the chemical plant because the hours of his first job did not leave him enough time to date the woman he later married. At Ciba-Geigy he turned down at least one opportunity for a promotion into management and then moved to a position in the company that promised to pay less well, but had better hours and less supervision. After moving to this department he avoided overtime assignments and promotion into a higher rank with better pay, but more unpleasant work duties. Since Ciba-Geigy's closing, although Gallucci is only fifty-six, he has retired.

Tony D'Abrosca, the only man who thoroughly rejected the success model (elsewhere he said, "Small things make me happy. Not money" [5:5]), in fact worked harder than anyone else in this group to earn a good living. This is not as inconsistent as it sounds, because D'Abrosca also had a larger family to support than any of the other men did. Still, in 1985 D'Abrosca reported an income significantly higher than that of my other blue-collar interviewees. Unlike Gallucci, D'Abrosca worked two jobs much of his life and chose a career path at Ciba-Geigy that gave him many overtime opportunities, which he took. Also unlike Gallucci, who retired when Ciba-Geigy closed, D'Abrosca, at sixty-one, went back to work.

In sum, explicit belief or disbelief in American success values is only weakly correlated with the actual behaviors of these five working men.[9] Why is this?

My explanation turns on the way success values were internalized as cognitive schemas by my interviewees. For most of them success values seem to be held as a relatively isolated, compact package of ideas that is only weakly linked to a larger picture of reality or sense of self. Connections of the latter sort may be necessary to motivate action.

Some evidence for the supposition that my interviewees hold the success model in a bounded way comes from the fact that their beliefs could be stated compactly, in the space of a few sentences. This suggests a correspondingly compact form of storage.[10]

Further evidence for the bounded way in which these beliefs were held comes from two men who stated the same ideas earlier in the course of the interviews. The earlier expressions of the model are given in the first column, the later expressions (from above) are given in the second column. Notice how similar they are.

12. [Jim Lovett is talking about the Amway sales organization, which he and his wife have been part of for many years] There's a, we used to have a little saying that if your mind can conceive it, then you can achieve it. It's like, you know, whatever your mind can conceive, you can achieve. But you only get out of *anything* what you're willing to put into it. And if you're going to lazy around, then you're going to lazy, that's what you're going to earn, is lazying around. But if you're going to work, you're going to earn something. (4:21)

[From 1. above] You, you are the one to blame. It's you. Because... you can achieve anything your mind can conceive. If you can thin—, if you have an idea. [del] And if you think about it hard enough. And you want it bad enough. Then you can achieve it. There's nothing on this, in this country or on earth that if you were willing enough to work at it, that you cannot achieve it. (6:17)

13. [Collins is talking about his plans to go to college for training in a new field] I see on TV where people sixty-five, sixty-eight years old, graduating from college, so that kind of inspires me to say, Yea, I can do it. If they can do it, I can do it... You know, it's just a matter of applying yourself. And *wanting* to succeed. (6:3)

[From 3. above] I believe if you put an effort into *anything*, you can get ahead. Just [like] myself, where I have to put the effort into learning, again. You know. If I want to succeed, I'll succeed. (6:27–8).

The largely unchanged way Collins and Lovett repeated their views is further evidence for a bounded form of storage.

An illuminating description of bounded storage was once given by Robert Abelson. He proposed the following:

Let us postulate the existence of self-contained cognitive units called opinion *molecules*... [which] give you something to say and think when the topic comes up... These sorts of opinions are often quite impervious to other levels of argumentation because of their complete, closed, molecular character. It is as if the opinion-holder were saying, "what else could there possibly be to add?" (1968a:27)

The bounded, packaged quality of this kind of knowledge was earlier described by Mikhail Bakhtin as a feature of "authoritative discourse": "It remains sharply demarcated, compact and inert . . . It enters our verbal consciousness as a compact and indivisible mass; one must either totally affirm it, or totally reject it" (1981:343).

Abelson's "opinion molecules" and Bakhtin's "authoritative discourse" are examples of knowledge that is held in an isolated, encapsulated, bounded way. Both theorists also describe knowledge that is less bounded.[11] Similarly, Rumelhart, quoted above from a 1980 publication as asserting the building blocks of cognition to be "packets of knowledge," is one of the propounders of a new theory of cognition, connectionism, which proposes the building blocks of cognition to be not large packets of knowledge but smaller units modeled after neurons (Rumelhart, McClelland, and the PDP Research Group 1986). Units can be joined in many different configurations, from bounded packages to unbounded networks. I argue below that beliefs represented in the latter way – especially when they include links to key childhood memories and self-understandings – do embed strongly motivating goals.

Before turning to unbounded beliefs, however, we should consider some beliefs that contrast with my interviewees' success values in a different way. As discussed above, their talk about getting ahead indicated a meta-awareness that these values are dominant social values. This contrasts with much of their discourse about their duties as the breadwinner in the family. The latter talk suggests that breadwinner values typically come to consciousness not as values, but as an inescapable reality.

Working men's breadwinner assumptions

These ideas were expressed in statements like the following:

14. [Collins is discussing the workers' fight against Ciba-Geigy's proposal mandating Sunday work] But when that changed and it was negotiated through a contract that you would work, so you had to change or keep losing that eight hours pay. With three children, I couldn't afford it. So I had to go with the flow and work the Sundays. (1:7)

15. [D'Abrosca is talking about why he worked at Ciba-Geigy] Lot of people getting cancer there. So – over the years. And . . . it's a risk. We know it. And – but the money's good. This state doesn't have too many good-paying jobs. So. We're sort of trapped. So. I wouldn't want my kid going there. If he had a choice. (1:5)

16. [Lovett is explaining why more workers don't report hazards at the workplace] And if you're making good money, <u>you're not going to</u> make no waves. Even if your buddy next to you is dying with whatever that caused it, that you *know*. You're still <u>not going to</u> make waves. I mean, if a guy's making a living, you now, <u>he's just not going to do that</u>, unless he's ready to make a move. (1:15)

17. [Gauvin is sixty-two and would like to stop working, but Ciba-Geigy has made it difficult for him to retire] <u>they keep me there, they keep me there</u>, and I want to leave, and now they want me to stay. (6:5)

Unlike the individualistic success model expressed in 1.–4., passages 14.–17. assume that the interests of the family come ahead of the interests of any individual, including the father/husband/breadwinner. Bellah *et al.* (1985) found that some of their white-collar informants carried their individualism to the extreme of not being sure they had any responsibility for their families. The individualistic focus on my interviewees' success model was also clear. Thus, Lovett said, "you can achieve anything your mind can conceive" (1.); Gauvin urged, "you've got to really try to better yourself" (2.); and Collins stated, "if you put an effort into anything, you can get ahead" (3.). By contrast, see 14. in this section, and 7. and 10. in the last, where Collins, Lovett, and D'Abrosca state explicitly their responsibility for their families, especially their children. The same assumption is implicit in 15.–17. above. Gauvin, for example, went on to say that he has to have Blue Cross coverage because his wife is sick.

Furthermore, this is not, as in the success model, a matter of putting upward mobility ahead of all else. The men were not talking about the possibility of upward mobility so much as the pitfall of downward mobility. Each man was considering a situation in which he or someone like him held a job that paid well – and the question was whether or not to keep it. If the alternative is another manufacturing job, this could easily mean, at least for the Ciba-Geigy workers, a much lower income. In 1985 most of the Ciba-Geigy workers I interviewed had incomes between $20,000 and $25,000. In Rhode Island as a whole, the average manufacturing wage in 1985 was only $15,860.[12] So it is not a question of striving for wealth above all, but of avoiding near-poverty.

These working men's breadwinner values have in common with middle-class gender-role expectations the idea than an adult male's income should be his family's primary source of support. My interviewees' norms differ from white-collar versions of these gender-role expectations, however, in three ways. First, it is not necessary for the breadwinner to advance his family's fortunes; it is sufficient if he has a steady paycheck that covers the bills. Furthermore, unlike the middle-class man's version, which is closely linked to the success model, the focus in the working man's model is not on the individual, but on the family. In the working man's model, the interests of the family come ahead of the interests of any one individual in the family.[13] It follows that getting and keeping a job that pays well enough (in wages and benefits) to ensure that his family is secure is more important than the breadwinner's self-fulfillment or personal needs. Also part of this model is the knowledge – for Rhode Islanders with a high-school education or less – that there are not many jobs in the state for men of their skills that pay a decent wage.

Thus far I have discussed only the content of this model. In comparing the way my interviewees talked about success in 1.–4. with passages 14.–17. above, I was also struck by the use of constructions in the former passages that indicated a sense of choice between values, as compared with constructions in the latter passages that indicated a sense of constraints imposed by inescapable realities.

Thus, in answering my questions about getting ahead, Lovett said, "if you're willing to work at it . . ." and "Everyone should have a goal" (1.). Collins said, "If I want to succeed, I'll succeed (3.). Gallucci said, "Some people don't want to get ahead" (4.). Finally, Gauvin exhorted a generalized "you" to "improve your job" (2.).

By contrast, in talking about the sorts of situations they or others have faced as breadwinners, Collins said, "I had to go with the flow" (14.). D'Abrosca said, "We're sort of trapped." Lovett asserted flatly that unless a worker is ready to leave the job, "You're not going to make no waves" (16.). And Gauvin said that the company "keeps me there" (17.).

Of course, these men are not literally trapped, without any choice, in jobs that are tiring, dangerous, and interfere with family life. They could report hazards on the job. But to do so would probably mean a drastic loss of income. The metaphors of necessity these men use hide the implicit value premise that downward mobility is bad, highlighting instead the day-to-day realities of their work lives.

This does not mean that these men are unable to see that they have a choice. On another occasion Collins was talking about how his life had become very routine:

18.   No, boredom did set in, I believe, after twelve or fourteen years, I was kind of getting edgy and said, Wish I would go somewhere else or go look for something. But I never did, the one factor was that the money was too good to, you know, to say, "I'm going to go somewhere else for $3 [an hour] less. So, I guess you get married to the job after a while . . . And I guess, that's kind of why you like to stay in that field because the money, the money is there. You know, you get to say, Well, I like putting a few dollars in the bank account and doing what I like to do. But if you go down and do some different type of work, especially in this state, the money isn't there. (6:5)

The first part of this statement shows a sense of constraint, similar to that exhibited in 14.–17. above ("you get married to the job after a while"). Then, however, Collins pauses and indicates that he *could* have left the job; it is just that he liked the wage scale there, which gave him the money for "doing what I like to do."

Similarly, a few minutes after Gauvin said that the company "keeps me there" (17.), he spoke in a different vein about making choices rather than being held against his will:

19.   And they want to keep me there? I'll stay. Okay. Otherwise, if I go, I lose my severance pay and my Blue Cross. (6:6)

So it is not quite the case that my interviewees *cannot* see that they have a choice. What is at stake is how they *tend* to think. Their tendency, as shown by the way they usually talked, is not to see the value of avoiding downward mobility as a value. This is quite different from the way they talked about success, which they consistently treated as a value.

There is also a clear difference between success and breadwinner values in their directive force. Knowing that the success model represents widely shared values led several men to respond verbally – defensively in some cases, with pride in others – to the imagined judgment that they had not been very successful. It may be that awareness of their failure to live up to these values has affected their self-esteem. However, this model was less effective than the breadwinner model at motivating action: only one of the blue-collar interviewees who endorsed the model acted on it consistently in his work life. Every man who spoke of breadwinner role expectations as an inescapable reality, on the other hand, assumed primary responsibility for supporting his family, subordinating his own interests to the need to keep a steady paycheck coming. For these four men at least, the values they felt constrained by were usually seen not as values, but as simple reality.[14]

Only Gallucci – the one man for whom I did not find a quote comparable to 14.–17. above – seems to have seen and acted on the belief that downward mobility is a real choice. In one sense Gallucci did subordinate his interests by going to work in as dangerous an environment as a chemical plant. (Although the long-term health effects of these chemicals were not publicized until recently, the risks of fire, toxic leaks, and explosion were obvious all along.) On the other hand, even though Gallucci had a family to support, he moved to a position in the plant that paid less well but allowed him to escape the close contact with chemicals, rotating shifts, and strict supervision he had faced as a chemical operator. This is consistent with his initial decision to work at the chemical plant, where he made less money initially than he had in his previous job but had more time to court the woman he married.

Personal semantic networks

My understanding of "semantic networks" relies on the significant insight of symbolic anthropologists that symbols draw their force from their links with concepts from diverse realms of experience (Good 1977).[15] The webs of significance that can stretch from house layouts to kinship structures and cosmology are good examples of outlooks represented in an unbounded way rather than as bounded "packets of knowledge." (Unbounded networks can be composed of smaller, bounded sets of beliefs; although the constituents may be bounded, the whole is not.)

Personal semantic networks are the idiosyncratic webs of meaning carried by each person, linking individually salient verbal symbols[16] to memories of significant life experiences and conscious self-understandings (Quinn, this volume). Everyone I interviewed had a different cognitive network of this sort. Each man's personal semantic network has directed him toward an idiosyncratic pattern of self-defining goals and styles of behavior.

How are cognitive links expressed in discourse? The following aspects of discourse may be indicative of strong associations in cognition:

> *Contiguity.* In the absence of any interruptions that change the topic of the conversation, if idea B follows idea A in a person's discourse, then B and A are linked for them.
>
> *Significant terms.* If a person talks about A and B using the same significant terms, then A and B are linked for them.
>
> *Shared "voice."* If a person talks about A and B using the same "voice" (Bakhtin 1981), i.e., with the same outlook and mode of expression, then A and B are linked for them. (In this paper lexical rather than paralinguistic features are used as the primary indicator of "voice.")[17]

These clues can help us construct part of Tony D'Abrosca's personal semantic network.

Tony D'Abrosca was fifty-nine when I interviewed him, married, with children and grandchildren. He had been working at Ciba-Geigy for twenty-five years, first as a chemical operator, then as a maintenance mechanic. His discourse revealed a personal semantic network that links up the following ideas: memories of growing up poor, concerns about social injustice in America, the conviction that his views about social injustice are very different from most people's, the idea that his values and beliefs are different from his siblings' and parents', the sense that his childhood asthma helped make him different, and the realization that his childhood asthma makes him now want to compete in marathons.

D'Abrosca, the oldest in a family of eleven children, grew up poor. His parents, immigrants from Italy, both worked in Rhode Island's textile mills, where D'Abrosca, too, worked for many years before taking a job at Ciba-Geigy. Although D'Abrosca has worked hard and had the highest income of the working men I talked to, he still identifies with the "poor."

20. [CS asks for TD's overall attitudes about business.]
    TD: Well, businessmen I think would sell us for a buck. [del] And ... well all my sisters and brothers are all in business. Most of them are and I shouldn't feel that way, but ... [del] That's my attitude on businessmen. Businessmen are, to me, are a shady bunch. That, that's my feeling, so. And ... I can't see soaking a poor guy. Because I was poor. I was one of eleven kids. The oldest. And we were all poor. (1:4)

21. CS: What do you think of the free enterprise system?
    TD: Well here I go. Free enterprise. I think ... too many guys have too much greed in them. And ... they want all they can get for – at the expense of others. You know? The *businessman* is out for one thing – money. (3:13–14)

D'Abrosca connects his criticism of businesspeople to a more general critique of American society. He is not hesitant to voice these opinions – whether in discussions at work or in his frequent, caustic letters to the editor of the Providence paper. The following letter, written after Ronald Reagan's re-election, is representative in both content and tone:

22. The results of the recent elections indicate to me that either there are 52 million rich Americans or else we have become a nation of insensitive, uncaring dolts with no social or moral conscience.
    Since this majority is so concerned with only number one and so infatuated with greed, superficiality, and tinsel, I wouldn't be surprised to see the following changes made soon:
    1. Move the US Capital to America's mecca, Disneyworld.
    2. Redesign the American flag to a fascimile of the dollar bill and pledge allegiance to same.
    3. Change the National Anthem to that inspiring tune, "Hooray for Hollywood" complete with chorus line and soft-shoe dance.

The use of the word "greed" and the references to money in this letter connect these ideas to D'Abrosca's criticism of businesspeople like his siblings (20., 21.). It is evident from 22. that D'Abrosca sees himself as different not only from his siblings, but also from most Americans. This theme, the consciousness of being different, was repeated often in the context of talking about his politics:

23. [CS asked who would agree with the statement, "People on top in society

don't really care about the little guy." TD agreed, then CS asked who else would agree with that.]

TD: I don't know, I'm unique I think, in a lot of these thoughts. I mean . . . Who would agree with me? [del] The working man is so busy working that he doesn't think about these things. Seems to me. (laughs) I don't know what it is. They've got no opinions – there's a vacuum in their head. The working guys . . . Like I told you, they voted Reagan in. That's – they don't think it out. (6:31–2)

24. [CS mentioned that TD has taken "different stands on certain issues."]
TD: Yea, I'm different.
CS: Yea.
TD: I'm one of a kind maybe. I don't know. (6:6)

As 23. indicates, D'Abrosca has particular scorn for his fellow working men: "there's a vacuum in their head." This theme, how uninformed his work-mates and other working men are, was also repeated often:

25. I'm not a Communist. I'm just a socialist. I'm not Communist. I like – I want the people to have a fair deal, so – fair break. I'm against what these people are doing here for the rich, you know. The rich get richer and the poor get poorer. Like the old saying goes, and it's true. And . . . I'm called Communist. At work. By a few guys. That's their scape word, you know. Copout. Try to talk to these guys and forget it. I may as well [just] talk Red Sox to them. (2:33)

D'Abrosca sees himself as being different from others (e.g., more bookish) since his childhood. He explains this as being the result, in part, of his severe childhood asthma:

26. [CS asked if TD "went with the crowd" more as a child.]
TD: I never did. I had my own way of thinking. If they want to jump off a bridge somewhere, I wouldn't do it. Unless I'd want to do it. When I was a kid I had asthma. Real bad. And when I was about nine I couldn't even walk. (6:10)

27. [CS asked if it was tough being a young boy and not being athletic.]
TD: I could never play. You know, with the other kids. So I took to books. (6:12)

D'Abrosca also connects his childhood asthma to his desire to compete in marathons now:

28. TD: It's different. Test yourself. I had asthma as a boy. I still have it and I wanted to see what I could do. Wanted to prove to myself I could do something because as a young boy I'd dream about Boston [Marathon]. Impossible dream then, you know? 'Cause of the asthma. Now I've done it three times. (2:12)

Finally, D'Abrosca links up his interest in running marathons to his critique of his family's concerns with money, closing the circle to the ideas with which we began:

29. CS: Do you think you pretty much lived up to your parent's expectations for you? What they would've hoped for you?
TD: I don't know. The boy – the other kids did. Went in business. They're all proud of them and bragging about them. Which is normal I guess. I'm not sure if they ever bragged about me or not. They never did in front of me. One time I was so proud, I ran in that 50-mile race, I won the New England championship. I called up, I was all excited you know? "Are you crazy? You're an old man. You should be in a rocking chair." That shot me down. But ... that's my mother. My father was dead. He died back in '68 I think. And ... that was the end of that. That was one thing I was really proud about, but ... no one else was I guess. Well my wife and kids were. It's a sense of values I guess. I guess if I told them I made a million dollars they'd be out of their minds but, it was only a race, so it didn't count. It counted to me. I was happy with it. So. I was happy when my kid ran his first marathon. You know. Small things make me happy. Not <u>money</u>. (5:5)

Fig. 9.1 summarizes the connections I have discussed above. Some of these connections were indicated by contiguity of topics within a passage (e.g., marathon running and making money in 29. or attitudes toward businessmen and attitudes toward his siblings in 20.). Cognitive links were also indicated by shared significant verbal symbols in different passages (e.g., "money" in 21. and 29. or "greed" in 21. and 22.). Finally, there is a shared "voice" – the same embattled, sarcastic tone – expressed in many of these passages (e.g., 22., 23., and 25.). These aspects of discourse, especially when they occur in combination, strongly suggest cognitive links.

Note how different this whole network of ideas is from the bounded success model each interviewee was able to express compactly in response to my standardized interview questions about getting ahead. There was no time in the interviews when D'Abrosca compactly described this whole set of ideas, indeed, he may never at any one time be aware of the whole set. The extensiveness of the ideas encompassed (and I could have described further linkages with, for example, his ideas about war or about family roles) probably makes it impossible to capture the whole within awareness. What we have here is not a bounded opinion, but an unbounded network (containing within it, to be sure, many bounded opinions).

Two elements of this unbounded network have acted as strong motives for D'Abrosca. He has published his political views in frequent letters to the editor – so many, that for the last two years he has been invited to attend the *Providence Journal*'s annual dinner for frequent contributors of letters to the editor. He has continued writing letters like the one quoted in

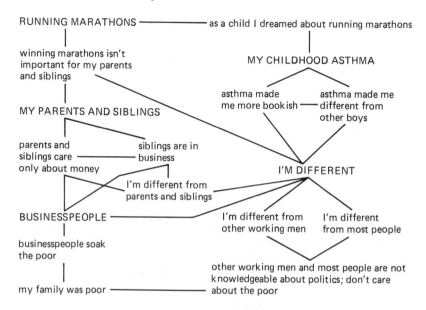

Fig. 9.1 Partial personal semantic network for Tony D'Abrosca.

22. despite threatening phone calls, vandalism to his home, and hostile reactions from his workmates.

D'Abrosca has also continued with his marathon running. His extraordinary accomplishments as a runner show just how powerful that goal has been for him. When D'Abrosca was a child he was so severely asthmatic that he could not walk more than a few yards without collapsing. His asthma improved as he grew older, but because he worked two jobs on rotating shifts most of his adult life, he did not have much time left for physical fitness programs. He did not begin running until he was fifty and his work was mostly on the day shift. Within two years he was running marathons, then ultramarathons, that is, races 50 miles or longer. Recently he won the New England Championship for his age group in a 50-mile race. In 1986 he was one of only six Americans to compete in a 40-mile race through the Swiss Alps.

Idiosyncratic networks are not important just for people who, like D'Abrosca, consider themselves to be unique. Everyone I interviewed had a personal semantic network that contained strong goals.

George Gauvin, like Tony D'Abrosca, had physical problems as a child. Unlike D'Abrosca, however, the memory of his disability is linked for Gauvin to pride in the skills that have enabled him to earn a steady living despite his problems, and to the belief that people should just do their best and not complain. He was quite contemptuous of the "radicals" at Ciba-Geigy who badmouthed the company. I mentioned above that Gauvin is the only working man I interviewed for whom (at least when he was young) making more money was a consistent, strong goal. In his case, the bounded, shared American success model seems to have been reinforced by the unbounded personal network of ideas just described.

Jim Lovett has a personal semantic network that links the key terms "responsibility" and "caring" to family concerns and unhappy memories of the absence of his father's companionship as a child. This family-centered model is in turn linked to Lovett's politics: many of his views about business and society can be paraphrased by saying that people should always treat each other as they would inside a family. The motivational force of these ideas can be seen in the energy he has devoted to his family and to caring for others. When Lovett was working he learned first aid and assumed responsibility for treating fellow workers' injuries. Now, although Lovett is out of work with an occupational disability, he has very little free time left in days devoted to providing assistance to his parents, inlaws, and children.

Anthony Gallucci's networks are very different. His views cannot be summed up easily, but one theme he expressed quite explicitly:

30.   [Thinking about who influenced him when he was growing up.] I really hated any kind of authority. (5:4).

This general dislike of authorities continued into adulthood, and is linked to specific views about his bosses at work and governmental authority in society. The directive force of these views can be seen in pranks that undermined authorities in the workplace. These ideas also influenced his decision to switch to a position at Ciba-Geigy where he earned less money than he had made as a chemical operator but was freer of supervision.

Daniel Collins, by contrast, believes in the need for strong leadership. His network links this idea to his concerns about working people's welfare, opposition to "selfishness" and "complacency," and remembrance of his mother's admonition to "speak your piece." These ideas have had strong motivational force for him. Until Ciba-Geigy announced its closing, Collins devoted much of his free time to the union local at the plant. He has also put aside concerns about his safety and welfare to "speak his piece" whenever he thought it necessary, whether to fellow workers, bosses, state bureaucrats, military commanders, or neighborhood toughs.

In sum, each man's personal semantic networks contain strongly motivating goals. The directive force of these goals is not just *stronger* than the force of the goals attached to other sorts of beliefs, however.

Each of the three types of belief I have described has had a different *sort* of directive force for my interviewees. The bounded success schema, which they were aware of as a widely shared value, may have had potent effects as an internalized social judgment affecting each man's self-esteem. Success values were much less potent, however, in determining career choices for most of them. Their breadwinner assumptions were likewise internalized social judgments, failure to satisfy which would also have affected their self-esteem. However, because these values were generally seen not as a matter of choice but rather as an inescapable fact of life, they were much more effective than the success schema in shaping the men's routine behavior. Finally, the goals contained in personal semantic networks, which are linked to emotionally salient individual experiences, have pushed each man to out-of-the-ordinary, self-defining efforts.

Conclusions

The main argument of this paper is that cultural models differ in not only the extent but also the kind of directive force they provide. American success values, though endorsed by four of the working men I talked to, motivated the actions of only one of the men who stated them. This is not to say that this ideology had no effect on the rest. The one man who thoroughly rejected success values may have been influenced in a less conscious way by them.[18] The others might be moved by political rhetoric that appeals to this model. Finally, the fact that success values can be seen *as* shared values meant that my interviewees all judged themselves by that standard. These recognized social values, however, did not determine their practice.

Working men's breadwinner values were apprehended differently by most of my interviewees. In talking about choices faced by breadwinners, they tended to speak not of what people *should* do, but of what they have no choice but to do. This is the form of belief that Clifford Geertz has called "the native's point of view":

People use experience-near concepts spontaneously, unselfconsciously . . . they do not, except fleetingly and on occasion, recognize that there are any "concepts" involved at all. That is what experience-near means – that ideas and the realities they inform are naturally and indissolubly bound up together. What else could you call a hippopotamus? Of course the gods are powerful, why else would we fear them? (1984:125)

Shweder (this volume) has developed this argument, pointing out that when experience is seen in this way, directive force naturally follows out of commonsensical adherence to the reality principle. Indeed, for the four men who saw the constraints of the breadwinner model as the constraints of reality, these ideas were a powerful predictor of their actions.

Geertz and Shweder overlook, however, the fact that "the native's point of view" is not at all uniform.[19] Some cultural constructs are indeed used in the "unselfconscious" way Geertz talks about. Others, however, such as the shared success model, are apprehended with a greater meta-awareness of the status of the constructs as cultural values.[20]

Parts of the personal semantic networks I traced were, like the success model and unlike the breadwinner model, seen as values. The unbounded cognitive storage of these networks, however, means that they are difficult to apprehend in their entirety. These networks embed self-defining goals consciously chosen and acted on by my interviewees (cf. Quinn, this volume) as well as less conscious personal styles of action.

Each of these three kinds of beliefs was expressed differently in discourse. The bounded, cognitively accessible success model was expressed fairly explicitly, as compact generalizations. This made my interviewees' statements of the ideology very similar to analysts' statements of the ideology. When repeated by two men, major elements of this model were preserved largely intact. The breadwinner model, on the other hand, was present more often in an implicit form. Its premises were just assumed in what Bourdieu has called a "discourse of familiarity, [which] leaves unsaid all that goes without saying" (1977:18). It is true that most of the statements of the success model quoted above were elicited by questions that asked for compact generalizations, while no questions of the sort that would have elicited a compact, explicit statement of the breadwinner model were asked. Yet, two informants also volunteered explicit statements of the success model (12. and 13.) before being asked the questions about getting ahead. Furthermore, as a member of this culture, I would have felt foolish asking something like, "What are the obligations of an adult man?" The mere fact that it would not have occurred to me to ask such a question, whereas it seemed reasonable to my interviewees and me to ask, "What things keep people from getting ahead in the world?" is itself some indication that success values and breadwinner role expectations are different types of culturally shaped beliefs.

Some elements in personal semantic networks were expressed in a similarly explicit, compact form in my interviewees' discourse. Explicit self-descriptions (e.g., "I'm unique I think, in a lot of these thoughts" [23.] or "I really hated any kind of authority" [30.]) are examples of this. The cognitive connections between these elements, however, can be seen only by tracing the order of topics in a speaker's discourse and the links between ideas expressed with the same significant terms or in the same "voice."

Some further points can be made about these three forms of belief. First, they were probably acquired by my interviewees in different ways. While they may have observed many people who tried to get ahead and even some who succeeded at it, their explicit verbal formulation of shared success values suggests acquisition from an explicit verbal source. Such sources are readily available in U.S. society in the mass media, advice books, fictional accounts, and popular discussion. Lovett mentioned another source: the slogans he learned at Amway sales meetings (12.). As evidence for the supposition that the success model is learned largely from verbal formulations, notice that when D'Andrade summarized his informants' ideas about success, he used several key terms ("drive," "works hard," and "goals") that also turned up in one or more of my interviewees' statements. The importance of these terms as explicit verbal symbols can also be seen in the way my interviewees emphasized them through repetition within a statement, verbal stress, or use as a one-word sentence (e.g., "Goals. Everyone should have a goal" [1.]).

These working men's breadwinner assumptions, on the other hand, were likely to have been acquired more through observation than explicit statements. Some aspects of this model are common enough in popular discussion (e.g., that men should be the main income earners in a family), but others (e.g., the need to sacrifice one's interests to keep a steady paycheck coming) were probably learned simply by observing other working men staying at boring or dangerous jobs.[21]

Personal semantic networks contain elements learned both in the explicit verbal manner of success values and the implicit, observational manner of breadwinner assumptions. Particularly important here, however, are the ideas and experiences that each man came to take as self-defining ones – often because they contrasted with the values of others with whom he interacted.

Each of these models represents different forms of knowledge and awareness – different *ways of believing*. These ways of believing are not reducible to differences in content, but involve different forms of cognitive representation and conscious apprehension. Thus, for most of my interviewees, success values are stored as the packets of knowledge postulated in traditional schema theory, while their wide-ranging personal semantic networks are stored in a less packaged way. The success model comes to their consciousness as a set of values, while the breadwinner model (though it contains values as well) often comes to their consciousness in a different way, as knowledge of reality.

It was also interesting that these three models are shared by increasingly narrow segments of American society – from the widely shared success model, to the more class- and gender-specific working man's breadwinner model, to personal semantic networks, which contain many culturally given elements, but include unique life events and, in any case, represent idiosyncratic combinations of shared elements. This is not surprising. The success model is acquired from ideological sources that are widely available in our society; the working man's breadwinner model is learned from observation of other working men; and personal semantic networks are shaped by the particular combination of experiences and ideas to which each individual is exposed, which are never exactly the same for any two people.

A few warnings are in order about the extent to which my findings could be generalized beyond my interviewees and the particular sets of ideas I described.

First, the separate effects of these different kinds of beliefs were probably easier to see with my blue-collar informants than they would have been with white-collar informants. In a white-collar working environment behaviors probably conform to the success model more than they do on the factory floor. Thus, observation learning would reinforce explicit ideological learning, making their separate effects harder to distinguish. In general, it is doubtless the case that differences between distinct kinds of cultural models will be easier to observe in the discourse and behaviors of non-dominant than of dominant social groups. (Furthermore, this paper has downplayed interactions, which did exist, between these different levels of belief. One example of this is the way the success model was reinforced for George Gauvin by the particular configuration of experiences and linked explanatory concepts in his personal semantic network.)

It is also possible that the distinct effects of these different models were enhanced by two peculiarities of industrialized western cultures. In the liberal western tradition there is a distinction between values, adherence to which is a matter of choice, and "hard" reality. Other cultures would not make the same distinction. Perhaps peculiar to western cultures is our metaphysical and moral construct of the self. I claimed that elements of personal semantic networks are strongly motivating. I do not know if this is because they are stored in an extensive, unbounded cognitive network (which would be the case in any culture) or because these ideas are attached to a distinct, valued self construct more limited to the West. (Probably both explanations are partly correct.)

Finally, although the focus of my argument has been on ways of believing, it has a bearing on what we assume culture to be. If we conceive of culture monistically – everything is symbols or discourses, which differ only in meaning and position in the ordering of experience – then it is difficult to talk about different *kinds* of cultural values and motivational force. As D'Andrade has noted (n.d.), we will not make progress in anthropological theory without a more differentiated model of culture.

ACKNOWLEDGMENTS

An earlier version of this paper was presented at the 85th Annual Meeting of the American Anthropological Association, Philadelphia, PA, December 1986, in an invited session, "The Directive Force of Cultural Models." I am grateful to Roy D'Andrade and Naomi Quinn for organizing this session. The two discussants in this session, Robert Weller and Edwin Hutchins, had comments that were helpful in rewriting my material. This paper has also benefited from comments by Ellen Basu, Bradley Levinson, Naomi Quinn, Robert Strauss, and Kathryn Woolard. My biggest debt is to the five men quoted here.

NOTES

1 D'Andrade does not take credit for the insight that schema theory can subsume motivation theory, citing Schank and Abelson (1977), Mandler (1984), and Gallistel (1985), among others, as sources for this idea.
2 Tony D'Abrosca asked that I use his real name. All other interviewee names here are pseudonyms.
3 Most of these questions came from Kornhauser (1965).
4 Every interviewee but one chose a pseudonym consistent with his ethnicity.
5 My other transcript conventions are the following:
[?] = unintelligible
[word?] = uncertain transcription
... = long pause
[del] = deletion
[ ] = paraphrase
" " = my reading of a standardized interview question
(X:Y) = utterance citation from my transcripts, where X is the interview number and Y the page number
(X.) = utterance citation from previous use in this paper
Punctuation reflects the speaker's intonation rather than rules of grammar, and transcripts were regularized for stammers, stutters, and verbal pauses.
6 Elsewhere, D'Abrosca stated that he and his siblings had all "turned out fairly good. Moneywise or otherwise." He added, "I hope my kids do well" (5:3,4). Conversely, the other four men, who endorsed the success model in response to my standardized questions, expressed doubts about the moral worth of riches and discussed inequality of opportunity in other discourse contexts. So their beliefs are more complicated than it would appear here (Strauss 1988, 1990).
7 I did not usually transcribe verbal pauses. This one seemed especially significant, however.
8 There were several examples of this speech in another's "voice" in Gallucci's discourse.

9 This is not to say that success values are rarely linked to action for working men in general. Beyond the obvious difficulty of generalizing from a sample of five people, there is the less obvious factor that some of these men fell into the working-class part of my interview group precisely because they had *not* been motivated by the success model. Two of the white-collar workers I interviewed started out life in circumstances much like these five, but then sought education and promotions that put them into management positions.

10 Gauvin's belief structure is the only exception here. His references to starting as a helper, then becoming a journeyman (2.) show that the general statements quoted are intimately linked to a broader set of ideas he has about his own career.

11 See Bakhtin on "internally persuasive discourse" (1981:345–6) and Abelson's cognitive consistency theories (1968b).

12 Based on $305 average weekly earnings in Rhode Island manufacturing industries (1987 Journal-Bulletin Rhode Island Almanac.)

13 This model is based primarily on my research. However, it fits with other accounts of American working-class culture, e.g., Halle (1984), Komarovsky (1987), and Miller and Riessman (1961).

14 However, in some contexts (see 7. and 10.) some of the men talked as if they were being judged by the breadwinner model. This was especially true when, as in the above two cases, the breadwinner model overlaps with the success model.

15 Good's "semantic network analysis" (Good 1977) captures at the cultural level what my "personal semantic networks" try to capture at the individual level.

16 In finding these symbols I used the methods outlined by Agar (1979).

17 For a more detailed discussion of all three criteria, see Strauss (1988).

18 In D'Abrosca's case the example provided by his hard-working immigrant parents may have been more significant than the success model as an explicit ideology.

19 Geertz's own view is not uniform either. Earlier works of his suggest a much more sophisticated understanding of different forms of belief.

20 These different forms of awareness are usually referred to as the difference between "overt" and "covert" or "explicit" and "implicit" culture (LeVine 1984). (See also Bourdieu's [1977] doxa/dogma distinction.) These terms do not capture all the degrees of opacity and transparency that exist, however (see Strauss 1988.)

21 The process here is much as Bourdieu (1977) describes for the formation of the habitus.

REFERENCES

Abelson, Robert P.
1968a Computers, Polls, and Public Opinion – Some Puzzles and Paradoxes. *Trans-action* 5(9):20–7.
1968b Psychological Implication. In *Theories of Cognitive Consistency: A Sourcebook*, R. P. Abelson *et al.*, eds. Skokie, IL: Rand-McNally.

Agar, Michael
1979 Themes Revisited: Some Problems in Cognitive Anthropology. *Discourse Processes* 2:11–31.
Bakhtin, Mikhail M.
1981 Discourse in the Novel. In *The Dialogic Imagination: Four Essays by M. M. Bakhtin*, Michael Holquist, ed., Caryl Emerson and Michael Holquist, trans. Austin: University of Texas Press. Pp. 259–422.
Bellah, Robert N., Richard Madsen, William M. Sullivan, Ann Swidler, and Steven M. Tipton
1985 *Habits of the Heart: Individualism and Commitment in American Life.* Berkeley and Los Angeles: University of California Press.
Bourdieu, Pierre
1977 *Outline of a Theory of Practice*, Richard Nice, trans. Cambridge: Cambridge University Press.
Casson, Ronald W.
1983 Schemata in Cognitive Anthropology. *Annual Reviews in Anthropology* 12:429–62.
D'Andrade, Roy G.
1984 Cultural Meaning Systems. In *Culture Theory: Essays on Mind, Self, and Emotion*, Richard A. Shweder and Robert A. LeVine, eds. Cambridge: Cambridge University Press. Pp. 88–119.
1990 Some Propositions about the Relations between Culture and Human Cognition. In *Cultural Psychology: Essays on Comparative Human Development*, James W. Stigler, Richard A. Shweder, and Gilbert Herdt, eds. Cambridge: Cambridge University Press. Pp. 65–129.
n.d. Anthropological Theory: Where Did It Go? (How Can We Get It Back?). Unpublished manuscript.
Gallistel, Charles R.
1985 Motivation, Intention, and Emotion: Goal Directed Behavior from a Cognitive-Neuroethological Perspective. In *Goal Directed Behavior: The Concept of Action in Psychology*, M. Frese and J. Sabini, eds. Hillsdale, NJ: Lawrence Erlbaum.
Geertz, Clifford
1984 "From the Native's Point of View": On the Nature of Anthropological Understanding. In *Culture Theory: Essays on Mind, Self, and Emotion*, Richard A. Shweder and Robert A. LeVine, eds. Cambridge: Cambridge University Press. Pp. 123–36.
Gerber, Eleanor R.
1985 Rage and Obligation: Samoan Emotion in Conflict. In *Person, Self, and Experience: Exploring Pacific Ethnopsychologies*, Geoffrey M. White and John Kirkpatrick, eds. Berkeley: University of California Press. Pp. 121–67.
Good, Byron J.
1977 The Heart of What's the Matter. *Culture, Medicine and Psychiatry* 1:25–58.
Halle, David
1984 *America's Working Man: Work, Home, and Politics among Blue-Collar Property Owners*. Chicago: University of Chicago Press.

Holland, Dorothy and Naomi Quinn, eds.
1987 *Cultural Models in Language and Thought*. Cambridge: Cambridge University Press.
Komarovsky, Mirra
1987 *Blue-Collar Marriage*, 2nd ed. New Haven: Yale University Press.
Kornhauser, Arthur
1965 *Mental Health of the Industrial Worker: A Detroit Study*. New York: John Wiley.
LeVine, Robert A.
1984 Properties of Culture: An Ethnographic View. In *Culture Theory: Essays on Mind, Self, and Emotion*, Richard A. Shweder and Robert A. LeVine, eds. Cambridge: Cambridge University Press. Pp. 67–87.
Mandler, George
1984 *Mind and Body: Psychology of Emotion and Stress*. New York: W.W. Norton.
Miller, S.M. and Frank Riessman
1961 The Working Class Subculture: A New View. *Social Problems* 9:86–97.
Providence Journal-Bulletin, comp.
1987 *Rhode Island Almanac*, 101st edn. Providence Journal-Bulletin.
Quinn, Naomi and Dorothy Holland
1987 Culture and Cognition. In *Cultural Models in Language and Thought*, Dorothy Holland and Naomi Quinn, eds. Cambridge: Cambridge University Press. Pp. 3–40.
Rumelhart, David E.
1980 Schemata: The Building Blocks of Cognition. In *Theoretical Issues in Reading Comprehension: Perspectives from Cognitive Psychology, Linguistics, Artificial Intelligence, and Education*, Rand J. Spiro, Bertram C. Bruce, and William F. Brewer, eds. Hillsdale, NJ: Lawrence Erlbaum. Pp. 33–58.
Rumelhart, David E., James L. McClelland, and the PDP Research Group
1986 *Parallel Distributed Processing: Explorations in the Microstructure of Cognition*, Vol. II: *Psychological and Biological Models*. Cambridge, MA: MIT Press.
Schank, Roger C. and Robert P. Abelson
1977 *Scripts, Plans, Goals, and Understanding: An Enquiry into Human Knowledge Structures*. Hillsdale, NJ: Lawrence Erlbaum.
Strauss, Claudia
1988 Culture, Discourse, and Cognition: Forms of Belief in Some Rhode Island Working Men's Talk about Success. Ph.D. dissertation, Harvard University.
1990 Who Gets Ahead? Cognitive Responses to Heteroglossia in American Political Culture. *American Ethnologist* 17(2):312–28.

10   Afterword

Roy G. D'Andrade

The preceding chapters have tried to explore the usefulness of the idea that cultural models can have motivational force. What now can be concluded about this idea? What issues have arisen from this work?

Practicalities of psychological assessment

At this point, several things stand out which were previously unseen or obscure. First, at the beginning, it was not known whether it would be difficult or easy to assess the motivational force of particular cultural models. It is one thing to argue that, on various theoretical grounds, some schemas, and therefore some cultural models, should have motivational properties, and that these properties should be assessable. It is another thing to identify, in a real ethnographic study, the motivational properties of a specific cultural model.

Overall, assessment of the motivational force of cultural models appears to be a feasible task. The authors had no special difficulty in determining the degree to which the models they were investigating functioned as active goals for specific individuals. These models ranged across a variety of domains; romance, marriage, gender, the self, emotion, childhood "stages," witches, gods, and water glasses. Based on the results of all the chapters, it seems fair to conclude that the assessment of the motivational force of a cultural model is well within the capacity of a competent ethnographer.

Why should this be? The usual account is that motives are hard to identify and even harder to measure. In the traditional approach one has to determine to what degree a person strives for – or would strive for if they could – a particular state of affairs, such as *self-actualization*, which has been defined by some theorist, and which may correspond to no schema, idiosyncratic or cultural, of the person being assessed. This task is further complexified by the frequent failure to distinguish between the ultimate energy sources which may activate many goals and the specific goals toward which the person strives. The difference between standard motivational analysis and the approach used here is that in the assessment of the motivational force of cultural models one begins with an understanding of some schema which is something defined by the person. Once one understands how some state of affairs is defined and conceptualized by the person, determining the degree to which that state of affairs serves a true goal for that person is a relatively direct operation involving the skills that most humans have developed to high degree by the time they are adults. If one knows how someone understands romantic love, determining if that schema is also a strong goal for that person involves finding out what activities the person engages in, what choices between alternative is typically made, etc. Such an assessment may not always be obvious, but it is generally feasible given the kind of intensive personal relationship that most anthropologists develop with their informants.

Multiple forces

The papers in this volume also make it plain that motivational force is just one of the kinds of psychological force that a model can have. Models may also have orientational force, redefining what certain kinds of events mean (e.g., the Harkness *et al.* stage model), evaluative force, functioning as standards by which the "goodness" or "badness" of things are assessed (e.g., the self model of Quinn's informants), or affective force, functioning as conditions which elicit strong emotional reactions (e.g., Holland's informants' romance model).

Furthermore, based on the material presented in the chapters in this volume, it appears that cultural models typically do not have just *one* psychological function, but rather tend to include a number of kinds of psychological force. The breadwinner model, for example, is not just a goal for Strauss's informants, it is also a measure by which they evaluate how well they have done in their life and can also be a source of strong feelings of satisfaction or dissatisfaction. It has been argued throughout this volume that one cannot know just from the description of a cultural model whether or not it has motivational force. This point can be generalized; from a purely cultural description one cannot tell whether or not a cultural model will have psychological force, or if it does have psychological force, which kinds of force will be most salient.

One might speculate that *as models become more deeply internalized, they tend to include more functions.* The so-called "master motive models" will probably turn out in almost all cases to be multifunctional. One might expect this on theoretical grounds; if something becomes a powerful motive, this something is likely to be included into the individual's self-schema, and hence be a strong source of self and other evaluation, and also a source of satisfactions and frustrations which will give rise to strong feelings. As Spiro's description of the different levels of internalization assumes, perhaps it will turn out that there is a sort of scale relating kinds of psychological force to levels of internalization; at the moderate levels of internalization models do little more than orient the individual, at deeper levels they act as standards of evaluation. At the deepest levels of internalization it would seem likely that cultural models have strong affective and motivational power.

Where motivational force comes from

Most of the chapters – especially the papers of Part II – present analyses of how the cultural models studies came to have motivational force. The most general conclusion appears to be that the force of a model comes from the conditions under which it is learned. If the model is (1) linked by socializing agents to pervasive and affectively laden rewards and punishments, and if (2) these agents link the accomplishment of goals inherent in the model to the self-schema of the individual, and if (3) striving for the model's goals has some chance of meeting with success, the model is likely to have strong motivational force.

A fourth condition, stressed in Shweder's paper, and also discussed by Quinn and Strauss, is that if the condition defined by the schema is firmly believed to be both natural and right, the motivational force of the schema is greatly enhanced. Shweder makes the point that once the vulnerability of children to physical harm schema becomes a tangible reality, as it is for many urban middle-class Americans, it has an enormous number of behavioral entailments ranging across things as different as the handling of drinking glasses to buttoning up when it is cold outside. The type example is witchcraft; if one believes in the existence of witches then various techniques of magical protection and cure become simple consequences of the belief, and one needs no further motivational source than the belief to account for the practices. The question then becomes "what accounts for the belief in witches?" This question has different answers – "because there *are* (in some sense) witches," "because humans frequently project their own malevolence onto others," "because humans are easily confused about cause and effect," etc. At this point one must "descend" into a deeper-level analysis, an analysis of the nature of human interpersonal existence, or an analysis of drives and mechanisms of defense, or an analysis of the capacities of human reason. All of these are problematic positions (although I believe that the primary cause lies with human hostility and mechanisms of defense, and secondarily with the lack of alternative social institutions for the binding of personal conflicts), and

Shweder rightly points out that it is an error to try to account for witchcraft practices without an emphatic understanding of the great motivational force of the reality created by the cultural model of witchcraft and an ethnocentric imposition to assume that if a cultural model differs from the investigator's own models that it is a fantasy to be explained by "descent" into deep levels of analysis.

On the other hand, if a cultural model is simply verbally presented as what one should believe, without the kinds of socialization and enculturation experiences described above, the model is likely to be only a cliché; something one says but something that is without motivational force for the individual. And finally, if socialization experiences of reward and punishment are present, but no cultural model is presented to "hold" or "incorporate" the goals being learned, the result is the kind of loosely connected personal model analyzed in Strauss' chapter.

These are analyses of "proximal" rather than "distal" causes of motivational force. However, this raises the next question – why were *these* conditions present, rather than some other conditions? What political, economic, and demographic factors created these particular conditions? This question depends on theories of social causation – theories connecting the chain of causation from specific social conditions that lead to internalization to more ultimate factors such as labor market conditions, migration, class position, etc.

These questions of social causation are outside the scope of this volume. There are a number of quite different theories of social causation – various conflict theories, a number of different Marxist theories, Parsonian functionalism, rational choice theory, etc., each of which would yield somewhat different answers concerning the chain of causation linking general social factors to the personal conditions necessary for internalization. The point to be stressed here is that *any* social theory needs to be able to link its variables to the kinds of conditions we have described here for the internalization of models if that theory is to be used to give an account of human striving.

Conceptual issues

The next issue to be discussed concerns the relation of the study of cultural models to the study of other things also called cultural, such as symbols or collective representations. Perhaps at this point it should be pointed out that the claim that cultural models have different degrees of psychological force directly contradicts the notion of symbolic hegemony, which presupposes that certain ideologies have power simply because they are encoded in some pervasive symbolic form. The claim here is that cultural symbols never have power just because they are symbols. Sometimes a set of cultural symbols – the outward manifestation of a cultural model – has an internal schema which has the power to define, to act as a standard of evaluation, and to influence feeling and action. Sometimes it does not. As we have argued, one must look to factors outside the symbols themselves to discover why a cultural model has psychological force.

There has long been a bifurcation in cultural anthropology: a division between those who prefer to center the study of culture on external representations or external symbols – things such as enacted rituals, recited myths, or written texts – versus those who prefer to center the study of culture on internal structures, i.e., cognitive schemas. This division has theoretical implications; one objection to the work collected in this volume is simply to say that this work does not really study culture because culture consists only of external representations and external symbols, such as myths and ritual, not things like understandings or internal schemas. This move effectively blocks any link between culture and motivation, or culture and psychology.

There are those who still wish to hold on to this dichotomy. Most of us, however – speaking at least for the authors in this volume, and I hope for the field at large – reject this dichotomy. As Quinn and Strauss say:

How could something be ideational, but not in someone's head? Based on what people say they think, but not about what they think? It is time for us to confront the contradiction in this definition of culture as meaningful, symbolic, signifying, conceptual, ideational, but not to anyone in particular, that has encumbered the analysis, and required circumlocutions in the analytic language of so many anthropologists. It is time to say that culture is *both* public and individual, both in the world and in people's heads. (Quinn and Strauss 1989)

Certainly a Beethoven quartet as played is something "cultural." And so are the skills needed to play the instruments. And so are the complex cognitive schemas by which the music is interpreted by listeners into affectively powerful forms and structures. These are culturally learned skills and culturally learned schemas, just as the actual performance is a cultural event.

It is notable how much less confusion surrounds the adjective "cultural" than the noun "culture." Perhaps the noun form leads to more intellectual confusions than the adjectival form because it is more reifying. To say something is "cultural" does not commit one to a belief in some unified structure or single thing in the way the noun "culture" does. Lots of things can be cultural, but culture can only be that *one thing* which *is* culture. The adjective "cultural" has less ontological baggage than the noun "culture."

Then what does it mean to say that something is *"cultural"*? As I understand how anthropologists generally use the term, to say something is cultural is – at a minimum – to say that it is shared by some significant number of the members of a social group; shared in the sense of being behaviorally enacted, physically possessed, or internally thought. Further, this something must be recognized in some special way and at least some others are expected to know about it; that is, it must be *intersubjectively* shared. Finally, for something to be cultural it must have the potential of being passed on to new group members, to exist with some permanency through time and across space.

The term "cultural model" as used here refers to shared, recognized, and transmitted internal representations, not to external forms such as symbolic objectives or events. Let us say that cultural models are part of the internal side of culture (to use that noun), and distinguish them from the external side of culture. We assume that these two sides of culture are *always* linked, otherwise we would have on one side external forms without meaning or sense and on the other side internal meanings without any forms to express or communicate them. Once this linkage is admitted, it does not matter which side is called "culture" – begin on either side, and investigation of the phenomena will lead one to the other. Obeyesekere, for example, in his analyses of cultural motivation, begins with the external symbol, such as actual "matted locks," and proceeds from there to identify the personal schemas which give meaning to the object (Obeyesekere 1981). In most of the chapters of this book cultural models are linked to various external forms. Mathews' chapter on the *La Llorona* folk-tale traces out in detail the way an external cultural representation is linked to internal schemas. The most ubiquitous of all external symbolic forms, of course, is *talk*. Most of the chapters in this volume are full of informant talk – the discourse that flows almost invisibly around people most of their waking hours. Talk, we believe, is the external matrix of all deeply internalized cultural schemas.

Further investigation

The overall theory presented in this volume links external cultural forms to internal representations, called schemas, and then links these schemas to other psychological functions of the human psyche such as motivation, evaluation, emotion, and orientation. The way the argument has been made has been to take a particular cultural model which the investigator already knows relatively well, and then to ask if the model has motivational force. In all cases the authors had worked out a relatively clear description of the cultural model before attempting any assessment of motivational force. And in all these cases it was relatively easy to make this assessment. One thing that remains untested is whether this procedure can be turned around; that is, can an investigator begin by looking for strong psychological forces in the lives of some group, and then trace these forces back to the cultural models which underlie them?

This problem arises if one wants to know what cultural models have the most important psychological forces in the lives of some set of people. One might think that an investigator could begin by investigating every cultural model, describing each model, then assessing its psychological force. But this is impractical because people have too many cultural models; a reasonable estimate is that an average person knows and uses thousands of cultural models learned over twenty years of enculturation. Of course, some of these models are very specific, such as the schema for the alphabet or the schema for basting turkey. Some are somewhat more general, such as the cultural schema for anger or the model of the mind. Some are very general, such as the cultural model for emotion discussed in Lutz's chapter, or for the different models of the self, discussed in Quinn's chapter.

One might expect that those models with greatest psychological force would also be the most general, since the more general models generally correspond to top-most levels of interpretation on which the individual depends to decide what to do (see chapter 1). If this is true, then one method of narrowing down the number of cultural models to be described is to limit the search to very general models. However, this is also difficult, since it is hard to know how general a model is until it is relatively well described.

A method which might be more practical comes from a consideration of the material in Quinn's chapter. In her chapter, Quinn explores the internal conflicts generated by the goals of the marriage model. Making use of the talk expressing the informants' experience of these conflicts, Quinn is able to identify and analyze the cultural models that generate the forces that conflict with or support marriage goals. Quinn finds, for example, that the cultural schema that defines self as a human being with certain inalienable rights generates forces that can conflict with the motives of the marriage model.

Quinn's method of exploring internal conflicts could be adopted as a search strategy for identifying those cultural models which have powerful psychological forces. The strategy goes as follows: begin work in a group with the analysis of one particular general cultural model. After determining the kinds and degrees of psychological force generated by this model, explore the kinds of inner conflict that occur as people try to accomplish the goals of this model. Then identify the cultural models that generate the forces that lead to these conflicts. Once these cultural models have been described, and their psychological force assessed, repeat the procedure by exploring the conflicts which occur as people try to accomplish the goals of these new models, and then identify the cultural models that generate the forces for these conflicts, etc.

A varient of this method would be to interview a sample of informants, using a modified life-history method, to try to determine the overall structure of their life goals, placing these goals within the models that contain them. Such an investigation would involve investigating both personal, idiosyncratic models and shared cultural models, along the lines developed in Strauss's chapter.

Finally

In summary, above and beyond the issues of what might be done next and what place the study of the motivational force of cultural models has in the general scheme of studying culture, three general conclusions have emerged from the chapters in this volume. First, it is an ethnographically feasible task to ascertain the motivational force of cultural models once the cultural model has been identified and described. Second, most cultural models which have motivational force appear also to have other kinds of psychological force, such as orientational force, evaluative force, and affective force. Third, specific kinds of linkages between socialization experiences and the cultural learning of the model are crucial for the development of the model's motivational force. Each of these conclusions is supported in detail in the preceding chapters. The gap between culture and action is not just theoretically bridgeable. In the cases described in these chapters, it has been shown that the connection can be made directly with empirical materials.

REFERENCES

Obeyesekere, Gananath
    1981 *Medusa's Hair: A Study in Personal and Cultural Symbols.* Chicago: University of Chicago Press.
Quinn, Naomi and Claudia Strauss
    1989 A Cognitive Cultural Anthropology. Paper delivered at the Annual Meeting of the American Anthropological Association, Washington, DC.

Index

Topics marked with an asterisk* are the focus of one or more whole chapters; see table of contents. Informants' pseudonyms are in quotes.

233

Rumelhart, David E., 199, 207; *see also* McClelland, Rumelhart, and the PDP Research Group; Rumelhart, McClelland, and the PDP Research Group
Rumelhart, David E., James L. McClelland, and the PDP Research Group, 12, 28, 207

sadness, cultural models of, 147, 151, 155–7, 191; *see also* emotion, cultural models of
Samoa, 198
"Sandy," 69, 74, 83
Sapir, Edward, 36
Schank, Roger C., and Robert P. Abelson, 34, 198, 221
schemas: definitions of, 28–9, 197–8, 230; goal-embedded, 29–31, 32–3, 34, 37, 90–2, 118, 198–9; *see also* cultural models
Schneider, David, 49
Schwartz, Theodore, 163
Scott, James, 4
Searle, J. R., 35–6, 124n.1
self, Western, 220
self-actualization, 225
self-attributions, 92–4, 110–16, 117, 120, 123
*self-understanding, 14, 91–4, 122–4, 135, 157, 207, 211, 226, 227, 231; *see also* identification; personhood; cultural models of; self-attributions; social role enactment; and specific cultural models, gendered human nature; human being
Semang, 49–51
seriation, 182, 183, 185
Shafer, Roy, 190, 191
shame, cultural models of, 133, 146–8, 149, 151–4, 156, 157; *see also* emotion, cultural models of
Shore, Bradd, 6
Shweder, Richard A., 3, 4, 13, 16, 31, 217–18, 227, 228
Shweder, Richard A., and Edmund J. Bourne, 93
Shweder, Richard A., M. Mahapatra, and J. G. Miller, 51
Shweder, Richard A., and J. G. Miller, 51
Shweder, Richard A., and N. C. Much, 51, 55
significant terms, 211, 214, 218
significant verbal symbols, *see* significant terms
Simon, Herbert A., 34
Singer, Jerome, and Peter Salovey, 28
singularity, 182, 183, 185

"Smith, Mrs.," 55–6
social forces, 191
social reproduction 4, 9–10; *see also* internalization
social role enactment, 92–4, 98–9, 102–4, 105–8, 110–13, 117–18, 123–4
socialization, 10, 37, 39, 95, 120–2, 123, 137, 139, 227, 228, 232; *see also* culture acquisition
sociocultural determinism, 1
sociolinguistics, 192
Sperber, Dan, 4, 6, 16
Spiro, Melford E., 6, 7, 11, 13, 14, 23, 36–8, 51, 61, 62, 68, 79–83, 84, 124n.2, 139, 157, 185, 194n.5, 227
stage, cultural models of, 11, 166–8, 177, 226; definitions of, 165, 169–70
Stinson, Charles, and Stephen Palmer, 28
Stoller, Paul, and Cheryl Olkes, 194n.2
story grammar, 128–36, 157
Strauss, Claudia, 11, 13, 14, 16, 32, 38, 39, 63, 91, 159, 221n.6, 222n.17, 222n.20, 226, 227, 228, 232; *see also* Holland and Strauss; Quinn and Strauss
structural functionalism, 8–9
structuralism, 4, 40
structures of meaning, 6
Suarez-Orozco, M. M., 32
subjectivity, collective, 51–2
success, cultural models of, 13, 32, 38, 141–2, 199, 200–8, 210, 214, 217–20, 221n.6, 222n.9; *see also* individualism, cultural models of
"Susan," 69, 70, 72–4, 75–7, 78, 80–1, 83, 87n.10
symbolic anthropology, 211, 229; *see also* interpretivism
symbols, cultural, 211, 228–9

thought-feelings, 2, 3, 7, 15
transformational generative grammar, 129–30
tristeza, see sadness, cultural models of
Trobrianders, 158

unconscious knowledge and desires, 15
universals, human, 1, 4, 14, 63, 93–4, 183; *see also* variability in cultural models

variability of cultural models: cross-cultural, 63, 198; situational, 3, 27, 33; within a culture, 9, 12, 27, 29, 39–40, 120, 185–6, 211, 220; *see also* pandemonium; personal semantic networks
vector model of motivation, 33
Vogt, Evon Z., 40